# The Plains Indians of the Twentieth Century

Edited and with an Introduction by
Peter Iverson

University of Oklahoma Press : Norman and London

To
David, Pat, and Laura Iverson
Paul, Yoko, and Ayuko Iverson

By Peter Iverson
*The Navajos: A Critical Bibliography* (Bloomington, 1976)
*The Navajo Nation* (Westport, Conn., 1981)
*Carlos Montezuma and the Changing World of American Indians* (Albuquerque, 1982)
(Editor) *The Plains Indians of the Twentieth Century* (Norman, 1985)

**Library of Congress Cataloging in Publication Data**
Main entry under title:

The Plains Indians of the twentieth century.

Includes bibliographies and index.
1. Indians of North America—Great Plains—History—20th century—Addresses, essays, lectures. I. Iverson, Peter.
E78.G73P53 1985     978'.00497     85–40475
ISBN 0–8061–1866–0 cloth (alk. paper)
ISBN 0–8061–1959–4 paperback

The paper in this book meets the guidelines for permanence and durability of the Committee on Production Guidelines for Book Longevity of the Council on Library Resources, Inc.

# Preface

In 1974, Vine Deloria, Jr., issued a challenge to historians to begin the study in greater detail of Indian life in the twentieth century. Speaking to an audience in Fort Collins, Colorado, he suggested in vintage fashion that historians were mired in the previous century. Deloria said that rather than rehashing what Lewis and Clark had for breakfast on the Bitterroot in 1804 or reliving Little Big Horn once again, we need to discover what has happened to Indians since the passing of the frontier.

I could not have agreed more completely, having recently returned to graduate school after living for three years in the Navajo Nation. Although the struggles of a hundred years past will command forever a certain fascination, it was time, surely, that we devoted more attention to the people and the events of more recent eras. We have made some headway in the right direction since Deloria's address, and I hope this book enhances understanding of Indian history as a continuing story. Above all, it speaks to a basic reality: the Indian people of the Plains will always be here.

The task of putting together an anthology of recent writings on Plains Indians has been rewarding but not without challenges and limitations. Defining the Plains proved to be one of the first problems, and eventually I realized that a precise definition has defied others for generations. I opted for a somewhat flexible boundary but kept within the limits of the traditional group of ten states: North Dakota, South Dakota, Nebraska, Kansas, Oklahoma, Texas, New Mexico, Colorado, Wyoming, and Montana. Four of those states, namely, Kansas, Texas, New Mexico, and

Colorado, were omitted because of the relatively small Indian populations in their Plains areas. Within the remaining states I have included the Northern Arapahoes of Wyoming, certainly a tribe within the Plains tradition even if the Wind River Reservation is a bit west of some Plains maps. This volume also contains portions of Alfred DuBray's commentary about the contemporary Winnebago Reservation in eastern Nebraska, another site on the edge of the Plains region.

In a book of moderate length it is impossible to include all Plains tribes during all periods of the twentieth century. I have attempted to provide a sampling of the best work in the field of modern Indian history, with attention to chronological, tribal, and geographical diversity. I have provided each chapter with a brief introduction that will, I hope, place it within the broader context of the period. I am grateful to the individuals who have contributed to this volume and to colleagues who suggested articles for inclusion. It should go without saying that many other articles could have been chosen.

Unlike many other anthologies, this one incorporates the footnotes accompanying the original articles. I have never been convinced by the argument that footnotes get in the way of the average reader. It is important, I believe, for readers to know where the writers obtained the information upon which they drew their conclusions. Also, these citations may inspire other students of Plains Indian history to broaden their own research.

I would like to thank John Drayton, Editor-in-Chief of the University of Oklahoma Press, for his enthusiastic support of this undertaking. Once again I am indebted to Diane Alexander, of Laramie, Wyoming, for her help in typing the manuscript. I also wish to thank my department secretary, Irene Walker, and my department chair, Deborah Hardy, for their assistance.

To my wife, Kaaren, reared in southern Oklahoma, and to all other members of my family, I express my love and appreciation. I am pleased to dedicate this book to my brothers, David and Paul; my sisters-in-law, Pat and Yoko; and my nieces, Laura and Ayuko.

*Laramie, Wyoming*                                    Peter Iverson

# Contents

PREFACE                                                            v

INTRODUCTION   They Shall Remain
  By **Peter Iverson**                                             3

CHAPTER 1   Adjusting to the Opening of the Kiowa, Co-
  manche, and Kiowa-Apache Reservation                            11
  By **William T. Hagan**
  Notes                                                           29

CHAPTER 2   Legacies of the Dawes Act: Bureaucrats and
  Land Thieves at the Cheyenne-Arapaho Agencies of
  Oklahoma                                                        31
  By **Donald J. Berthrong**
  Notes                                                           50

CHAPTER 3   From Prison to Homeland: The Cheyenne River
  Reservation Before World War I                                  55
  By **Frederick E. Hoxie**
  Notes                                                           73

CHAPTER 4   The *Winters* Decision and Indian Water Rights:
  A Mystery Reexamined                                            77
  By **Norris Hundley, Jr.**
  Notes                                                          100

CHAPTER 5   The Indian New Deal and the Years That
  Followed: Three Interviews                                     107
  Conducted by **Joseph H. Cash** and **Herbert T. Hoover**

CHAPTER 6    Fighting a White Man's War: The Extent and
    Legacy of Indian Participation in World War II          149
    By **Tom Holm**
    Notes                                                  166

CHAPTER 7    Federal Water Projects and Indian Lands: The
    Pick-Sloan Plan, a Case Study                          169
    By **Michael L. Lawson**
    Notes                                                  183

CHAPTER 8    "What They Issue You": Political Economy at
    Wind River                                             187
    By **Loretta Fowler**
    Notes                                                  216

CHAPTER 9    Tribal Leaders and the Demand for Natural
    Energy Resources on Reservation Lands                  219
    By **Donald L. Fixico**
    Notes                                                  233

CHAPTER 10    The Distinctive Status of Indian Rights      237
    By **Vine Deloria, Jr.**
    Notes                                                  248

CHAPTER 11    Power for New Days                           249
    By **Peter J. Powell**
    Notes                                                  263

The Contributors                                          265

Index                                                     269

# Illustrations

Boarding school, Cheyenne River Agency, 1890.                    133
Major James McLaughlin, n.d.                                     134
Quanah Parker and council, n.d.                                  135
Sioux cattlemen, Cheyenne River, 1911.                          136
Typical housing, Crow Reservation, ca. 1900.                    137
Police on Crow Reservation, ca. 1900.                           138
A gathering on the Crow reservation, ca. 1900.                  139
Farming at Cantonment, late 1930s.                              140
Meeting in Anadarko, Oklahoma, 1940.                            141
Sioux men enlist during World War II, 1940s.                    142
Comanche machinist, 1940s.                                      143
Fort Berthold land ceded, 1948.                                 144
Relocation of Indian family, 1957.                              145
Arnold Headley, Arapahoe powwow, 1984.                          146
Wyoming Indian High School team, 1984.                          147
Nowah'wus sacred to the Cheyenne people.                        148

## Maps

1. Land Openings in Oklahoma                                       9
2. Plains Indian Lands                                            10

# The Plains Indians of the Twentieth Century

# They Shall Remain

### BY PETER IVERSON

The Indian peoples of the Plains are an important, integral part of the region's past, present, and future. From Oklahoma to the Dakotas and throughout the Plains, Indians have helped shape the character and destiny of all who have resided in this area. Instead of vanishing before the onslaught of the land rushes at the end of the nineteenth century, Indians have endured. Despite impressive challenges to their lands and lives they have maintained changing, adaptive cultures, responsive to the needs and demands of each generation. Theirs is a story of failure and success, of defeat and triumph—but, above all, of continuation.

Historians usually date the end of the frontier at 1890, in accordance with Frederick Jackson Turner's judgment made in the final decade of the nineteenth century. In the snows of December 1890, Sioux men, women, and children were killed at Wounded Knee, South Dakota, a tragic event that is often considered to mark the end of hostilities between the United States and various Indian nations. Until recently 1890 also marked the point at which teachers and students of western and Indian history concluded their studies.

Those who lived in the American West in 1890, including Indian peoples, would have been surprised at such a clear-cut demarcation between the Old West and the New. In parts of Wyoming and in other forbidding locations, frontier settlement continued well into the twentieth century. Up to this very day many Indians have resisted forced assimilation into the larger American culture and society. Despite the image of the modern West as a mobile, rootless society, there are within the more rural West countless families, both Indian and non-Indian, who have lived in the same area since the late nineteenth century. Some of them, indeed, occupy the very ground that their great-grandfathers and great-grandmothers walked upon a hundred years ago.

Nonetheless, while there has been continuity, there has also been change. The world of the late twentieth century doubtless looked rather different from the way that citizens of a century earlier would have imagined or preferred it. While the Plains region has remained predominantly rural, its residents are very much affected by the demands of their urban counterparts and by other impositions upon them, particularly those of the federal government, an institution often viewed as a somewhat foreign enterprise. Still, when one drives today from Carnegie to Lone Wolf on Highway 9 through southwestern Oklahoma, or from Faith to Eagle Butte on Highway 212 through western South Dakota, one is impressed by the same earth and the same sky—and by the presence of Indians.

Indeed, one of the most remarkable features of the history of the modern Plains is that Indians have remained a part of it. In 1887 the Congress of the United States passed the General Allotment Act, popularly called the Dawes Act after its congressional sponsor, Henry Dawes of Massachusetts. The division of tribal land into individual holdings represented only one part of an overall program designed to assimilate American Indians as rapidly as possible. The practice of Christianity, the use of the English language, the imposition of Anglo-Saxon names, the schooling of children—all were supposed to encourage a quick transition into the mainstream national culture. Simultaneously the practice of traditional religion, the use of tribal languages, the maintenance of tribal names, and the customary instruction of the young by the elders were at the least discouraged and were generally repressed.

Throughout the Plains the non-Indian population expanded overwhelmingly during the final decade of the old century and the first decades of the new, placing pressures on Indian peoples in areas such as Oklahoma, the Dakotas, and Montana. As non-Indians swarmed into the region, "surplus" Indian land was made available to them. What remained of individual and tribal holdings came under increasing attack. Indians were informed repeatedly that large reservations were not in their best interests. Reservations

thus appeared to be only temporary creations, and within a generation, some speculated, they would vanish. The country as a whole
was absorbing immigrants from beyond its shores; why could it not
also absorb the first occupants of this land? For varying reasons
employees of the Bureau of Indian Affairs, missionaries, land
speculators, town organizers, farmers, and ranchers were all tempted to believe that Indians as Indians might soon disappear.

They did not disappear, of course, but neither could they remain
the same. While it is important not to overemphasize the negative
aspect of that era, it clearly was in many ways a very difficult
period. Many of the children taken eastward to Carlisle Indian
Industrial School and other similar environments died or dis-
appeared; others who did return were often unable to adapt to the
place in which they had been reared. The status that previously
could be gained in warfare or on the hunt could no longer be
achieved. The Sun Dance and other ceremonies were prohibited.
Even the land itself could not be preserved as an undivided entity.
To respond to this new age, the Indians had to develop new
strategies and find new leaders.

It is important to recognize the Indian cultures before the late
nineteenth century were not static. To cite the most obvious example, the introduction of the horse dramatically altered the lives
of most Plains Indians. People had made long migrations before
(from the eastern woodlands, for example, or southward from a
northern region); thus change was not considered foreign or forbidden. Within the "Americanization era," as it is sometimes termed,
the question no longer was whether or not to change but what kinds
of changes could be usefully incorporated into Indian life.

One of the most significant and perplexing issues involved
leadership. What skills, what qualities were needed? In some
instances, for example, knowledge of English and of some of the
white man's ways could assist in negotiations over land, water, and
other central concerns. Even if unanimity could not be achieved,
still the pressing needs of the day demanded action and resistance.
In South Dakota a reservation might be preserved as the base for an
evolving cultural homeland. Yet, given the demographic and economic pressures within Oklahoma, such could not be the case
(except for the Osages' mineral resources, which are held in
common). The loss of reservations in Oklahoma by no means
ended tribal identity, but it did make a difference.

Religious faith was another basic question. Traditional tribal ceremonies could not be killed off easily, and many survived. Some individuals, however, turned to Christianity; still others embraced the Native American Church, which sanctioned the ritual use of peyote. Some people adhered to more than one practice. By the time of World War I, nonetheless, the Native American Church had gained members throughout the Plains, in part because that church offered a sort of accommodation between the two worlds, Christian and Indian, within its rituals and symbols.

By participating in the Native American Church or in new associations such as the Society of American Indians, Plains Indians could seek and gain a sharper sense of themselves as a people with ties and allegiances not only to a community or to a tribe but also to a larger identity: the American Indians. Santee Sioux Charles Eastman, Yankton Sioux Gertrude Bonnin, and Northern Arapahoe Sherman Coolidge figured prominently in the affairs of the society and spoke out on contemporary issues. A brother and two sisters from an Omaha family also became nationally known: Francis LaFlesche, an anthropologist; Susan LaFlesche, a physician; and Susette LaFlesche, a writer. Fred Lookout served for many years, both during and after this era, as Osage principal chief and was a member of the Native American Church.

By the end of the 1920s the Americanization program had waned, and it came to an end with the installation of John Collier as commissioner of Indian affairs during the administration of Franklin D. Roosevelt. The passage of the Indian Reorganization Act in 1934, the subsequent legislation affecting Oklahoma Indian tribes, and Collier's own actions apart from congressional sanction all combined to swing the pendulum away from assimilation. Collier and his associates advocated greater protection of Indian lands, consolidation of Indian landholdings, and promotion of Indian arts and crafts and in general were sympathetic to the important elements of tribal cultures, including languages and cultural traditions.

As Indian critics of the time and historians within the past decade have reminded us, Collier's record was not spotless, and some of his efforts as commissioner were hardly greeted with unanimous approval. The Indian Reorganization Act had emerged in modified form, and vested interests opposed its full implementation. Despite

the good intentions of those who wished to reform Indian education, teachers either opposed the Collier plan or were ill-prepared
to implement it. Under the act, tribal governments could become
promoters of factionalism rather than self-rule.

Still D'Arcy McNickle and other Indian supporters of and participants in the Indian New Deal would soften that criticism by noting
the vital achievements of the 1930s. For example, even with its
shortcomings the Indian Reorganization Act was applicable to a
particular tribe only if that tribe approved it, a policy certainly
worthy of commendation. Indeed, as McNickle has asserted, the
bureau's past record doubtless caused greater opposition to the
legislation than it may have deserved. Perhaps the two most crucial
accomplishments were the halting of land allotment and the halting
of religious persecution and harassment.

With the onset of World War II federal policy began to shift once
again. Indians participated in the war effort in remarkable numbers
and with important results, as chapter 6 demonstrates. The experiences of Indians in the armed forces and in war-related industries
away from home had far-reaching consequences. A new generation returned from the war with heightened expectations of what
the country could offer and of what was needed to take part in
national life. Sometimes frustrated by limited opportunities at
home, they moved to towns and cities in search of more lucrative
employment, better education, and generally enhanced opportunities. The federal government aided and abetted that transition
through a relocation program in the 1950s designed to push
thousands of people into more urban residences. In addition,
through legislation intended to withdraw federal services from
tribal communities and to delegate more reponsibilities for Indian
affairs to the states, the federal government reemphasized the goal
of assimilating Indians into the social and cultural mainstream of
the United States.

Those federal programs, however, like so many others in Indian
history, did not always achieve the intended results. Many Plains
Indians did not remain in the cities. Many fought against potential
federal termination of trust responsibilities, and Indian opposition
did play an indispensable role in turning back that counterproduc-
tive policy after the Eisenhower administration. Moreover, Indians
began at this time to take advantage of public laws designed
initially to aid public school districts encumbered with military

installations, and Indians began to build viable public school systems on many reservations. Even while many Plains Indian children were being shipped to such large multitribal boarding schools as Chilocco, in northern Oklahoma, the seeds were being sown for the abandonment of these institutions in the 1970s and 1980s.

The years since World War II have brought more than one fluctuation in general policy, as the Reagan administration illustrated after the somewhat more progressive era of the 1960s and 1970s. Economic development is a good case in point. In the 1950s, Indians in the Plains and elsewhere were informed by bureau agents and power company officials that nuclear power was just around the corner, and coal resources soon would become obsolete. Coal leasing thus could take place for minimal rates made ludicrous in later years by spiraling inflation. Through hard-won experience, however, Indian people have now gained a more thorough understanding of the value of their minerals. They have attempted to assess whether leasing and mining should take place; if it is to take place, they seek a maximum return for these nonrenewable resources. Water rights, critical to economic development, have increasingly been safeguarded in the contemporary arena. Tribal abilities to control and tax corporate interests on the reservation have been tested in the courts. Economic development schemes do not win ready and immediate acceptance.

Through efforts to enable a greater percentage of Indian people to remain at home and survive economically, through promotion of tribal languages in the schools, through wider if not universal participation in tribal government, and through higher education and the training of more people in needed skills and occupations, Plains Indians are determined to remain within the region. That goal will be difficult, given the demands of white neighbors and of other interests within the Plains. On the other hand, when we compare the overall picture in the mid-1980s with that of the early twentieth century or even that of the mid-1950s, we may discern a brighter future. Severe and complicated problems loom large in the present and will hardly vanish in the years to come. Yet, as we approach the twenty-first century, we may predict with confidence that Indians will continue to be a vital force in the Plains. For too long and for too many observers the visible problems of these people have obscured their resilient spirit. The record of the twentieth century demonstrates that the Plains Indians shall remain.

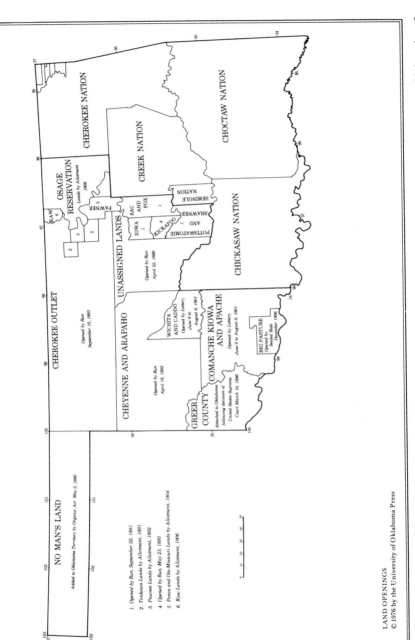

LAND OPENINGS
© 1976 by the University of Oklahoma Press

Land Openings in Oklahoma. Reprinted from John W. Morris, *et al.*, *Historical Atlas of Oklahoma*, 2d ed. (Norman: University of Oklahoma Press, 1976), p. 48.

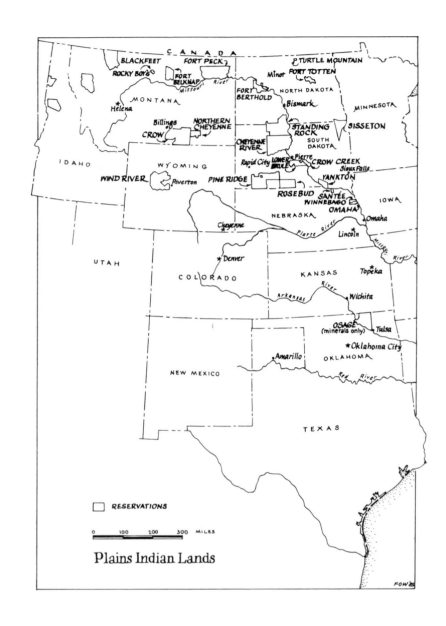

CANADA

BLACKFEET    FORT PECK    ⌐TURTLE MOUNTAIN
ROCKY BOY'S          FORT         Minot ◦FORT TOTTEN
                  BELKNAP   River
                          FORT     NORTH DAKOTA
       MONTANA         BERTHOLD
   Helena                    ◦Bismark
                         STANDING   SISSETON
       Billings   NORTHERN   ROCK
               CHEYENNE
       CROW              CHEYENNE   SOUTH
                         RIVER      DAKOTA      MINNESOTA

IDAHO          WYOMING   Rapid City LOWER  ◦Pierre  CROW CREEK
                              BRULE          Sioux Falls
WIND RIVER    ◦Riverton  PINE RIDGE     YANKTON
                                 ROSEBUD  SANTEE
                              WINNEBAGO
                                   OMAHA        IOWA

                       NEBRASKA          ◦Omaha
UTAH           ◦Cheyenne        Platte River
                              Lincoln◦

                    ◦Denver              River

           COLORADO    KANSAS    Topeka◦
                           River
                    Arkansas         ◦Wichita

                              OSAGE       ◦Tulsa
                              (minerals only)
                              ★Oklahoma City
               ◦Amarillo   OKLAHOMA
NEW MEXICO                    Red River

                    TEXAS

   ☐ RESERVATIONS

   0   100   200   300  MILES

   Plains Indian Lands

                              F.O.W.'85

# CHAPTER 1

# Adjusting to the Opening of the Kiowa, Comanche, and Kiowa-Apache Reservation

## BY WILLIAM T. HAGAN

*The Dawes Act (or General Allotment Act) of 1887 signaled that large Indian reservations, such as the one shared by the Comanches, Kiowas, and Kiowa-Apaches in Indian Territory, could and would be reduced in size in the immediate future. Private property was the order of the day; through individual landholding, Indians were supposed to become more a part of contemporary America. In addition, of course, a division of the tribal estate made more likely the incursion of non-Indian people into that land.*

*By the end of the 1880s, Indians in Indian Territory were under tremendous pressure to have their lands allotted. As William T. Hagan describes in* United States-Comanche Relations: The Reservation Years, *important tribal leaders either resisted allotment or sought to delay its enactment. The Cherokee Commission, headed by David H. Jerome, began formal negotiations with the Comanches, Kiowas, and Kiowa-Apaches in September, 1892. Eventually, through the Jerome Agreement, the Indians agreed to sell their "surplus" land, potentially for two million dollars, after individual parcels had been carved out for them.*

*The Jerome agreement was not ratified by the United States Congress until 1900. According to Hagan, the Comanches prospered in the interim period, in part from substantial leases to cattlemen using reservation grazing lands. At the same time boomers steadily increased their demands that the reservation be*

From William T. Hagan, *United States-Comanche Relations: The Reservation Years* (New Haven, Conn.: Yale University Press, 1976): 262–85. Reprinted by permission.

*opened immediately for their use. The Rock Island Railroad
crossed a portion of the reservation; Chickasha and other communities were established nearby. Only cattlemen who benefited from
their leases on the reservation opposed rapid ratification of the
agreement. The Comanche leader Quanah, the Kiowa leader,
Lone Wolf, and hundreds of other Indians protested to Congress
that the agreement had not been presented accurately to them.*

*The final version of the Jerome Agreement contained a guaran-
tee for at least a quarter of the original two-million-dollar sum and
allowed the Indians to keep almost half a million acres of land.
Congressional action paved the way for the next stage of the
drama. How should residents of the reservation respond to the
opening of their lands? Was resistance still feasible? Or would
essential cooperation be the best approach?*

*The following selection, by William T. Hagan, describes the
adjustments made by various Indian individuals and groups to the
opening of the reservation. The chapter includes consideration of
the important United States Supreme Court decision in* Lone Wolf
v. Hitchcock *in 1903 that reaffirmed congressional power over
Indian affairs, regardless of stipulations made in previous treaties
and agreements. It was, indeed, a new era for the Indian people of
the Plains.*

SIX years elapsed between Congress's ratification of a version of
the Jerome Agreement in 1900 and the dissolution of the 480,000-
acre tract that was the last land the Comanches and associated tribes
held in common. During this period the Comanches suffered
heavily from a smallpox epidemic as well as from the temptations
and persecutions attendant upon the introduction among them of
several thousand whites. Comanche unity, never a strong feature
of tribal life, was damaged by another bitter controversy when
some Comanches sided with Lone Wolf's Kiowa faction in a
last-ditch fight to stop the opening of their reservation.

In June, 1900, Agent James F. Randlett broke the news to the
Indians of Congress's action on the Jerome Agreement, presenting
it as the best deal they could get under the circumstances. Speaking
for the Comanches, Quanah and Eschiti accepted it. However, at a
meeting a month later there were rumblings of discontent from

Eschiti. The agent decided that it would be best if the Indians sent a delegation, at their own expense, to Washington to have what he had said confirmed by higher authority. The delegation included Eschiti, Quanah, and William Tivis; representing the Kiowas were Apiatan and Delos Lone Wolf. Delos, the Carlisle-educated nephew of Lone Wolf, was on the agency payroll as a district farmer, the best job held on the reservation by an Indian.

In Washington the delegation had a brief interview with President McKinley, but Quanah's plea that the opening of their reservation be postponed another five years and the individual Indian allotments be increased to 320 acres was cut short.[1] Congress had spoken and the Indians must conform.

The principal chiefs of the three tribes, Quanah, Apiatan, and Apache John, and most of their followers appeared resigned to their fate. The Kiowa faction headed by Lone Wolf, with Delos by his side, was not ready to submit, and it soon secured the support of some Comanches who followed the lead of Eschiti and his main henchman, William Tivis. The latter, like Delos, was Carlisle trained. These irreconcilables wanted to hire an attorney to continue the fight, and the name of John T. Hill, the shady character who had helped negotiate the Jerome Agreement eight years earlier, was bandied about. Then the Supreme Court in December, 1900, quashed the Choctaw and Chickasaw claims to the $1.5 million Congress had authorized in 1900 for the purchase of the surplus land, and the Lone Wolf faction's bargaining position improved.

In the spring of 1901 the irreconcilables took action. On their own initiative Lone Wolf and Delos proceeded to Washington and retained an attorney, not Hill but William M. Springer. Springer was well known in the nation's capital. A member for twenty years of Illinois's delegation to the House of Representatives, when he was defeated for reelection in 1894, he had been consoled with a federal judgeship in Indian Territory. Springer left that position in 1900 to practice law in Washington. As Lone Wolf's attorney his first move was to seek an injunction from the Supreme Court of the district of Columbia blocking the opening of the reservation. Springer also drafted a memorial, which he sent back to Anadarko by Delos with instructions to secure enough signatures to give weight to Lone Wolf's request for an injunction.[2]

This set off a tug of war on the reservation between the Lone Wolf faction and the three principal chiefs backed by Agent Randlett. The agent had Delos fired from his government job and replaced him with William E. Pedrick, a Kiowa squaw man and the brother-in-law of Apiatan. Attorney W. C. Shelley, who had some ties with the Lone Wolf faction, responded by urging the removal of Apiatan from the Court of Indian Offenses for being a polygamist. Complaints were also made against Laura Pedrick, Apiatan's sister and William's wife, that were designed to get her discharged from her position as field matron in the Indian Service. But unlike the days when he seemed responsive to any suggestion from Attorney Shelley at the expense of Agent Frank Baldwin, Indian Commissioner Jones supported Agent Randlett in this struggle.

The agent was able to hold the principal chiefs in line with his advice "to make the most of the good bargain" Congress had provided,[3] although Delos managed to secure numerous signatures on the memorial Springer had drafted. Lone Wolf led a group of Indians who presented it to President McKinley early in June, 1901. Attorney Springer also added the name of Eschiti and seven other Indians to Lone Wolf's petition to the District of Columbia Supreme Court, but to no avail. The court denied the injunction, reasoning that it could not intervene because the Indians were subject to the control of Congress.[4] Attorney Springer promptly announced that he would appeal and expressed confidence that he could obtain for the Indians at least twice the sum the United States had agreed to pay them for their land. In September, Springer requested the Oklahoma Territory Supreme Court to stay the opening of the reservation, and again was denied. By that time all the Indians had been allotted homesteads and the surplus land had been opened for settlement.

Allotment had begun in late July, 1900, and was completed within a year. Throughout the 1890s agents had enouraged the Indians to select their homesteads, and many had done so. These areas were now confirmed to them if they did not intrude upon the tracts reserved for the military reservation, the agency, or the religious groups functioning on the reservation. If an Indian already had established himself on section 16 or 36 of a township, he could remain there; otherwise these tracts were reserved for the support of public schools. With few exceptions the Indians were able to select the land they wished, and an effort was made to assist them in obtaining the best land available. Unfortunately, most of the reservation was suited only for grazing, and some Indians ended up with allotments of this variety. The location of the Indian homesteads tended to follow previous residential patterns. The Comanches generally selected homesteads south of the Wichita Mountains, while the Kiowas and Kiowa-Apaches clustered to the north.

When the Indians had first learned of the additional 480,000 acres available to them, they hoped that this meant an additional 160 acres per capita, making a total of 320.[5] They were speedily disabused of this, since Congress had not intended that they should retain so much good land. The 480,000 acres would be selected from the inferior lands left after the round of 160-acre allotments and would be held in common.

Although the Indians were disappointed in their hopes for 320-acre homesteads, seventeen squaw men were able to pull it off in a patently unfair fashion. The Treaty of Medicine Lodge had provided that heads of families prepared to undertake careers as farmers could have up to 320 acres set aside for them. Joseph Chandler had applied as early as 1871, acting in the name of his Comanche wife Tomasa, who after Chandler's death married George W. Conover. Other squaw men recognized this as a possible loophole that would enable them to double the size of allotments permitted under the Jerome Agreement. In 1898 three squaw men applied for 320-acre allotments, and two of them, William Wyatt and John Nestell, retained William C. Shelley to represent them. Fourteen others, including Quanah's son-in-law Emmett Cox, also filed for 320 acres. Despite Agent Randlett's protest that the Indians would be upset "and the world will decide with them, that there is no justice in making such allowance,"[6] the squaw men retained their double allotments. It was yet another illustration of the white man's ability—and drive—to exploit the system to satisfy his lust for land. The Indian not only lacked the knowledge to manipulate the system, he lacked the white man's powerful urge to do so.

The 480,000 acres Congress assigned to the Comanches and associated tribes to hold in common sparked a last battle among the white ranchers seeking to exploit the Indians. But whereas they once had been using two-thirds of the reservation, they now were reduced to quarreling about one-seventh of it. The bone of contention was referred to as the Big Pasture, a tract of about 400,000 acres fronting on Red River. The other 80,000 acres were in three tracts, two of them convenient to the Comanches, who had more cattle than the other two tribes.

Agent Randlett subdivided the Big Pasture into four units, which were then leased at ten cents an acre to four ranchers who had been on the reservation for years, E. C. Sugg, Samuel B. Burnett, Daniel Waggoner's son Tom, and Asher Silberstein. With the possible exception of Silberstein, no one was happy with the arrangement. Each could point to corrals, tanks, fences, and bunkhouses that he had constructed and maintained but was now forced to give up. In the confusion surrounding the opening of the reservation other ranchers pushed herds across Red River and intruded on pastures that Sugg, Burnett, and Waggoner had been leasing. Tom Waggoner damned them as ''little cattle men that has no right whatever there.'' His piteous ''I have no chance to do any thing only starve to death''[7] would have inspired more compassion had the Waggoner family not been one of the wealthiest in Texas. The trouble was that the ranchers' nearly twenty years' preferential status on the reservation had given them a sense of proprietorship which was outraged by the other whites seeking the same advantages.

It was inevitable that with the total amount of land available drastically reduced the ranchers should fall to quarreling among themselves about the disposition of the Big Pasture. Sugg and Burnett took their frustrations out on each other. Since Sugg's new pasture had been carved largely from Burnett's old lease, Burnett did his best to prevent Sugg's men from constructing the necessary fences. The major battle was fought in Washington, where both enlisted help. Sugg was aided by Representative Charles Curtis of Kansas and by an attorney for the Rock Island Railroad. But Burnett brought up even heavier artillery in the person of Texas Senator Joseph Bailey, who accompanied him on a visit to the commissioner of Indian affairs. Burnett also was helped by a congressman who interceded for him with the secretary of the interior. Agent Randlett, a stern old man used to having his own way, protested in vain when Burnett went over his head, and he expressed ''sorrow and shame because of the degradation to which I have been subjected.''[8]

Agent Randlett was not a man to trifle with. In an attempt to increase profits for the Indians, he further subdivided the Big Pasture so that more cattlemen could bid for leases, thus incidentally getting back at Burnett. He also was able to successfully oppose Senator Bailey's attempt, supported by eleven other members of the Texas delegation, to extend for five months the existing leases. The new leases, which ran for three years beginning July 1, 1902, required Burnett and Waggoner to pay an average of nearly thirty cents an acre. This they did, despite protestations of impending economic ruin, thereby suggesting what a fine bargain the reservation grass had been for them in the earlier years. For the Indians the new lease meant annual grass payments of over $130,000.

Of the other three pastures, no. 3, which included 22,500 acres and lay directly west of the railroad town of Duncan, also caused controversy. The Duncanites were appalled at the creation of the pasture where they had hoped to see hundreds of homesteads occupied by potential customers. They appealed to Randlett to save them from financial disaster, pointing out how the towns competing with them were advertising their plight.[9]

Pursuing tactics that whites had found successful in other situations, the Duncanites sought help from the Indian factions. Quanah declined to become involved, but Eschiti permitted his name to be used in a statement deploring the location of pasture no. 3.[10] So desperate were Duncan's businessmen that they offered to lease the land for agricultural purposes at higher rates than cattlemen were able to pay. In the spring of 1902 the secretary of the interior approved a plan by which pasture no. 3 was leased in units of 640 acres at a minimum of forty cents an acre, the lessee to fence it and the fences to revert to the Indians on the expiration of the lease. Duncan businessmen who comprised most of the lessees subdivided the land into 160-acre tracts and sublet them to actual farmers.

The deliberations on the disposition of the 480,000 acres had taken place over a period of eighteen months, during which sooners had invaded the reservation. Within three weeks after the passage of the amended Jerome Agreement in June, 1900, Agent Randlett estimated that there were as many white intruders in the Wichita Mountains as there were Indians on the reservation, with more whites on the way.[11] Those posing as prospectors used the agreement's provision relating to mineral law as an excuse for their activities. Their real intention was to scout out the best land in anticipation of an opening by a ''run'' such as had been employed elsewhere in Oklahoma.

In the thirteen months before the actual opening, the Indians were constantly harassed by the sooners. The public roads through the reservation were open to them, and the troops at Fort Sill were too few to be of much assistance. The cavalrymen did help clear the Wichita Mountains on one occasion, but the sooners quickly returned when the troops retired to their barracks. On the eve of the opening Agent Randlett estimated that at least 50,000 intruders were on the reservation.[12] Included along with the honest homeseekers were a number of thieves who stole Indian cattle and ponies and bootleggers who dispersed to the Indians what Randlett referred to as ''bottled consolation.''

William Kinman, who had been one of the most persistent sooners, had set himself up in business as an agent for those seeking homesteads. Out on bond in a case involving sale of liquor to the Indians, Kinman was now operating from a post office of which his wife was postmistress. As a result of Randlett's complaints against the Kinmans' new activities, an investigation resulted in charges filed against them for mail fraud. Randlett was rewarded for his industry in trying to protect the Indians by a legal suit that produced an injunction restraining him temporarily from interference with the squatters.[13]

In December, 1900, after six months of constant harassment from sooners, Agent Randlett suggested to the Indian commissioner, who forwarded his proposal through channels to the General Land Office, that the reservation be opened by a lottery instead of a run.[14] This would reduce the incentive for the sooners to infiltrate the reservation. Whether or not Randlett initiated the idea, the president's proclamation of July 4, 1901, adopted the lottery procedure for the Kiowa, Comanche, and Kiowa-Apache Reservation.

This proclamation divided the reservation into two land districts for filing purposes, with one office at El Reno and another at Lawton. Between July 10 and July 26 individuals could register for the approximately 13,000 homesteads, and more than 165,000 did so. About 50,000 of them anxiously witnessed the drawings at El Reno from July 29 to August 1. Those names were selected in the drawings were entitled to choose allotments in the order in which their names were drawn. The first two selected, from the only available land adjacent to the Lawton town site, allotments valued in excess of $20,000.[15]

The next major scene of activity was the tent city of 10,000 adjacent to the site of Lawton, where an auction of town lots was held August 6. Within hours Lawton was a frantic scene of new owners pitching tents on their property while trying to fend off squatters. The Comanches must have been bemused by the hectic activity which transformed the dusty prairie into a bustling frontier town that within a week featured banks operating under canvas and sported fifty saloons, including one called the Carrie Nation.[16]

The Carrie Nation may have provided solace for some of those whites who did not draw one of the approximately 13,000 lucky numbers in the lottery or whose number came up too late to claim one of the good tracts available. A year later nearly 23,000 acres still had not been filed on, most of it in the barren Wichita Mountains.[17] Meanwhile, disappointed boomers were trying to stake out mineral claims on Indian allotments or challenging the authenticity of Indian title to valuable tracts.

The mineral claims stemmed from an ambiguity in the June 6, 1900, law opening the reservation. It could be construed to permit filing on Indian allotments under mineral law, and many whites did just that. Agent Randlett quickly sought a ruling from Washington to squelch such efforts, but it took over two weeks for the Interior Department to rule that the whites were trespassers and should be removed. Even then, Randlett was directed that "it is not deemed advisable . . . to resort to harsh force."[18] As usual the government was more sensitive to white than Indian needs, and the trespassers were to be given time to withdraw after proper notification.

Such attitudes encouraged other whites to challenge Indian allotments, particularly those that were held in the names of the 163 Comanche victims of the smallpox epidemic in the winter of 1900–1901. Squatters also camped on some of the 320-acre allotments of adopted squaw men and their children, as well as on the homesteads of Mexican captives of the Comanches and associated tribes. The latter individuals were taken in their youth and now considered by the Indians as members of their tribes. Nevertheless, if the Mexicans had been allotted good land, there were unscrupulous whites who hoped to swindle them out of it on a technicality. Even two deputy United States marshals were among the squatters.[19] In October, 1901, President Theodore Roosevelt authorized the use of troops to remove the squatters, but more than sixty legal challenges ultimately required rulings from the Department of the Interior. As late as December, 1902, troops were still being called upon to evict trespassers from Indian allotments.

Some of these squatters could have been honestly mistaken about the legality of their claims. There were whites, however, who were common thieves, and they made drastic inroads upon Indian cattle and horses. The livestock likewise suffered from the application of the terrritorial herd law, whose effect was accentuated by the failure of the Indians to properly care for their animals. The law was designed to protect farmers from stock running loose and provided that they could impound animals intruding on their land and force their owner to compensate them for their care. Because few Indians were content to constantly remain on their allotments and care for their cattle, they frequently lost them when confronted by white men with large bills for the maintenance of their stock. Some whites were suspected of permitting Indian cattle and horses to enter their fields and graze on poor crops and then holding the animals and demanding damages from their owners.

The sharp decrease in Indian herds in the years immediately following the opening of the reservation was partially due to the diminishing level of support provided the Indians by the government. Hungry tribesmen were being fed from the herds of friends and relatives. Beginning in 1901, no Indians administered by the Kiowa, Comanche, and Wichita Agency received government rations unless they could be classified as dependent because of age or infirmity.[20] This was part of a general effort to force the Indians to become more self-reliant. However, the United States continued to assist the Indians on a modest scale. Funds previously used to purchase rations were now being assigned to the employment of Indians at $1.25 per day to do road work and other necessary chores for the agency. As of 1905, Congress was still appropriating about $25,000 a year for the support of the Comanches and associated tribes, most of it going into salaries and wages for agency employees, but a few sets of harness and some wagons and plows were being issued to the Indians.[21]

Despite the decline in the level of support provided by the government and the constant preaching of agency officials, few of the roughly 1,400 Comanches worked their land or cared for their livestock to the satisfaction of their supervisors. They continued to derive income from the 480,000 acres the Indians retained, a total of about $136,000 a year to be divided among 2,800 Comanches,

Kiowas, and Kiowa-Apaches.[22] In addition, families collected rent varying from $0.25 to $3.00 per acre from the allotments of their children. Moreover, most adults chose to rent their own allotments rather than work them, retaining a few acres on which to reside. The hundreds of small frame houses constructed by the government in recent years were more often than not occupied by the families of the white renters. The Indian owners lived in camps, as they had since time immemorial. In the five years following the opening, the Comanches also shared in the $500,000 that the 1900 law provided should be paid them, with the $1.5 million balance being held in the treasury to draw 4 percent interest.

The $500,000, plus the income from the 480,000 acres, was turned over to the Indians in a series of per capita payments. Coming at intervals of several months, they ranged from $20 to $60. Each payment was a bonanza for the local merchants, the whiskey vendors, and the loan sharks. A Lawton paper reported the impact of one payment in 1904:

Every store in the city has been full all day and the red men have bought everything from an ice cream soda to the finest vehicles offered for sale. The Indian has little conception of the value of a dollar and so long as it will last there is nothing too good.[23]

Unaccustomed to handling cash and bolstered by the knowledge that their allotments were held in trust for them by the United States, the Indians indulged their desires during the payments. In the long intervals between payments they lived on credit extended by the local merchants, turned to the loan sharks, or depended upon more fortunate friends and relatives. Although their homesteads could not be seized for debt, other property could, and it was not unusual for a merchant to secure a court order requiring the seizure and sale of an Indian's property to satisfy indebtedness. The Indian's ignorance of the language and the law made him easy prey to such actions.

The loan shark problem was particularly bad, with local bankers active in the role. The Indian would borrow at usurious rates of interest, signing a chattel mortgage on his stock and farm equipment. Agent Randlett was especially incensed at the operations of one Anadarko banker:

This man has been of more damage to the moral character and well being of the Indians of this Agency than all the barrooms, gambling houses and houses of female prostitution that ever have been established in Caddo County. As a usurer he . . . equals the atrocious attributes of Shylock in his cold-blooded, inhuman methods of making collections. . . . I will not permit him to come upon the reserves of this Agency to do any kind of business with the Indians.[24]

This white man was one of several charged by Randlett with trying to slip into the reservation disguised by blankets and shawls as Indian women. The agent was pleased to report in 1905 that one banker in Kiowa County had been found guilty and fined $1,000 for charging Indians interest rates of 150 to 3,360 percent.[25] But the practice persisted. An Indian desperate to feed his family, or as was too often the case anxious to get in a card game or buy a bottle of whiskey, was an easy victim for the pawnbroker or banker.

Gambling always had been a popular pastime with the Comanches, but alcohol was a new vice. Agent Randlett inveighed against the bootleggers who circulated among the Indian camps with their "bottled consolation." He was even more indignant that the town officials of Lawton and Anadarko made no effort to reduce the temptations for the Indians and denounced them publicly. The situation at Anadarko Randlett found particularly revolting:

Any day at almost any hour Indians are seen drunk . . . and without any apparent effort to drag the drunken Indians to jail and police court for fine. Several of the boys of the Riverside School have become thoroughly demoralized and are able at any time they go into town to procure whiskey. . . . They have to be sought for and brought home in a wagon.[26]

Quanah had not developed a drinking problem, although the opening of the reservation had produced changes in his life-style. No longer did he have access to almost unlimited range for his cattle. Now, like other Comanches, Quanah had to pay $1 an acre to graze more than the few head his allotment would support. Furthermore, the chief was not the recipient of income from Texas cattlemen on the scale that he once enjoyed, and his standard of living fell proportionately.

The Comanche chief did continue to play the role of the progressive leader, and his agent was grateful. Quanah set a good example by sending his children to Carlisle and Chilocco and cooperated with agency employees in settling domestic quarrels and property disputes. As a member of the seven-man Business Council through which Agent Randlett tried to administer the affairs of three tribes, Quanah followed the progressive line and backed Randlett against the Lone Wolf-Eschiti faction among the Kiowas and Comanches.

There were compensations for Quanah. The agent strengthened his hand by having the chief's warrant of Quanah's rival Eschiti recalled. When Quanah wanted his daughter Wanda returned from Carlisle before her term was up, this was arranged, and two years later the chief was able to secure for her a position as assistant matron at the Fort Sill School. In 1904, Quanah himself went on the government payroll as an assistant farmer at $240 per year.[27] Randlett justified this in terms of both the services he called upon Quanah to perform and the Comanche's dimininished fortunes.

Quanah had his share of the penalties as well as the rewards of leadership. A missionary charged him with being prominent in the peyote cult, and the polygamy issue again was raised against him. Agent Randlett denied Quanah was a leader of the peyote cult while tacitly admitting that the chief was a participant. An investigator from Washington confirmed that Quanah was living with three wives but concluded this was a reduction from seven. The white man went on to explain Quanah's leadership role as a result of sheer ability rather than government favoritism:

If ever Nature stamped a man with the seal of headship she did it in his case. Quanah would have been a leader and a governor in any circle where fate may have cast him—it is in his blood.[28]

The investigator also pointed out that the chief's much-criticized pigtails were just "double the number affected by George Washington."[29] On another occasion Randlett cited Quanah to defend the Indian practice of wearing their hair in braids, which violated the government's mandate against long hair. He said he had chided the chief about it only to have Quanah remind him that the agent's own Chinese servant wore his hair in a pigtail.[30]

As one of the most publicized Indians in the United States, Quanah was a logical choice to be included among the five tribesmen to ride in Theodore Roosevelt's inaugural parade in 1905. And when Roosevelt came to Oklahoma a few weeks later to hunt wolves and coyotes in the Big Pasture, Quanah was singled out again for special attention. Arriving at Anadarko, the president saw Quanah in the crowd and summoned him to his side. The Comanche later brought members of his family to meet Roosevelt at his hunting camp and took the opportunity to discuss some of his people's problems. The president was sufficiently impressed to urge the commissioner of Indian affairs himself to visit Anadarko. "My sympathies have been much excited and I have been aroused by what I have seen down here," wrote Roosevelt, "and I am concerned at the condition of these Indians and the seeming helplessness of their future."[31]

Quanah could secure an audience with the president of the United States; however, he was discovering that allotment and the opening of the reservation had not brought him all the privileges of citizenship. When his son Harold died in 1902, Quanah had inherited his allotment. When he chose to sell it, he learned to his discomfiture that he could draw on the income only in amounts and at times acceptable to the Indian Office. The Indian would have the protection afforded by wardship, but only at the cost of his economic freedom.

The decision of the United States Supreme Court in *Lone Wolf* v. *Hitchcock* in January, 1903, vitiated efforts of the Lone Wolf-Eschiti faction to overturn the Jerome Agreement and clearly established the wardship status of the Indian by reaffirming Congress's "plenary authority over the tribal relations of the Indians." The court dismissed the complaint that the Jerome Agreement had been altered by Congress by holding that Congress had the power "to abrogate the provisions of an Indian treaty."[32] The Indian Rights Association recognized the significance of the Lone Wolf decision: "It is now distinctly understood that Congress has a right to do as it pleases; that it is under no obligation to respect any treaty, for the Indians have no rights which command respect."[33]

The association had involved itself with the case in its last stage and in the process antagonized Agent Randlett. The association had decided to act after the original decision by the Supreme Court of the District of Columbia was upheld by the Court of Appeals and employed a Philadelphia lawyer to assist William Springer in presenting the case to the United States Supreme Court.

As Agent Randlett saw it, Attorney Springer and the Indian Rights Association were sniping at him from the flanks while he was absorbed in trying to defend the Comanches and associated tribes from the squatters, usurers, and bootleggers. Randlett also resented a reference made at the 1901 Lake Mohonk Conference to the drunken Indians in Anadarko. Although he had been as critical as anyone of the conditions at Anadarko, reference to them at Lake Mohonk was taken by him as implied criticism of his administration. In his next annual report the agent denounced the Indian Rights Association for having become "the allies of grafting attorneys" and suggested that the time had come "when the righteous should, in praying for the interests of his agency, plead, "God, save them from their friends.' "[34]

Even the Agent Randlett's superiors were pondering charges of improper conduct brought against him by Senator Matthew S. Quay at the suggestion of the Indian Rights Association. The senator proposed that an investigator be dispatched to Anadarko and that he specifically be instructed to include Lone Wolf, Big Tree, and Eschiti among those whom he interviewed.

In 1903, Agent Randlett and his agency were subjected to two thorough investigations as a result of charges brought by dissident Indians and Senator Quay. In January and February, Inspector James McLaughlin, who had been to Anadarko on a comparable mission in 1898, carried out a thorough probe of the agency. McLaughlin's report was a ringing vindication of Agent Randlett:

I am convinced that it has been of vast benefit to the Government and fortunate for the Indians . . . that a strong, fearless and just man, such as Col. Randlett, was agent here during the opening of this reservation to settlement.[35]

Nevertheless, President Roosevelt felt impelled by accusations that Agent Randlett had taken bribes in the course of allotting the reservation to dispatch yet another investigator to Anadarko. Roosevelt's choice was Francis E. Leupp, a personal acquaintance and a New York journalist who had once served the Indian Rights Association as its Washington-based lobbyist. Later he would be the president's choice as commissioner of Indian affairs. Leupp also gave Randlett a clean bill of health, defending him in a statement that graphically portrayed an agent's problems:

When an Agent has sat in one swivel chair for four consecutive years, practically every day from eight in the morning 'til five in the evening, hearing complaints, issuing orders, writing letters, opening bids, signing leases, supervising accounts, drawing checks, settling domestic disputes, exercising the functions of a guardian for orphan children, unravelling the intricacies of heirship . . . adjusting debts and credits between individual Indians, preparing cases for the prosecution of dram sellers or the ejection of intruders, devising forms for legal instruments which will save some remnant for the Indian after the white man gets through stripping him—performing these and a hundred other kindred duties day in and day out—who will cast the first stone at him if his spirit revolts now and then. . . . How many men in private life could endure such an unremitting grind as this, and meet with a smile a daily accusation of fraud, conspiracy, and misappropriation of funds, often from the very persons whose poor little possessions he is trying to save for them?[36]

What apparently shocked Leupp the most at Anadarko was something that had bothered Inspector McLaughlin in 1898: the casualness with which sworn statements had been made. "Among a certain class of citizens affidavits are to be had on any side of any subject, and in quantities as wanted," Leupp said.[37] After a strenuous six weeks at Anadarko, the investigator concluded:

I must be content with the satisfaction of adding one more testimonial to the worth of an admirable but much maligned public servant, and with instituting certain criminal proceedings through the United States court which may make perjury a little less profitable as a trade hereafter in the neighborhood of the Kiowa Agency.[38]

James F. Randlett had less than two years to serve as agent for the Comanche and associated tribes at the time Leupp composed his final report. In his last months at Anadarko, Randlett was trying to salvage for the Indians as much as he could of the 480,000 acres held in common by them under the 1900 act. The white man's campaign against the 480,000 acres had commenced before the ink was dry on the legislation setting it aside for the benefit of the Indians. Several bills were introduced into Congress in the period 1902 to 1905 to open the land for settlement. Texas Congressman John H. Stephens was one of the leaders in this effort. His hometown, Vernon, was just across the Red River from the Big Pasture and definitely would profit from the opening. Speaking in behalf of his bill in 1903, Stephens stressed the theme popular in Congress that if the Indians were able to sell their land, "no appropriations will have to be made for them in the future."[39]

Randlett vigorously opposed the legislation. He argued that under the terms of the proposed legislation the Indians would be selling for $600,000 land bringing them an annual lease income of $136,295. The $600,000, the agent emphasized, held in the Treasury at 5 percent, would yield them only $30,000 a year. Randlett also pointed out that the Indians would be losing the use of more than 50,000 acres of pasture that they had reserved for their own cattle, thus reducing them to complete dependence on the inadequate 160-acre homesteads.[40]

The agent's counterproposal was that all children of the Comanches and associated tribes born since the 1900 opening be allotted 160-acre homesteads, and that the remaining land continue to be leased to white farmers and ranchers. Also, Randlett reminded his superiors that the Lone Wolf decision clearly established the Indians as "the wards of the nation":

Congress, the guardian, may deal with the lands of the Indian wards of the nation precisely as an individual legal guardian would deal with and dispose of the lands of an infant or other incompetent person, being careful at all times that no injustice was visited upon the ward.[41]

However, congressmen took their role as representatives of their white constitutents more seriously than their role as guardians of the Indians.

Randlett retired in 1905 due to age and infirmity; he was over seventy and had been in ill health for some time. His handpicked successor, his chief clerk John P. Blackman, kept plugging for Randlett's proposal of allotments to Indian children, but he discouraged Eschiti from circulating a petition against another opening. Like his predecessor, Blackman believed he could represent the Indians better than they could represent themselves. Quanah accepted Blackman as he had Randlett and became an advocate of the plan to allot the childern. As usual, however, the decisions were to be made in Washington.

Early in 1906 a Stephens bill to open the 480,000-acre Indian tract, plus 25,000 acres that had been set aside as a wood reserve for Fort Sill, began to move in Congress. It passed the House and received a favorable report from a Senate committee. Despite a protest from Agent Blackman that the $1.50-an-acre minimum price set by the bill was far too small compensation for the Indians, the Stephens proposal was approved by Congress and sent to the president on March 20.

The Indians' interests finally found an effective advocate in President Roosevelt. On the recommendation of the commissioner of Indian affairs, Roosevelt threatened to veto the bill unless it were recalled for further consideration.[42] This Congress did and rewrote the bill to provide for allotments for the 517 Indian children born since the 1900 opening and for a minimum price for the remaining land of not $1.50 per acre but a substantial $5. In this form it was signed into law by Roosevelt on June 5, 1906.[43]

Even this victory for the Indian was not unalloyed. Agent Blackman wished to select the 160-acre allotments for the children from the relatively fertile pasture no. 3 adjacent to Duncan. However, the white farmers who had been leasing this land were given preference over the Indians who had owned it. On June 18, 1906, Roosevelt approved a law permitting the white lessees to purchase their farms at a price established by an evaluation board, only one of whose three members would be an appointee of the agent representing the Indians.[44]

By September, 1906, Agent Blackman had selected allotments for the Indian children, and the remaining 2,531 tracts were opened for sale to the public. The Indians had $4,015,785.25 added to their account in the United States Treasury as a result of the sales.[45] The Comanches and associated tribes had finally entered an era in which they would own land solely as individuals. Only in that respect was it the situation anticipated by the government officials who had drafted the Treaty of Medicine Lodge. The Indians were still far from the 1867 vision of independent farmers ready for assimilation into the mainstream of American society.

# Notes

1 *Woodward News*, August 10, 1900.
2. *El Reno News*, June 27, 1901; James F. Randlett to Commissioner of Indian Affairs, June 1, 1901, K87:329, Oklahoma Historical Society (hereafter OHS).
3. Randlett to Quanah, June 3, 1901, K88:111, OHS.
4. *New York Times*, June 21, 1901.
5. Indians to Commissioner of Indian Affairs, September 17, 1900, Indian Office—Letters Received (46605–1900) (hereafter IOLR).
6. Randlett to Commissioner of Indian Affairs, December 10, 1900, K81:197, OHS.
7. Daniel Waggoner to Randlett, September 11, 1901, Special Cases, no. 191, National Archives; hereafer NA.
8. Randlett to E. C. Sugg, November 2, 1901, K92:318, OHS.
9. Alexander Gullet and W. I. Gilbert to Randlett, June 6, 1901, Kiowa Agency Files: Cattle Grazing, OHS
10. Randlett to Commissioner of Indian Affairs, June 12, 1901, K89:157, OHS.
11. *Daily Oklahoman* (Oklahoma City), June 28, 1900.
12. Randlett to Secretary of the Interior, July 25, 1901, K90:165, OHS.
13. Commissioner of Indian Affairs to Secretary of the Interior, October 19, 1900, Indian Office Letter Book (Land), 228:261 (hereafter IOLB).
14. Commissioner of Indian Affairs to Commissioner of the General Land Office, December 31, 1900, IOLB (Land) 464:83.
15. "Drawing Homesteads in Oklahoma," *Independent*, August 8, 1901, p. 1826.
16. For the opening see "Drawing Homesteads in Oklahoma," *Independent*, August 8, 1901, p. 1826; William Hymen Murphy, "A History of the Opening of the Wichita-Caddo-Kiowa-Comanche-Apache Reservation"; John Curry Haley, "The Opening of the Kiowa and Comanche Country"; Berlin B. Chapman, "Land Office Business at Lawton and El Reno."
17. Chapman, "Land Office Business," p. 19.
18. Commissioner of Indian Affairs to Randlett, September 9, 1901 IOLB (Land) 499:429.
19. Randlett to Commissioner of Indian Affairs, October 7, 1901, K92;160, OHS.
20. Randlett to Commissioner of Indian Affairs, October 2, 1901, K89:426.
21. Commissioner of Indian Affairs to Agent, June 28, 1905, Kiowa Agency Files: Finance; Randlett to Commissioner of Indian Affairs, January 21, 1906, K119:80, OHS.
22. Annual Report of Randlett, 1904 (Serial 4798), p. 294.
23. *Lawton Daily News Republican*, August 25, 1904.
24. Randlett to Commissioner of Indian Affairs, October 21, 1904, K118:102.
25. Annual Report of Randlett, 1905 (Serial 4959), p. 300.
26. Randlett to Horace Speed, December 30, 1902, K101:412.
27. Randlett to Commissioner of Indian Affairs, February 1, 1904, IOLR (8733–1904).
28. 58th Cong., 2d sess., 1903, S. Doc. 26 (Serial 4646), p. 468.
29. Ibid., p. 469.

30. Randlett to Commissioner of Indian Affairs, July 30, 1902, K101:95, OHS.

31. Roosevelt to Commissioner of Indian Affairs, April 14, 1905, IOLR (37866-1905).

32. 187 U.S. 553 (1903).

33. *Twenty-first Annual Report of the Executive Committee of the Indian Rights Association* (Philadelphia: Indian Rights Association, 1904), p. 24.

34. Annual Report of Randlett, 1902 (serial 4458), p. 289.

35. James McLaughlin to Secretary of the Interior, February 11, 1903, McLaughlin Papers, R 25:263.

36. 58th Cong., 2d sess., 1903, S. Doc. 26 (serial 4646), p. 473.

37. Ibid., p. 495.

38. Ibid., p. 497.

39. *Cong. Rec.*, 57th Cong., 2d sess., p. 2291.

40. Annual Report of Randlett, 1904 (serial 4798). p. 294: Randlett to Commissioner of Indian Affairs, April 5, 1904, K119:369, OHS.

41. Annual Report of Randlett, 1904 (serial 4798), p. 294.

42. *Cong. Rec.*, 59th Cong., 1st sess., p. 4739; John P. Blackman to Commissioner of Indian Affairs, April 2, 1906, K129:304.

43. 34 *U.S. Stat.* 213.

44. 34 *U.S. Stat.* 550.

45. *Annual Report of Commissioner of Indian Affairs, 1907* (serial 5296), p. 113.

# CHAPTER 2

# Legacies of the Dawes Act: Bureaucrats and Land Thieves at the Cheyenne-Arapaho Agencies of Oklahoma

## BY DONALD J. BERTHRONG

*Indian land has always been central to the continuation of Indian* M~p?A.
*identity. As Donald J. Berthrong demonstrates in the following arti-
cle, philanthropists allied with individuals who wanted Indian land
achieved their common goal in early-twentieth-century Oklahoma:
the significant reduction of the Indian land base. The Cheyenne-
Arapaho Reservation in Oklahoma is used here as a case study.*

*While the Dawes Act was an important piece of legislation,
Berthrong shows here that it was not solely responsible for the loss of
Indian land. Other legislation, such as the Burke Act of 1906, helped
implement the goals for allotment. Both those who were charged with
helping the Cheyennes and the Arapahoes and those who simply
sought to use or profit from their land combined to alienate tribal
holdings.*

*As with the previous chapter it is important to recognize that the
dilemmas faced by the Cheyennes and Arapahoes were not confined to
the time period analyzed in the following section. Berthrong's* The
Cheyenne and Arapaho Ordeal: Reservation and Agency Life in
the Indian Territory, 1875–1907 *(Norman, Okla.: University of
Oklahoma Press, 1976) provides a detailed account of the problems faced by the two tribes once they had been placed within the
boundaries of a reservation in Indian Territory in 1875.*

*In reading either account, one is impressed with both the rapid-
ity and the overwhelming extent of the changes confronting the
Cheyennes and the Arapahoes. Within a generation startling
transformations were expected to take place in Indian attitudes*

From *Arizona and the West* (Winter, 1979): 335–54. Reprinted by permission.

*toward religion, schooling, authority, land ownership, and land use. The non-Indian population in Indian Territory increased dramatically. As "free" or open land quickly was becoming part of the American past rather than the present, and as Indian tribes throughout the West met defeat in their military conflicts with the United States, Indians confronted unprecedented demands upon their lives and their lands.*

*While it is beyond the scope of this particular essay, the adaptive nature of the Cheyennes and the Arapahoes is an important concern in the final pages of Berthrong's longer work. He notes that the Native American Church would emerge as an alternative form of religious practice for the Cheyennes. Even though the loss of land was devastating, an altered yet continuing identity could be maintained. Berthrong concludes: "Chiefs were still respected, the love of earth and nature were undiminished, children and elders were cherished, friends were welcome and food was hospitably shared. In western Oklahoma there were individuals who softly and with quiet dignity informed a new neighbor: "I am a Cheyenne.' "*

DURING the Progressive Era, the ideals of nineteenth-century Christian reformers continued to influence the Indian policy of the United States. Assimilation of Native Americans into the mainstream of American life remained the principal goal. However, in implementing the larger outlines of Indian policy, both reformers and government officials invariably encountered obstacles. One of the major obstacles that blocked progress was the leasing of Indian allotments. The Dawes Act of 1887 had made allotments to tribesmen who, instead of starting small farms, had leased their land and soon were drawing a substantial income from farmers and ranchers. Reformers, imbued with the work ethic, pronounced this arrangement an evil and reasoned that if the Indians owned less land, they would be forced to gain a livelihood directly from farming or some other employment. If allotted land were sold, the money obtained could be used to buy farm machinery, provide houses, and generally assist an Indian to begin farming. To achieve such a program, Congress enacted legislation between 1902 and 1910 which permitted the sale of all Indian lands allotted under the

Dawes Act. Poorly administered by misguided bureaucrats, these statutes created myriad opportunities for whites to defraud Indians of their land and property. By 1921 more than one-half of the individuals within tribes affected by the Dawes Act were landless, rural, and economically devastated people. The impact of this national disgrace was vividly illustrated by the alienation of Indian lands on the Cheyenne-Arapaho Reservation in Oklahoma during these years.

Christian reformers and humanitarians, allied with government officials, believed by 1900 that the "Indian question" would soon be solved. Their naïve assumption resulted from the anticipated efficacy of the General Allotment (Dawes) Act of 1887. Key features of the act provided for the allotment of reservation land, the eventual sale of nonalloted land to whites, and citizenship for all Indian allottees. Allotted land would remain in trust for twenty-five years. While the federal government served as trustee for these allotments and other restricted Indian lands, the benefits of private property and citizenship would be supplemented by vocational education emphasizing farming, stock raising, and manual skills, and by religious instruction stressing individualism over tribalism. In a generation, it was assumed, Indians would possess all the requisites for full participation in American society. Labor, thrift, and the accumulation of private property would swiftly transform tribesmen into self-supporting farmers and stockmen who would have no need for federal paternalism.[1]

Congress, responding to western land demands, had enacted legislation to implement the intent of the Dawes Act. A clause in the Indian Appropriation Act passed in March of 1889 authorized the appointment of a commission to negotiate with various tribes for lands in central and western Indian Territory. The Unassigned (Oklahoma) District was opened on April 22, 1889, and quickly occupied by land seekers. A year later, on May 2, 1890, Congress created the Territory of Oklahoma and immediately sought to expand the new political unit by opening land on adjoining Indian domains. To accomplish this objective, a three-man commission, chaired by David H. Jerome, in June initiated talks to implement the allotment program and purchase unoccupied reservation land.[2]

The Jerome Commission met with the Southern Cheyennes and Arapahoes during July and October of 1890. Hard bargaining, threats, deception, and bribery were employed to break down the resistance of several Cheyenne and Arapaho chiefs to the concept of allotment and loss of unused land. When the cession agreement was worked out, every Cheyenne and Arapaho listed on the 1891 tribal roll would be allotted a one-hundred-sixty-acre homestead— eighty acres each of crop and grazing land—and the surplus land would be sold to the government. In time, when the allotting process was completed, 3,294 Cheyennes and Arapahoes had acquired a total of 529,682 acres of land, out of slightly more than four million on the reservation, to be held in trust for twenty-five years by the government. Approximately 3,500,000 surplus acres of their reservation were signed over to the federal government for $1,500,000. Of that sum $500,000 was distributed to tribal members in per capita payments, while $1,000,000 was deposited at five percent interest in the United States Treasury for the tribes' benefit.[3]

Even before the Cheyennes and Arapahoes had accepted the allotment program, Congress began modifying the Dawes Act. The modification was necessary because in setting aside allotments the 1887 statute made every conveyance or contract touching trust lands "absolutely null and void" during the trust period. On March 10, 1890, Senator Henry L. Dawes, the sponsor of the original act, introduced a bill to authorize Indians, subject to the approval of the secretary of interior, to lease their allotments. In 1891 statutory authority to lease land was extended to allottees who "by reason of age or other disability" could not personally benefit from the occupation of cultivation of the allotment. Congress broadened the leasing criteria in 1894 by amending the defining phrase to read "by reason of age, disability or inability" and by extending the lease periods.[4]

With these modifications Indian agents began arrranging leases. By 1900 approximately 1,100 leases had been signed for the Cheyennes and Arapahoes, who realized $42,120.83 for the 1899– 1900 fiscal year. These leases, which covered approximately one-third of their allotted land, increased Cheyenne-Arapaho income by slightly more than 40 percent. Leasing of allotments was more prevalent at the Cheyenne-Arapaho Agency than in other jurisdictions in 1900, when it was estimated that 13 percent of land allotted to all tribes was leased.[5]

The Dawes Act, however, did not eliminate tribalism. Allotted Indians continued to live together in extended families and small villages, resisting the white man's education, Christianity, family structure, and concept of private property. Furthermore, marginal soil fertility and rainfall, minimal capacity to operate agricultural machinery, and deep aversion to agricultural labor prevented most tribesmen from becoming farmers. A Cheyenne-Arapaho Indian agent reported that eight years after allotment only 15 to 18 percent of the adult male population was "actually occupying and cultivating their own lands." Other tribal members were dependent upon rations, per capita payments from interest on funds deposited in the United States Treasury, and lease income. An insignificant fraction of tribal adults was gainfully employed at the agency or as clerks in traders' stores. Commissioner William A. Jones complained in 1900 that the widespread practice of leasing Indian allotments undermined the goals of the Dawes Act. "The Indian," wrote Jones, "is allotted and then allowed to turn over his land to whites and go on his aimless way." Leases not only fostered "indolence with its train of attendant vices" but also provided white settlers and realtors an effective means to exploit Indian lands. When an allottee became discouraged by unsuccessful efforts to farm, he usually leased his land and returned to camp life.[6]

The sale of allotted lands soon was being pushed. If lease income permitted Indians to live without engaging in physical labor, then legislation amending the Dawes Act was necessary. A lease only temporarily abridged an allottee's property rights, but if this land could be removed from a trust status and opened for sale, Indians would have less land to lease. Indians could use the money derived from the sale of whole or partial allotments to aid in building houses, barns, and fences; buying draft animals, cattle, and swine; and providing the necessities of life while bringing smaller and more manageable acreage into cultivation. Congress would also be relieved of approving larger appropriations to support Indians.

Westerners also wanted to see Indian allotments sold to whites. The editor of a newspaper in Watonga, the seat of Blaine County, Oklahoma Territory, alleged that 69 percent of the original Cheyenne and Arapaho allottees were dead and their land was idle and unproductive. Nothing, the editor argued, could benefit Blaine County more than to have those allotments belonging to "dead Indians" owned and cultivated by white farmers.[7]

In 1902 the Dawes Act was modified to free inherited allotments from trust status. According to the act, when an allottee died, his homestead would be held in trust for his heir or heirs for the remainder of the twenty-five-year trust period. However, tucked obscurely into the Indian Appropriation Act of 1902 was a little-discussed provision which altered this requirement. Section 7 stated that adult heirs "of any deceased Indian to whom a trust or other patent containing restrictions upon alienation has been or shall be issued for lands allotted to him may sell and convey lands inherited from such decedent."[8]

Congress also responded to pressure from western townsite promoters to approve alienation of allotted land. In March of 1903, the secretary of interior was "authorized and directed" to dispense patents in fee (unrestricted titles) for eight acres each in four Cheyenne allotments. These lands were covered by restricted patents issued in 1892 to No-wa-hi, Darwin Hayes, Red Plume, and Shoe. Their property had become extremely valuable because it lay adjacent to the intersection of four railroads, including branch lines of the Rock Island and Frisco railroads. Despite the provisions of the Dawes Act, Congress was prevailed upon to vote under Section 9 of the Indian Appropriation Act to free 320 acres of allotted land belonging to the four Cheyennes from all "restrictions as to the sale, encumbrance or taxation" of the specified tracts. The Indians received $6,200 for their tracts. When divided into town lots, the land was sold for more than $150,000 by Thomas J. Nance, who had obtained title to the four tracts. While the acreage involved in this case was small, Congress willingly had set aside provisions of the Dawes Act to satisfy the economic ambitions of western entrepreneurs.[9]

When Congress began debating the need for a major modification of the Dawes Act, reformers, legislators, and western residents expressed differing feelings regarding goals. Reformers saw no harm in issuing fee patents for allotments to those Indians who by reason of education, intelligence, industry, and thrift appeared competent to manage their own economic affairs without supervision of the Bureau of Indian Affairs (BIA). Legislators hoped that Indians who received fee patents would drift away from their people and into white society, so that congressional appropriations supporting Indian affairs could be reduced. Westerners knew that few allotted Indians, regardless of competency criteria, would be sufficiently adroit in business matters to protect their property.[10]

The Burke Act of May 8, 1906, significantly modified the Dawes Act. Under this legislation, competent Indians, at the discretion of the secretary of interior, could be issued fee patents freeing their allotments from all restrictions "as to sale, encumbrance or taxation," except that the land was not liable for any debt contracted before the issuance of the unrestricted patent. The new law also stipulated that thereafter citizenship would be granted only to Indians who received fee patents for their allotments. Those allottees with restricted property still needed BIA supervision and remained "subject to the exclusive jurisdiction of the United States" until they were issued a fee patent.[11]

Less than a year after the passage of the Burke Act, Congress made possible the additional alienation of allotted land. The 1907 Indian Appropriation Act included a section which permitted noncompetent Indians to sell both their original allotments and inherited land under rules and regulations promulgated by the secretary of interior. Funds obtained from land sales were to be used for the benefit of noncompetent allottees or heirs, under the supervision of the commissioner of Indian affairs.[12]

Thus, two decades after the passage of the Dawes Act every square inch of land used and occupied by Indians was subject to alienation. How much land Indians would retain depended upon the rapidity with which the Dawes Act and its modifying legislation would be applied administratively to Indian tribes or individuals.

In part, the land base of Indians diminished because reformers and government officials were blinded by their ideologies. They tied the destiny and lives of Indians to white institutions regardless of the Indians' ability or desire to adapt to a new way of life. It was disturbing to see Indians living on reservations or allotments without labor. If Indians dissipated their funds and resources, they would be forced, one commissioner of Indian affairs commented, "to earn their bread by labor." Albert K. Smiley, long influential in the Lake Mohonk Conference and on the Board of Indian Commissioners, expressed similar sentiments in 1905, when he wrote, " . . . work is the saving thing for the Indians. We have coddled them too much. . . . Put them on their mettle; make them struggle, then we will have some good Indians." Reformers and government officials agreed that assimilation and termination must be the goals of Indian policy, even though many Indians would suffer, "fall by the wayside and be trodden underfoot."[13]

Although some Indian Service field personnel were cautious in stripping land from Indians, pressures grew for the sale of Indian land. Old or incapacitated Indians needed money for life's necessities, young heirs of original allottees required money for education, Indians attempting to farm needed homes, teams, machinery, and barns. Policy changes by the BIA, meanwhile, made alienation easier, and agency administrators who were indifferent to the Indians' interests or who profited by corrupt acts willingly acquiesced to white pressure for the sale of valuable allotments.

Since land was the only significant capital resource the Indians possessed, its retention was imperative. Unlike white Americans, Indians could not replenish their capital resources for a number of reasons: limited employment opportunities, inadequate and inappropriate education, a high incidence of debilitating disease, an inability to protect property through legal actions, a hostile white population that preyed upon their property, and a tenacious Indian adherence to traditional social and cultural customs. The Cheyennes and Arapahoes of Oklahoma, for example, were systematically impoverished as the Dawes Act and subsequent legislation affected young and old, healthy and infirm, competent and non-competent tribal members alike. Once the act was applied to tribal lands, the allotted land base continued to decrease until many tribal members became landless and indigent. Would the reformers have insisted upon their legislative program if they had known its consequences? If Albert K. Smiley's 1905 judgment reflected the opinion of other like-minded reformers, the answer, deplorably, would have been yes!

Beginning in 1908, Cheyenne and Arapaho chiefs protested the sale of allotments. Cloud Chief, Little Bear, and Big Wolf, Cheyenne chiefs from the Darlington Agency, insisted that "it isn't right for old Indians and young ones to draw patents in fee, it makes [them] worse and poor." According to Indian customs, complained the chiefs, "those who have secured patents to their land, sold them and wasted the proceeds, are without home and food . . . [and] the burden of their existence would fall upon those who have held their lands." The chiefs fully comprehended the detrimental economic impact upon other members of extended families when allotments were alienated. In May of 1909 tribal representatives presented their objections to Washington bureaucrats. The discussion ranged over many topics, but the land question was of greatest concern, especially to the older, uneducated chiefs. Mower, a Dog Soldier chief from the Cantonment Agency, best expressed the attitudes of the traditional chiefs when he asked Acting Commissioner R. G. Valentine to tighten rather than remove restrictions "because we don't know how to use our money, and speculators take money from us. . . . They are standing ready to grab our land and money the moment it is in our possession."[14]

Arapaho spokesmen stated that some tribesmen desired increased land sales to relieve existing hardships for their families. The ration system had been abolished, and allotted Indians were dependent upon tribal or individual income to survive. Cleaver Warden, a Carlisle-educated Arapaho and peyote leader, favored increased land sales to alleviate poverty among families that could not live upon lease income and distributions from the sale of inherited land. Warden argued that an Indian should be "treated like a white man and let him suffer the consequences if he does make a mistake." Frank Harrington, another educated Arapaho from Cantonment, suggested that five members from each of the two tribes could be appointed as a committee to screen fee patent applications. Since the Cheyennes and Arapahoes knew the personal habits and abilities of their people, committee members should determine whether applicants were competent to manage their money and property and could advise a superintendent concerning endorsements.

Regardless of educational status, all Cheyenne and Arapaho delegates insisted that their people needed more money in order to buy the necessities of life. Families could not subsist on the ten-dollar disbursements each month from the restricted Individual Indian Accounts. Little Raven, an Arapaho chief, informed Commissioner Valentine that Indians without money signed promissory notes to cover the costs of food and clothing purchases. When the notes could not be redeemed, merchants foreclosed on the Indians' nontrust property. To increase the amount of money available, all Cheyenne and Arapaho delegates advocated that more Indians be allowed to lease their land and receive the income directly from the lessee. Negotiating leases and expending their own money, it was suggested, would enhance the Indians' ability to deal with the white community.[15]

Leasing of land independent of governmental supervision would not have solved the economic problems of the Cheyennes and

Arapahoes. Even if lease and other incomes were maximized, the average annual per capita income for all Cheyennes and Arapahoes at this time would have been approximately $160. Only a few fortunate individuals, or families with multiple inherited allotments, lived far above subsistence level. Since Congress accepted the reformers' view that lease income hindered the inculcation of steady work habits and agreed that Indians should support themselves, the sale of original or inherited allotments was the only means of preventing starvation. But the amount of allotted land was finite, and land sales merely postponed the day of permanent poverty and deprivation.

The May, 1909, conference prompted the Indian Office to send Indian Inspector Edgar A. Allen to investigate how Indian policy was affecting the welfare of the Cheyennes and Arapahoes. Allen's report, confined to the Darlington Agency, was shocking. He found that ninety-seven fee patents had been issued to the "most promising allottees" to test their capacity to manage their property, and at the time of his report in November all but two of the patentees had sold their land—in most instances at far below market value. Furthermore, they had signed over title to cancel debts or in exchange for horses, buggies, and other merchandise at inflated prices, and had received little cash for their land. None of the property acquired remained in their possession, and few permanent improvements were visible on their remaining lands. "The granting of these patents," Allen concluded, "brings joys to the grafter and confidence man and abject poverty to the Indian. No good reasons exist from the standpoint of Indian welfare, for removing restrictions from another allotment, in advance of the trust period. The most capable do not desire such action."[16]

Many Cheyennes and Araphoes were in dire need by November of 1909, despite the sale of almost 22 percent of all inherited and original allotments and extensive land leasing. Without funds or credit, Indians had "nothing to tide them over during the cold weather." Even Indian farmers were in straits. Corn crops, for example, for the 1909 season produced only from five to twenty bushels per acre because of hot, dry weather. Agency Superintendent C. E. Shell apologetically explained that he never favored issuing fee patents; his recommendations had simply conformed to Indian Office instructions. No more fee patent should be approved, Shell recommended, unless exceptional circumstances existed.[17]

Commissioner Valentine saw no immediate reason to change existing policy by "laying down hard and fast rules." He merely cautioned the Darlington superintendent to give fee patent applications "more carefuly scrutiny and recommend only those who have shown by past performances that they are qualified to care for their own affairs." Investigations in 1911 at agencies where fee patents had been issued revealed that 60 percent of all Indians who had received fee patents had sold their land and wasted the sale money. Valentine, annoyed by the "carelessness and incompetence" of Indians who had received fee patents, maintained that any "liberal policy of giving patents in fee would be strictly at cross-purposes with other efforts of the Government to encourage industry, thrift and independence."[18]

Valentine's land-sale program shifted from issuance of fee patents to competent tribesmen to the alienation of inherited land and the trust land of noncompetent allotted Indians. Since those lands could be sold under governmental supervision, he maintained that prices would be equitable and the proceeds would remain on deposit for the Indians' benefit as restricted funds. Valentine also judged that leasing was injurious to the Indians' welfare. Only if an Indian had begun to farm and needed lease money to attain full production on the cultivated portion of an allotment should leasing be recommended. Even then, Valentine believed that if market conditions were favorable, it might still be more advantageous to sell land and use the money for permanent improvements on the remaining trust land.[19]

The lack of agricultural progress by the Cheyennes and Arapahoes disturbed Valentine. At the Cantonment Agency he noted that only 2,587 acres were cultivated out of a total of 92,859 acres of trust land, while 80,320 acres were leased to non-Indians. He encouraged Superintendent Walter G. West to expedite the sale of inherited land to provide agency Indians with funds to improve their farming operations. Even if a family had not inherited land, portions of original allotment should be sold to buy farming equipment.[20]

Such recommendations reflected Valentine's bureaucratic  blindness. The Cheyennes and Arapahoes of Cantonment were the least likely groups of the two tribes to adapt to agriculture. After two decades of BIA efforts to implant the work ethic in these tribesmen through agricultural pursuits, their per capita cultivated acreage in 1912 was 3.38 acres. Agricultural machinery purchased for them would be abandoned, stolen, sold, or mortgaged, despite laws which prohibited the disposal of trust property. Therefore, if their agricultural land was sold, lease money would diminish and the Indians would be forced to work, thereby fulfilling the reformers' ideals, or starve.

Superintendent West hoped that younger Cheyennes and Arapahoes would become productive citizens after they were provided with farming machinery. More than 50 percent of the tribal population at the Cantonment Agency still lived in tipis and in camps consisting of from two to fifteen families. Some would fail to earn a living after their lands were sold, but West rationalized that "in any case, the Government will have done its part and the Indians will be no worse off than he [sic] would otherwise be . . . [and] will be benefited by the experience afforded them." Toward the older people, West was more compassionate. He optimistically predicted that the government could "conserve their health and make them as comfortable and happy as possible during the remainder of their days." When lease income of an elderly person was insufficient, West suggested the use of tribal shares and the sale of trust lands, reserving only enough land for the elderly to live on and to raise a garden.[21]

During the administration of Woodrow Wilson, the onslaught against allotted lands increased. No new legislation was necessary; the reformers had provided all administrative statutory authority required to strip land and property from allotted Indians. This power was seized by Franklin K. Lane, a Californian, and Cato Sells, a Texan, who as President Wilson's secretary of interior and commissioner of Indian affairs, respectively, viewed Indian affairs from a pro-western perspective. Arable land in the public domain was becoming less plentiful immediately before and during World War I, making unused Indian allotments attractive to non-Indian land speculators, farmers, and ranchers. The policies of the Theodore Roosevelt and William Howard Taft administrations of selling Indian allotments required only different emphases to decimate further the land base of many allotted tribes.

Cheyenne and Arapaho chiefs and spokesmen quickly perceived that more of their people were receiving fee patents and selling trust land. They were also worried that tribal restrictions would not be renewed in 1917, when their twenty-five-year trust period expired.

When Wolf Chief, an uneducated Cheyenne chief from the Seger Agency, heard in 1914 that Commissioner Sells intended to turn the Cheyennes and Arapahoes "loose to be civilized," he began "to moan aloud" and traveled to Washington to protest Sells's proposal. To Assistant Commissioner E. B. Meritt, Wolf Chief insisted that his people were not prepared to be severed from governmental supervision. "I am kind of afraid," Wolf Chief explained, "to take the white man's ways yet—I don't know how to write, I don't know how to manage my affairs the white man's way . . . when I look around amongst my tribe, my people, my school children—none of them are able to work like the white man, none of them can be doctors, none lawyers, none clerks in stores, and other work like that—they are too far behind yet." Alfrich Heap of Birds, a Carlisle graduate, told Meritt: "Some of our school boys thought they were educated enough to manage their own affairs and they received patents to their lands. As soon as the white man saw this they jumped on them and took all their land and money. Today they have nothing."[22]

Evidence abounds that few Cheyennes and Arapahoes were prepared to be declared competent under the 1906 Burke Act. During a 1916 inspection tour of the Concho Agency, Supervisor H. G. Wilson learned that none of the 173 persons who had been issued fee patents since 1906 retained any of their allotted land. Only one patentee had invested his money by purchasing other land and buying good livestock. The others had sold their allotments for less than market value and spent the money for unneeded merchandise. Wilson recommended that the Cheyenne and Arapaho land "be held in trust for them for many years to come."[23]

Ignoring information received from field personnel, Commissioner Sells in January of 1917 sent a competence board to the four Cheyenne-Arapaho agencies to prepare a list of Indians to whom fee patents should be issued. While the board members were en route to Oklahoma, a Cheyenne-Arapaho delegation made a futile appeal to Commissioner Meritt to have the board's proceedings delayed. Victor Bushyhead, a Haskell-educated Cheyenne, explained that even the younger educated people were not able to assume control of their land and money. "We young people," Bushyhead declared, "are always tempted to fall back and adopt the customs of the older people. We realize that if we were given . . . the right of conducting our own business affairs and our land turned over to us, that then all of our property and money would fall into the hands of grafters. We are not ready to prepare ourselves to compete with civilized people in a business way.'' Commissioner Sells made no concessions to the delegation, indicating only that he would recommend a ten-year extension of the trust period for those judged noncompetent. The younger people and mixed-bloods would have to take their chances with white merchants, bankers, and lawyers.[24]

On January 19, 1917, the competency boards began hearings on the ''business competency'' of the Cheyennes and Arapahoes. The board was concerned primarily with the level of education, the amount and value of trust land, the degree of Indian blood, employment, the number of dependents, marital status, and the ability of the Indians to read, write, and speak English. At the conclusion of the hearings, the board recommended that 177 Cheyennes and Arapahoes be issued fee patents. By executive order on April 4, 1917, President Wilson directed that 167 patents be issued from the list the board submitted.[25]

The allottees recommended as competent had attained at least a fourth- or fifth-grade education. A significant fraction had attended programs at nonreservation schools such as Carlisle, Haskell, Chilocco, and Hampton. Of the individuals recommended for fee patents, 26.5 percent were of mixed Indian, white, black, or Mexican ancestry, and 73.5 percent were full-blood Indians.[26]

The board's criteria of business competency were unclear. A few Indians recommended for fee patents worked as laborers or store clerks, held agency positions, or were craftsmen. A large majority of the younger people, however, pursued no vocation and lived on lease money. Among the fee patents subsequently issued, 54 percent were for full allotments, while 46 percent were issued for fractional allotments to individuals whose land had been partially patented or sold under the noncompetency provisions of the 1907 Indian Appropriation Act. Individuals on the board's fee patent list frequently retained inherited land or a portion of their original allotment, while a spouse's land often continued to be restricted. Of the 167 whose restrictions on land were removed, 76.5 percent were between the ages of twenty-one and thirty-nine. Regardless of age, 58.2 percent refused to sign applications for the removal of restrictions from their land. As the board's journal and recommendations indicate, little consideration was given to the allottee's previous record of handling his or her money and property.[27]

The fears of the Cheyenne and Arapaho chiefs and spokesmen soon became realities. Land thieves, grafters, merchants, bankers, lawyers, and realtors prepared to profit handsomely from land which the Cheyennes and Arapahoes would be free to sell. An estimated $660,000 worth of land was available for plundering. Superintendent J. W. Smith of the Seger Agency warned Commissioner Sells that many younger Indians had purchased automobiles, giving the dealers undated mortgages on their lands which could be recorded after the fee patents had been received. If the "reckless disposition" of the money affected only the young men, Smith complained, he would not protest so vigorously. But in many instances the Indians were the "father[s] of several children and most often have wives who do as much as they can to discourage such practices." W. W. Scott, superintendent at Concho and a competency board member, although displeased, was not as indignant as Smith at what was transpiring with the patented land. Scott also had learned that many Indians had "pledged" or mortgaged their allotments in anticipation of receiving a fee patent. In a matter of a few weeks after the patents had been received, Superintendent Smith claimed that all patented land had been sold. The Indians rarely acquired full value for their land and spent their money for automobiles and other purchases which soon disappeared from their possession.[29]

On April 17, 1917, Commissioner Sells announced a new Indian policy. Among all allotted tribes, any individual of one-half or more white ancestry, every Indian twenty-one years of age or older who had completed a full course of instruction in a government school, and all other Indians judged to be as competent as the "average white man" would be given "full control of his property and have all his lands and money turned over to him, after which he will no longer be a ward of the government." Sells decreed the sale of land for noncompetent Indians to increase, liberalized regulations controlling the sale of inherited land, and encouraged land sales for the the "old and feeble." He also permitted and accelerated use of tribal funds and Individual Indian Account money. The depletion of the Indian land base quickened even more when Indians who escaped the judgments of competency boards had trust restrictions removed from their property and money. Although Sells described his program as the "beginning of the end of the Inidian problem," the reverse was correct. Once the land sales closed and the money received was expended, allotted Indians and their dependents faced lives of endless poverty.[29]

Wherever allotted Indians lived, whites schemed to defraud them of their holdings. One center of white conspirators was the small community of Watonga, around which hundreds of Cheyenne and Arapaho allotments were concentrated in Blaine and adjacent counties. As early as 1908, Thompson B. Ferguson, former governor of the Territory of Oklahoma and editor and publisher of the Watonga *Republican*, warned that "sharks . . . have commenced to lay plans to beat the Indians out of their lands." At the heart of the ring of land thieves was Ed Baker, a Blaine County lawyer and judge, who was assisted by livestock dealers, merchants, bankers, county officials, four or five Cheyennes and Arapahoes, and at least one agency superintendent. Baker ingratiated himself with Cheyennes and Arapahoes by acting as their attorney for moderate fees in criminal and civil suits before local courts. He also loaned money at ten percent interest to Indians whom he believed would be granted fee patents, keeping complete records of their indebtedness to him.[30]

Baker never loaned Indians more than one-half of the value of the land for which a fee patent would be issued. When Indians first obtained money from him, the attorney secured their signatures on undated mortgages which were recorded against their land and dated at a later time. The Indian spent the borrowed money for horses and merchandise (at highly inflated prices), feasts for his friends, and trips to visit relatives in Wyoming or Montana. When the mortgage fell due and Baker demanded repayment, the Indian had run through all of the money and could not borrow more from any source. Threatening foreclosure, Baker obtained the individual's signature to a deed to the patented land for a small additional sum. Merchants who cooperated with Baker sold the Indians horses, buggies, wagons, and other goods valued higher than the amount borrowed from Baker, obtaining a promissory note for the differnce. When a note fell due and the Indian was unable to redeem it, the merchant foreclosed and seized the chattel property before a cooperative county court.[31]

From 1908 to 1917, Baker cleverly concealed his operations and avoided damaging legal actions. Only once, in 1914, was he sued successfully in a county court and forced to pay partial restitution for an illegal sale of two horses which were trust property. Prior to 1917, investigations by agency superintendents and BIA personnel dispatched from Washington failed to accumulate sufficient evidence against Baker and his fellow conspirators to present before a grand jury or a federal court. Following the 1917 hearings of the Cheyenne and Arapaho Competency Board, and Commissioner Sells's widespread issuance of fee patents, Baker's successful evasion of serious legal action emboldened him to embark upon numerous fraudulent ventures. Eventually, his activities and those of his friends became too flagrantly criminal for even Sells to ignore. Indian Inspector H. S. Traylor was sent to the Concho and Cantonment agencies to initiate another investigation of Baker. Traylor obtained sufficient evidence from R. H. Green, a wealthy white farmer, to prosecute. Baker had double-crossed Green on an arrangement to acquire a valuable fee-patented allotment. The irate farmer's testimony and the evidence Inspector Traylor gathered induced a grand jury to indict Baker for conspiracy to defraud the United States Government in its capacity as trustee of restricted Indian land and property.[32]

The grand jury indictment led to a criminal case tried in the United States District Court for the Western District of Oklahoma. Tried with Baker were Ernie Black, a forty-five-year-old, full-blooded Cheyenne educated at Carlisle, and W. W. Wisdom, a former superintendent of the Cantonment Agency. The United States attorney, using evidence compiled by Inspector Traylor and testimony of Cheyennes, Arapahoes, and BIA employees, demonstrated that Baker and Black had defrauded the federal government through purchases of scores of patented Indian allotments for grossly unfair considerations. Baker and Black on June 13, 1919, were found guilty as charged. Baker was sentenced to four months in jail and fined $1,000, while Black received a two-month jail sentence and a $250 fine. Baker appealed his conviction, but the district court's verdict was affirmed in the September, 1921, term of the United States Court of Appeals, Eighth Circuit. The judicial victory, however, did not restore one acre or one dollar to the Cheyennes and Arapahoes who had lost their land, money, and property to Baker and other looters.

In an attempt to recover the lost allotments or their monetary

value, four actions in equity were brought in 1919 before the
United States District Court. Baker and secondary purchasers—a
banker and insurance companies who had loaned money to Baker—were named defendants in the legal actions. The court returned
a judgment against Baker alone, forcing the four Indian plaintiffs to
look to the lawyer for recovery of their land or money. The
secondary purchasers, the banker (who certainly had full knowledge of Baker's operations) and the insurance companies, were
held by the court to be innocent and not liable to share in any
judgment against Baker. In 1920, Baker moved from Oklahoma to
Missouri, where in 1925 he stated that he was unable to pay the
judgments handed down against him. Inquiries into Baker's financial status confirmed that he owned no property and that all of his
family's assets, including his home, were registered in his wife's
name. Although judgments were rendered against Baker for his
crimes, the lawyer never repaid one cent of the money he had
defrauded from over one hundred Cheyennes and Arapahoes.[33]

The economic potential of the Cheyennes and Arapahoes was
severely crippled during Cato Sells's administration. A total of
181,500 acres, or 34.3 percent, of all their allotted lands was
alienated. By adding land sold during the Roosevelt and Taft
administrations, 297,214 acres, or 56.3 percent of all land allotted
to the tribes, had passed from their possession. Criticism of Sells's
policies surfaced in 1921, when the Board of Indian Commissioners concluded that the actions of the competency boards seemed to
be "a shortcut to the separation of freed Indians from their land and
cash." What happened to the Cheyennes and Arapahoes, unfortunately, also occurred at other western agencies. With less land
to sell and reduced demand during the 1920s, allotted land sales
declined sharply. Because much of the productive agricultural land
had been sold, income from leases and crops decreased at the
Cheyenne and Arapaho agencies. And since Individual Indian
Accounts were depleted even before Sells left office in 1921, the
economic future of the tribesmen was bleak.[34]

The attempt to transform the Cheyennes and Arapahoes into
self-sufficient farmers and stock raisers during the Progressive Era
had been a failure. The Dawes Act and its modifications led
directly to the destruction of a viable land base for the two tribes,
and bureaucrats wasted little sympathy on Indians when their land
and money slipped away. Horace G. Wilson, supervisor of farm-

ing, commented with remarkable callousness in early 1919 that some Cheyennes and Arapahoes were "probably better off now than they were before, as they made little or no use of their lands, and now that the land is gone and they receive no rentals, they are compelled to go to work." Land thieves such as Ed Baker, ready to defraud the Indians, profited from the blind adherence of reformers and bureaucrats to the work ethic. Misguided idealism, crippling legislation, destructive Indian policy and BIA regulations, hostile or indifferent courts, and white greed sapped the economic vitality of the Cheyenne and Arapaho peoples. That they have survived and multiplied in the twentieth century in spite of the policies of reformers and bureaucrats is a singular testament to their inner strength and a way of life based upon time-honored customs and spiritualism.[35]

# Notes

1. The origins and significance of the Dawes Act are in Loring B. Priest, *Uncle Sam's Stepchildren: The Reformation of United States Indian Policy, 1865–1887* (New Brunswick, N.J.: Rutgers University Press, 1942); Herny E. Fritz, *The Movement for Indian Assimilation, 1860–1890* (Philadelphia: University of Pennsylvania Press, 1963); and Francis Paul Prucha, *American Indian Policy in Crisis: Christian Reformers and the Indian, 1865–1900* (Norman: University of Oklahoma Press, 1975).

2. 25 *U.S. Stat.* 1004; 26 *U.S. Stat.* 81. More information on the Jerome Commission is in Roy Gittinger, *The Formation of the State of Oklahoma, 1803–1906* (Norman: University of Oklahoma Press, 1939); Arrell M. Gibson, *Oklahoma: A History of Five Centuries* (Oklahoma City: Harlow Publishing Corp., 1965); and Prucha, *American Indian Policy*, pp. 389–90. The Dawes Act was applied to Indian tribes with injudicious rapidity. The Iowas, Sacs and Foxes, Potawatomis, and Shawnees came to terms with the Jerome Commission in June, 1890, but the Kickapoos adamantly rejected all offers for a land cession. Finally Kickapoo lands were allotted and ceded under a fraudulent agreement which Congress ratified in 1893. William T. Hagan, *The Sac and Fox Indians* (Norman: University of Oklahoma Press, 1958), pp. 256–58, 268–76; Arrell M. Gibson, *The Kickapoos: Lords of the Middle Border* (Norman: University of Oklahoma Press, 1963), pp. 292–304.

3. Donald J. Berthrong, *The Cheyenne and Arapaho Ordeal: Reservation and Agency Life in the Indian Territory, 1875–1907*, (Norman: University of Oklahoma Press, 1976), pp. 148–65, 169–75, 364n.; 26 *U.S. Stat.* 1022.

4. Members of the Lake Mohonk Conference and the Indian Rights Association protested that the 1894 leasing act made protection of Indian allotments difficult. Their objections led Congress in 1897 to delete the word "inability" from leasing criteria, so that "age or other disability" were again the only legal grounds for leasing allotments. In 1900, however, Congess restored "inability" as one of the leasing criteria. 26 *U.S. Stat.* 795; 28 *U.S. Stat.* 305; 30 *U.S. Stat.* 85; 31 *U.S. Stat.* 229; D. S. Otis. *The Dawes Act and the Allotment of Indian Lands*, ed. by Francis P. Prucha (Norman: University of Oklahoma Press, 1973), pp. 111–14. 139, 149; Prucha, *American Indian Policy*, pp. 261–62.

5. *Annual Report of the Commissioner of Indian Affairs, 1900* (Washington, D.C.: U.S. Government Printing Office, 1900), 326; Berthrong, *Cheyenne and Arapaho Ordeal*, pp. 203–204; 256; Prucha, *American Indian Policy*, pp. 261–62; Otis, *Dawes Act*, pp. 139, 149.

6. *Annual Report of the Commissioner of Indian Affairs*, 326; Otis, *Dawes Act*, pp. 121–22.

7. *Watonga* (Oklahoma) *Republican*, March 6, 1902.

8. Minor heirs could sell their inherited land only athrough court-appointed guardians, and all conveyances were subject to the approval of the secretary of the Interior. Lands held as homesteads were exempted from trhe provisions of the statute during the lifetime of the "father, mother or minority of any child or children." 32 *U.S. Stat.* 245, 275; *Annual Report of the Commissioner of Indian Affairs, 1902*, pp. 64–66. Congress in 1910 gave the secretary of the interior the authority to determine the heirs of deceased allottess. 36 *U.S. Stat.* 855; Depart-

ment of the Interior, *Federal Indian Law* (Washington, D.C.: U.S. Government Printing Office, 1958), 814–15, & n.

9. *U.S. Stat.* 982, 1009. J. H. Seger to Commissioner of Indian Affairs, August 31, 1903; Affidavits of C. H. Lamb, Homer K. Dodder, and Charles H. Goodwin, January 2, 1908, Classified File (hereafter CF) 71315–1907–312, Seger Agency, Records of the Bureau of Indian Affairs (hereafter RBIA), Record Group 75, National Archives. Red Plume's allotment had been inherited by Night Killer, her granddaughter. The act also provided for the sale of Yankton, Potawatomi, Kiowa, Comanche, and Apache allotments.

10. Berthrong, *Cheyenne and Arapaho Ordeal*, pp. 300–302. Senator John C. Spooner, a conservative Wisconsin Republican, understood the consequences of removing restrictions from Indian land. In 1905 he predicted that unless Indians were protected "the white man will have the money, and the Indian will have the experience." *Cong. Rec.*, 58th Cong., 1st sess., pt. 4, p. 3518.

11. The Burke Act (1906) did not alter the citizenship status of those Indians previously allotted under the Dawes Act, but it did exempt all Indians living in Indian Territory from its provisions. 34 *U.S. Stat.* 182–83.

12. 34 *U.S. Stat.* 1015, 1018.

13. John F. Berens, "Old Campaigners, New Realities: Indian Policy Reform in the Progressive Era, 1900–1912," *Mid-America* 59 (January, 1977); 53, 58, 61.

14. Cloud Chief, Little Bear, and Big Wolf to C. E. Shell, April 12, 1908, CF 25811-1908-306, Cheyenne-Arapaho Agency; Wolf Robe, Circle Left Hand, and Sage to Commissioner of Indian Affairs, May 28, 1909; and Transcript of Statements by Cheyenne and Arapaho Delegations, Washington, D.C., May 28, 1909, CF 15976–1909-056, Cantonment Agency, RBIA.

15. Transcript of Statements, May 23, 1909, CF 15976-1909-056, Cantonment Agency, RBIA.

16. Report of Edgar A. Allen, November 12, 1909, CF 91477.2-1909-312, Cheyenne and Arapaho Agency, RBIA.

17. Shell to Commissioner of Indian Affairs, December 4, 1909, CF 98020-1909-312, Cheyenne-Arapaho Agency, RBIA.

18. R. G. Valentine to W. B. Freer, January 11, 1910, CF 98020-1909-312, Cheyenne-Arapaho Agency, RBIA.

19. *Annual Report of the Department of the Interior, 1911* (Washington, D.C.: U.S. Government Printing Office, 1911), pt. 1, pp. 20–21, 24–26.

20. Valentine to W. G. West, July 12, 1912, CF 288.1-1912-150, Cantonment Agency, RBIA.

21. West to Valentine, August 22, 1912, CF 288.1-1912-150, Cantonment Agency, RBIA.

22. Conference of Cheyenne and Arapaho Delegates with E. B. Meritt, n.d., CF 20733-1914-056, Seger Agency, RBIA.

23. In 1913 the old Darlington Agency had been replaced by new facilities at Concho, Oklahoma. Report of H. B. Wilson, n.d., CF 13101.8-1916-300, Cheyenne-Arapaho Agency, RBIA.

24. Transcript of Hearings with Short Man; Bird Chief, Sr.; Bird Chief, Jr.; Cut Finger; Hail Grant Lefthand; and Jessie Bent before E. B. Meritt, January 17, 1917, CF 5805-1917-056, Cheyenne-Arapaho Agency, RBIA; Transcript of Hearings with Magpie, Howling Water, Hicks, Three Fingers, Victor Bushyhead, Alfred [Alfrich] Heap of Birds, Cleaver Warden, Alex Yellowman, Bull Tongue, Deforest Antelope, Little Man, Tobacco, and Ernie Black before E. B. Meritt, January 22, 1917; Cato Sells to Magpie et al., January 27, 1917, CF 7692-1917-056, Cheyenne-Arapaho Agency, RBIA.

25. The board consisted of O. M. McPherson, Special Indian Agent; C. R. Trowbridge, Supervisor of Indian Education; and W. W. Scott, Superintendent of the Cheyenne-Arapaho Agency at Concho. The full board reviewed cases at the Concho and Cantonment agencies, but only McPherson and Scott reviewed cases at the Seger and Red Moon agencies.

26. The mixed-blood group included 3 percent of people of Indian, black, and Mexican descent.

27. A survey of fee patents of other age groups indicated: 17.4 percent were between the ages of forty and forty-nine; 6 percent were fifty or more years of age; and one person was less than twenty-one years old. Record of Proceedings of the Cheyenne and Arapaho Competency Board, O. M. McPherson, C. R. Trowbridge, W. W. Scott, January-February, 1917, CF 39488-1917-465, Cheyenne-Arapaho Agency, RBIA; McPherson to Franklin K. Lane, February 24, 1917, Cheyenne and Arapaho Competency File, Indian Archives, Oklahoma Historical Society (hereafter OHS), Oklahoma City. The extension of the trust period is in Executive Order 2580, April 4, 1917, Presidential Executive Orders.

28. J. W. Smith to Commissioner of Indian Affairs, April 25, 1917, CF 46287-1917-314, Seger Agency; Scott to Commissioner of Indian Affairs, June 20, 1917, CF 61165-1917-312, Cheyenne-Arapaho Agency; Typescript Annual Report, 1917, Narrative Section, 15, CF, Seger Agency, RBIA.

29. *Annual Report of the Department of the Interior, 1917*, 2: 3–4.

30. *Watonga Republican*, August 20, 1908.

31. Shell to Commissioner of Indian Affairs, December 19, 22, 1908, Cheyenne and Arapaho Letterbooks, Indian Archives, OHS.

32. Rodolphe Petter to W. W. McConihe, February 2, 1911, CF 15327-1911-154; and McConihe to Commissioners of Indian Affairs, March 27, 1911 (2 letters), CF 30629-1911-253 and CF 30600-1911-310; H. M. Creel to Commissioner of Indian Affairs, October 13, 1911, with subsequent correspondence and documents, CF 55978-1913-175, all in Cantonment Agency; Freer to Commissioner of Indian Affairs, May 10, 1910; CF 91351-1910-312; H. S. Traylor to Commissioner of Indian Affairs, May 15, 1915, CF [no file no.]1915-150; R. E. L. Daniel to Commissioner of Indian Affairs, July 11, 1917, with subsequent correspondence and documents, CF 67681-1917-126; R. E. L. Daniel to Commissioner of Indian Affairs, October 31, 1917, with other correspondence and doocuments concerning Traylor's 1917 investigation, CF [no file no.]-1917-150; all in Cheyenne-Arapaho Agency, RBIA. The Cheyenne and Arapaho Ernie Black and Ed Baker File, Indian Archives, OHS, contains important correspondence about Baker's activities and the court action taken against him.

33. Daniel to Commissioner of Indian Affairs, February 25, 1918, and July 15, 1919; John A. Fain to Daniel, July 2, 1919; Duke Stallings to Daniel, July 9, 1919; C. H. Burke to Secretary of the Interior, November 8, 1922; Frank Ransdell to U.S. Attorney General, September 6, 12, 1919; F. M. Goodwin to U.S. Attorney General, November 11, 1922; Ed Baker to Dr. Samuel Blair, December 8, 1925; Burke to L. S. Bonnin, January 15, 1926, all in Black and Baker File, OHS.

34. By 1921 probably only 68,510 acres of fee-patent land had been sold. Between 1921 and 1928 another 34,345 acres (6.5 percent of the land) were sold. A clearer picture of tribal land alienation emerges in 1928, when 62.8 percent of all Cheyenne and Arapaho land had been sold. A breakdown of the 332,599.02 acres alienated by June 30, 1928, reveals: 200,037.2 acres (37.8 percent) has been sold as inherited land; 71,827.63 acres (13.6 percent) had been released as fee-patented land; and 60,694.19 (11.5 percent) had been sold as noncompetent Indian trust land. By 1951 the Cheyennes and Arapahoes retained 174,667 acres (33 percent) of the 529,688.05 acres allotted to the tribesmen in 1892. The acreage alienated

between 1902 and 1921 is from statistics in the published reports of the Com-
missioner of Indian Affairs and from typescript annual reports of the Cheyenne and
Arapaho agencies in RBIA. The 1928 statistics are in H. D. Milburn to Bonnin,
June 30, 1928, appended to the 1928 Annual Report, Cheyenne and Arapaho
Agency, CF, RBIA. The 1951 figures are in Dover P. Trent, "Western Oklahoma
Indians in Agriculture," January [12], 1951, Box 379,307, Anadarko Area Office
Files, Fort Worth Federal Records Center. Trent also indicates that in 1951 allotted
land retained by Indian tribes within the jurisdiction of the Shawnee and Anadarko
(Oklahoma) Area offices varied from 69 percent by the Kiowas, Comanches, and
Apaches to 2.8 percent by the Potawatomis. Angie Debo, *A History of the Indians
of the United States* (Norman: University of Oklahoma Press, 1970), pp. 266,
283–85, discusses the general impact of Sells's administration policies upon
Western Indians.

35. Title to allotted trust land, as provided by the Dawes Act, was increasingly
held by multiple heirs, none of whom could profitably farm a share of an allotment.
In 1951, Woodrow Wilson, a full-blooded Cheyenne and chairman of the Cheyenne and Arapaho Business Committee, pointed out that some trust land was
shared by as many as 150 heirs. Wilson also stated that out of a population of 3,102
there were 2,000 completely landless, and that less than "a dozen of the fee
patented allotments now remain in Indian ownership." Typescript of Woodrow
Wilson Statement before House Sub-Committee on Indian Affairs, July 16, 1951,
Box 379,307, Anadarko Area Office Files, Fort Worth Federal Records Center.
Report of Horace G. Wilson, Supervisor of Farming, January 27, 1919, CF
8566-1919-300, Cheyenne-Arapaho Agency, RBIA.

CHAPTER 3

# From Prison to Homeland:
# The Cheyenne River Indian Reservation
# Before World War I

## BY FREDERICK E. HOXIE

*Donald Berthrong's concluding statement for chapter 2, about the
enduring nature of Cheyenne life in Oklahoma, serves also as a
transition to the following selection. In this piece by Frederick Hoxie
we move from the early-twentieth-century southern Plains to the
northern Plains in the same era. The issues confronted by the Sioux
people of the Cheyenne River Reservation in South Dakota, however,
remain essentially the same as those of the Cheyennes and Arapahoes
in Oklahoma.*

*The reservations in South Dakota were perceived as temporary
phenomena by most white Americans of the age. The Sioux began
their transition to life on the reservation with, at best, reluctance. The
Sioux agreement of 1889 and the tragedy of Wounded Knee at the end
of the following year appeared to be harbingers of decay and decline.
The white population in South Dakota, like that in Oklahoma, continued to grow with remarkable speed, and land speculators, politicians,
ranchers, and farmers clamored for the opening of reservations.*

*Even if the Sioux did not succeed in keeping all of their land within
the state, they kept a sizable portion of it. Clearly the situation within
South Dakota was not identical to that within Oklahoma; at least the
results proved different. Frederick Hoxie's article attempts to de-
lineate some of the reasons for the relative success of the Sioux on one
reservation not only in preserving some of their land base but also in
taking steps to adapt within the reservation to the different world in
which they found themselves.*

From *South Dakota History* (Winter, 1979): 1–24. Reprinted by permission.

55

*If we accept Hoxie's argument, we are forced to alter our perception of what reservations meant to Plains Indian peoples at that time, let alone what the reservations potentially could mean in the future. In addition Hoxie encourages us not to think about the first years of the twentieth century as merely a time when Indian people bore the brunt of assimilative forces.*

*The early twentieth century is a period that until recently attracted minimal attention by historians of American Indian life. The more the era is studied the more complicated it appears, and the image of unrelieved gloom that we are tempted to accept unquestioningly begins to shatter. If we give Plains Indians of another age the credit they deserve for their adaptability and their stubbornness, then we may begin to recognize this period as one in which Indians not only staved off disaster but started to build a foundation for their lives in the United States as we now know it. Without their struggle, so often ignored, James Fraser's statue* The End of the Trail *might have accurately foretold the Indian future.*

*Obviously there are variations from one Indian community to another, but the essential thrust of Hoxie's article is one of Indian continuity and flexibility under the most difficult circumstances: part of a continuum that has characterized postfrontier Plains Indian life.*

THERE should be no doubt that the Great Sioux Agreement of 1889 was designed to destroy what remained of the Teton bands' traditional way of life. The eastern reformers who drew up the agreement and the politicians who approved it were committed to replacing the old ways with new ones. Hunting, living in bands, accepting the rule of elders, following the wisdom of religious leaders, and traveling in an annual cycle across a large territory—these were all targets of the new law. Senator Henry L. Dawes, the author of the 1887 general allotment act that bore his name and the principal architect of the 1889 agreement, believed there was no alternative. As he wrote, ''We may cry out against the violation of treaties, denounce flagrant disregard of inalienable rights and the inhumanity of our treatment of the defenseless . . . but the fact remains. . . . Without doubt these Indians are to be somehow absorbed into and become a part of the 50,000,000 of our people.

There does not seem to be any other way to deal with them."[1] By
1889, Dawes was convinced of his own wisdom. South Dakota had
become a state. New rail lines were snaking across the plains, and
thousands of settlers—some of them freshly arrived from Europe—were traveling west to share in America's last great land
boom.[2]

Dawes promised that the new land would satisfy white land
hunger while it started the Sioux on the road to total assimilation.
The agreement provided that (1) the tribes would cede 11 million
acres west of the Missouri River to the United States; (2) five
reservations would be established on the remaining lands (Standing Rock, Cheyenne River, Lower Brule, Rosebud, and Pine
Ridge); (3) the government would create a fund to provide individuals with farming equipment, supplies, and schools; and (4)
each reservation eventually would be allotted among the people
who lived there.[3]

Secretary of the Interior John Noble welcomed these steps. He
wrote that "the breaking up of this great nation of Indians into
smaller parts and segregating . . . separate reservations for each of
said parts marks a long step toward the disintegration of their tribal
life and will help them forward to . . . civilized habits."[4] Like
Dawes, the secretary believed that the pace of white settlement in
South Dakota made it possible for the Teton bands to maintain their
old ways. The 1889 law would force the tribes into the modern
world.

Not surprisingly, tribal leaders among the Sioux agreed with
Senator Dawes and the secretary. Still angry over the theft of the
Black Hills and the government's refusal to live up to the 1868 Fort
Laramie Treaty, tribal headmen wanted no part of additional land
cessions. To them it was obvious that further reductions in the size
of their nation would mean the arrival of still more whites, along
with increased pressure from missionaries and educators, and more
demands that they turn to farming.

The 1868 treaty had stipulated that three-fourths of the adult
male members of the tribes must approve all future land sales.
Seven years and four different congressional delegations were
required before the tribes approved this new agreement. While
several leaders won significant concessions during these negotiations, the 1889 agreement was a major defeat for the tribes.[5] Its
ratification was met with anger and depression. It is probably no

accident that the announcement of the 1889 agreement and the fighting at Wounded Knee occurred within a year of each other.

But the events of 1889 and 1890 did not mark the last days of the Sioux Nation. Surprisingly, Lakota culture survived the programs designed to kill it. The 1889 agreement failed to destroy all the old ways. It failed to turn red men into white men. It failed to achieve the complete "disintegration" of tribal life. And the supreme irony: the reservations forced on the tribes did not become vehicles for "civilizing" and assimilating them; instead they became cultural homelands, places where a native identity could be maintained and passed on to new generations. Rather than graveyards for culture the reservations created in 1889 eventually became centers for awareness and even for hope. To describe this paradox is to beg the question—why? How did the prisons of the nineteenth century become the cultural homelands of the twentieth?

When Cheyenne River Indian Reservation was established in 1889, it contained four distinct Lakota bands whose ways of life had not changed fundamentally for generations. Prior to 1889, the native people living near the Cheyenne River had been confined to the area around old Fort Bennett and urged to farm and adopt Christianity. But despite these restrictions and demands, there was little direct pressure on the Indians to break up their camps and leave the protected river bottoms where they had made their winter homes.[6]

The bands had little contact with one another. Minneconjous lived on Cherry Creek in what would become the western end of the reservation. Sans Arc communities could be found along the Moreau River at places such as White Horse and On the Trees, running near what would become the northern border of the preserve. The Blackfeet and Two Kettle bands hugged the Missouri, spreading out between Fort Bennett and the Moreau. Most of these camps had a headman and some sort of government day school that operated sporadically during the year. Of course, allotment had not yet begun.[7]

While game was growing scarce and the government's rations were not always reliable, farming and stock raising had not yet become essential to the people's livelihood. Five district farmers visited the various communities, but as the superintendent reported in 1890, "they usually [had] very little to show for their work."[8] People at the Cheyenne River Agency survived on a combination of rations, money from odd maintenance and freighting jobs, and whatever they could hunt or gather on the prairie.

The 1889 agreement undermined this peaceful routine. The government stepped up its efforts at the agency and broadened the scope of its activities. As Senator Dawes had promised, the campaign to "absorb" the Sioux into American society began in earnest. First, the Cheyenne River Agency was moved from Fort Bennett—which lay outside the new reservation—to Charger's Camp on the Missouri River. While the Minneconjous living on Cherry Creek were farther than ever from the superintendent's office, the Blackfeet and Two Kettle bands on the Missouri and the Sans Arcs on the Moreau were now close at hand. Second, a large boarding school was built next to the new agency. By 1904, this school had space for 130 students. In addition, up to 200 children began to be sent to BIA schools in Pierre and Rapid City and to the mission school at Oahe. These institutions, coupled with the day schools at Cherry Creek, Thunder Butte, Green Grass, On the Trees, and White Horse, could accommodate all of the approximately 650 school-age children on the reservation. Consequently, the agency could now step up its campaign to force all young people to attend school. By the early 1900s, it was almost impossible for a family to avoid sending its children away for an education, the principal goal of which was to separate the children from their traditions and their past.[9]

School attendance also increased in response to the expansion of the Indian police and the Courts of Indian Offenses. In 1890, when the reservation was being organized for the first time, the superintendent at Cheyenne River noted that "many of the best Indians will not serve" on the police force. Whether this was because of the low pay offered them (as the superintendent thought) or because of the controversy surrounding the arrest and killing of Sitting Bull at nearby Standing Rock is unclear. What is certain, however, is that within ten years the Indian police were active in every part of the reservation. In 1896, policemen began to be selected from the districts, and police stations were erected at Cherry Creek and White Horse. The tribal courts, with judges selected from the four bands, met regularly and passed judgments on all but the five major crimes.[10]

A third feature of the government's activism on the new reservation was the practice of stationing farmers in each district. During the 1890s, subagencies were constructed at Cherry Creek and White Horse. Thunder Butte was added in 1909. These installations were permanent homes for the farmers who supervised individual family gardens and monitored the cattlemen who leased tribal pastureland. Through the efforts of these men, the area being cultivated at Cheyenne River began to grow. In 1895, only 700 acres had been planted in crops. Two years later that figure had nearly doubled, and by 1907 the superintendent reported that "at no time has there been so much farming . . . at this reservation." The gains in stock raising were equally impressive. In 1890, 500,000 pounds of Indian cattle were sold to the agency for rations. In 1899, *that* figure had doubled.[11]

The year 1900 marked the beginning of allotment at Cheyenne River. Crews of surveyors worked methodically across the entire preserve. By 1909, they had made more than twenty-one hundred homestead assignments.[12] This process not only pushed families out onto their own land but it brought home to each member of the reservation the fact that a new era had begun and that the government was determined to change their old way of life. The new reservation environment demanded that the Indians respond or perish.

Changes in Indian ways of life were apparent almost from the beginning of the government's assimilation drive. One of the most obvious of these was the dispersal of the population across the reserve. Rather than camping in concentrated areas and keeping to the place where their band had originally settled, young people began moving out on their own. For example, a man born near Fort Bennett in 1885 remembers today that "they allotted land to us and wherever our land was, was our homestead."[13] As a result, he moved to faraway Iron Lightning and began farming his allotment. Men like him thus opened up new areas of the reservation. In addition to Iron Lightning, Thunder Butte in the extreme northwest and Red Scaffold in the southwest were both settled during these years. People lived near their land and began to think of themselves as part of something new—the Cheyenne River Sioux Tribe. As the superintendent reported in 1897, "the Indians of this reservation, while composed of what were formerly known as the Blackfeet, Sans Arc, Minneconjou and Two Kettle bands of Sioux, are now regarded as one people, without any distinction as to band."[14] While the superintendent was overstating things—band designations are important even today—his perception was accurate. People on the reservation were now being defined as a single tribe. It was logical that they would begin defining themselves in the same way.

The second area of change involved the organization of reservation life. The Indian police and courts functioned as a unified whole and helped foster the idea of a reservation unit. Whether they were admired or hated, the policemen affected everybody, and they made it clear that Cheyenne River was a single place.

Another feature of this new tendency to organize the four bands into a single structure was the creation in 1903 of a twelve-man tribal business council. Prior to 1903, two kinds of councils had operated. The first was a general council open to all adult males assigned to the agency. This was the group that had been assembled to approve the 1889 agreement. The second council was an executive body made up of principal headmen. The new business council changed the old pattern in significant ways. First, members of the business council were elected from different parts of the reservation. Four men were chosen from each of the districts: White Horse, Cherry Creek, and the Agency District (Thunder Butte was added in 1909). And second, each councilman was elected by a local council, meeting at the subagency. These district councils also had to ratify all decisions involving money or the leasing of tribal property. While elders and traditional band leaders could still be chosen, this new system allowed younger people to rise to positions of influence. Nineteen hundred and three marked an important step in the gradual shift of leadership away from band leaders and toward people chosen for their ability to represent their  constituents in a unified tribal government.[15]

As the reservation neared its twentieth anniversary, in 1908, the people of Cheyenne River were surviving in their new environment. They were farming and raising cattle, relying less and less on government rations. Their children were attending school. Many of them were living in new settlements, and all of them were gaining a fresh image of themselves. They were a part of the Cheyenne River Tribe. While the members of this new tribe were themselves responsible for the changes that were taking place, it was clear that the government's programs had started the process.

But did the presence of these new institutions and new ways of life signify rapid assimilation? Does the fact that the tribes' adaptation began with the creation of the reservation mean that the Cheyenne River people were straying from their traditions and giving in to the white man? How did they respond to the erection of schools, the spread of allotment, and the rising power of the tribal police? Were the councilmen, the farmers, and the policemen all people who had been absorbed into the modern world? The behavior of the tribe during the remainder of the period before World War I reveals that answers to these questions should not be taken for granted. While first accepting a number of changes in their tribal organization and way of life, the people of Cheyenne River soon demonstrated that there were limits to their flexibility. They intended to remain a tribal people.

For the non-Indians of South Dakota, the twenty years following the passage of the Great Sioux Agreement brought unprecedented growth. White population in the state rose by over 60 percent. New branch lines linked small towns to major railroads, putting cattlemen and farmers within easy reach of eastern markets. South Dakota's boosters imagined that soon the state would finally live up to its publicity. This feeling intensified as the region emerged from the depression of the 1890s, and wheat and beef prices began to climb to new heights. After bottoming out at fifty cents in 1895, wheat rose to almost a dollar a bushel in 1908.[16]

Good times and the prospect of future prosperity brought new demands that the Teton reservations be reduced in size. Rosebud was the first to feel this pressure. In 1901, the tribe agreed to sell a large portion of its reservation to the government. The territory was not opened immediately, however, because a dispute arose in Congress over whether or not the government should pay for it. Some legislators argued for ratification of the agreement (and payment of the amount promised) while others suggested that they simply seize what they needed for settlement. The two groups were deadlocked until 1903, when the Supreme Court decided *Lone Wolf* v. *Hitchcock* and specifically authorized the national legislature to exercise its "plenary authority" in the disposition of all Indian lands.[17] There was now no legal reason for Congress to pay the Rosebud tribe the money it had been promised. Armed with this invitation, the advocates of seizure won out, and a large portion of the Rosebud preserve was soon open to white settlement.[18]

With Rosebud behind them, it did not take long for South Dakota's merchants and farm speculators to turn their attention to

Cheyenne River. Opening the reservation to settlement would —in the words of one Pierre newspaper—be "the impetus of the development of Central South Dakota." "It means," the editorial continued, "the building of a great city right at Pierre."[19] On December 9, 1907, Senator Robert Gamble (whose South Dakota backers called him "the empire builder") introduced a bill to take a portion of the Cheyenne River reserve for homesteading. At the same time, Philo Hall, the state's lone Congressmen, introduced a second bill that proposed to open *all* of the reservation's unallotted land.[20] Both bills were forwarded to the secretary of the interior for his comments. Within a few days, the secretary had instructed James McLaughlin, a thirty-five-year veteran of the Indian Service, to go to South Dakota and convince the residents of Cheyenne River to approve the idea.[21]

But people on the reservation did not wait for McLaughlin before they let their feelings be known. Lest than a month after the two bills were introduced, the tribe's general council met and spoke out against them. The group also appealed to the Indian Rights Association (IRA) for help. Writing on behalf of the general council, James Crow Feather noted that "we . . . consider ourselves incapable of plunging into the whirl of citizenship."[22] The business council sent a second letter to the IRA that listed four reasons for opposing Gamble's and Hall's bills:

1. Our consent was never asked.
2. In our reservation we think the lands are rich in mineral deposits. We want these lands to be examined before opening for settlement.
3. The bill is not satisfactory to us.
4. What former treaties promise is not fully carried into effect yet.[23]

After approving the texts of these two letters, the tribe's leaders decided to choose one delegate from each district to visit Washington. They selected Allen Fielder (Agency District), Percy Phillips (White Horse), and Ed Swan (Cherry Creek).

While willing to accept the government's schools and farming campaigns, the council rejected further land cessions out of hand. When Inspector McLaughlin arrived at Cheyenne Agency on March 16, 1908, he found James Crow Feather, the chairman of the business council, there to meet him. Bad weather kept most people from attending the conference with McLaughlin, but the inspector (with his BIA orders in his pocket) presented his case anyway. Crow Feather, speaking for the council, reponded sharp-

ly, "There are many more of us people than are here today, . . . and
we have a way of doing business in matter of this kind. . . . It is our
business council. . . . This matter is of interest to the whole tribe. I
am chairman of the business council and we have rules regarding
this matter, and I would like to carry them out. . . . I would like to
have all the people together when we do business regarding
land."[24]

McLaughlin ignored Crow Feather. He told the group that "Congress has the right to open the Indian reservations by legislative
enactment without obtaining the consent of the Indians" and that
they would be better off if they agreed to the change.[25] After
two days of fruitless speechmaking, the inspector returned to
Washington.

McLaughlin's prediction that Congress would act on its own
quickly came true. Less than two weeks after he left South Dakota,
the Senate Indian Affairs Committee endorsed a bill to open nearly
half the reservation to white homesteaders. Again, James Crow
Feather protested. In a letter to the commissioner of Indian affairs,
he minced no words: "I do not like this way of doing business,
because it is not according to the rules of the Indian Office, both
here and in Washington. Mr. McLaughlin made a story of my
people that did not represent them correctly. . . . As the bill now is
it [is] against our will. This is not honest."[26]

The tribal business council immediately dispatched the delegation they had selected in January. These men argued their case at
the Indian Office, offering to open a small portion of the reserve but
demanding the retention of mineral rights on whatever lands were
taken. Unfortunately their efforts were in vain. They arrived in
Washington during the first week of April. On April 15, the
homestead bill passed the full Senate; five days later, it was
approved by the House Indian Affairs Committee. At that point, its
ultimate passage was a foregone conclusion. President Roosevelt
signed the bill on May 29, 1908.[27]

Despite their defeat, the tribal leadership continued to protest the
new law. At its next meeting, the general council adopted a
resolution declaring that "the members of this reservation have
been treated unjustly in the opening of a portion of this
reservation."[28] A year later, the superintendent reported that "the
people of this reservation cannot become reconciled to the idea that
they did not have a proper voice in the recent ceding of the lands of

this reservation to the United States.''[29] The tribe had lost a battle, but it was gaining valuable experience in dealing with assaults on its territory. Tribal spokesmen had met the government's agents with effective arguments. Delegates representing the three districts on the reservation had presented their case in Washington. The business council had responded quickly to the crisis and presented a unified position to opponents. If the tribe had more time to organize when the next attempt was made to push a homestead bill through Congress, perhaps then their protests would be heard.

The people at Cheyenne River did not have long to wait for a new attack. In 1909, within a few months of the arrival of the first homesteaders on the freshly opened lands, South Dakota's merchants and politicians began lobbying to open still more territory to white settlement. This time they wanted all the remaining tribal lands. Their goal was nothing less than the "final absorption" that ✳ 1909 Senator Dawes had predicted. South Dakota's Senator Robert Gamble introduced his bill to authorize the sale of all unallotted land on the Cheyenne River Reservation in December. The politicians' argument was by now familiar: "It is a matter of the utmost importance to the development of the state."[30] While no one in Washington immediately opposed the idea, it was soon apparent that the new bill would not be rushed through as quickly as the first one had been. Homesteads opened by the 1908 law were only beginning to be settled, and it was obvious that they would go slowly. By the end of 1911—two years after the first filing—only a quarter of the available land had been claimed.[31] Neither Congress nor the Indian Office felt any overriding need to go along with Gamble and his backers.

This time the tribe would have more time. The general council began its resistance by passing a unanimous resolution opposing the measure and authorizing a delegation of eight to go to Washington. Before this group left, Inspector McLaughlin reappeared but got nowhere. Only thirty-six people showed up for the "council" he summoned.[32] With Congress eager to adjourn for the 1910 elections and the tribe unified in its opposition, it seemed clear that the bill would not come up for a vote. Gamble decided to put off the battle until 1911.

When the legislators reassembled in the fall of 1911, the senator was ready with a new version of his bill. Once again resolutions were passed at Cheyenne River condemning the idea, and once again Major McLaughlin appeared to argue his case. But the tribe refused to continue this now familiar charade. Percy Phillips, who had represented the White Horse district in trips to Washington in 1908 and 1910, was the first to speak when the representative from Washington arrived. "A delegation went to Washington concerning the same bill a year ago last winter," he exclaimed. "We went down there and we . . . would not have anything to do with the bill."[33] Why, he asked, should the tribe discuss it again? Others spoke up. Charles La Plant, who was aware that the meeting was being recorded, protested that from McLaughlin's speech someone reading the transcript might get the impression that an official council was taking place. He reminded the inspector that "this is not what we call a general council."[34] John Last Man was the most eloquent. Turning to McLaughlin, he said, "This bill has been before Congress for the last four years and you come every time to present it to us. . . . It seems like this bill called for the rest of our reservation being sold and the money to be used for the benefit of the whites. . . . [With the bill] this reservation is opened up and gone and used to the benefit of the white men and for them until the Indians die of starvation."[35]

Finally, after listening to the inspector's familiar arguments, Chairman James Crow Feather announced that the business council had decided that "a delegation should be sent to the Indian Office . . . to discuss this matter with them face to face. . . . We are all well acquainted with you," he told McLaughlin, "and . . . we have come to the conclusion of sending a delegation to the Indian Office and that is our answer to this bill."[36] Immediately after Crow Feather spoke, the meeting was adjourned. The next day, November 23, 1911, McLaughlin left the reservation. Three weeks later a new delegation was appointed by the tribe's general council. It consisted of representatives from each of the reservation districts. What is more, the tribe enlisted the support of the Cheyenne River superintendent and the head of the local boarding school. Both men wrote to Washington opposing the new bill, the school principal arguing that its passage would "be disastrous to these Indians."[37]

In early April, the tribal delegation arrived at the Indian Office to make its case in person. It consisted of Ed Swan from Cherry Creek (who was making his third trip to the capital); Oliver Black Eagle from Thunder Butte; Bazille Claymore from the Agency District;

Straight Head, probably from White Horse; and Charles Jewett. The group not only opposed Gamble's bill but also presented six counterproposals to the commissioner. These ranged from a suggestion that he join them in fighting against further homesteading bills, through requests that full payment be made for lands already opened, to demands that the Indian Office improve health care, education, and administration on the reservation.[38]

Whether they realized it or not, the delegation's elaborate statement succeeded in so confusing the situation that passage of Gamble's bill was now almost impossible. The BIA would have to study their counterproposals and review the current management of the reservation before the commissioner could recommend that Congress pass the measure. And with so little pressure from potential settlers, Congress would not pass the bill unless the BIA approved it. The slow pace of the BIA bureaucracy now became an asset to the tribe. By the time an opinion could be offered, Congress was eager to adjourn and the proposal was buried. In the years to come, more attempts would be made to pass this bill, and while a similar effort was successful at Standing Rock in 1913, it never succeeded at Cheyenne River.

There is no written record of the tribe's reaction to its victory over Senator Gamble and South Dakota's boosters. In fact, because the bill was simply delayed and not voted down, reservation leaders might not have realized that they had won. For many, it must have taken a winter without a visit from Major McLaughlin to convince them of their success. Less obscure were the dramatic changes that had occurred during the last generation in the tribe's style and system of leadership. Leaders were now chosen by districts and picked—at least in part—for their ability to deal with the business and political details that confronted them. In this respect, it is significant that the 1910 and 1912 delegations to Washington both included men like Ed Swan and Percy Phillips, who had been to the capital before. Experience and familiarity with "white ways" had become another qualification for leadership. The business council, with four representatives from each district, had become an effective and flexible body. It could respond quickly to crises and speak credibly for the entire tribe.

Few would claim that the 1908 law that opened nearly half the Cheyenne River Reservation to white settlement was a blessing to the tribe, or that the struggle to retain their remaining unallotted lands was beneficial. But what should be recognized in these events is the way they sparked people on the reservation to organize themselves to respond. The conflict heightened their commitment to the reservation and forced them to produce effective leaders. Senator Gamble's campaign to abolish the Cheyenne River preserve had a unifying and strengthening impact on the people who lived there. Equally significant, resistance to the Gamble bills was led by the business council—an institution created by white men. The white men had created it, but the tribe was now operating it.

Disputes over homesteading were not the only source of conflict between the tribe and the outside world during this period just prior to World War I. Law and order, education, and agriculture were also areas in which the hostility of outsiders allowed (and sometimes forced) the people at Cheyenne River to develop and maintain their own way of life. The final disposition of these issues was also a measure of the tribe's adaptation to their reservation environment.

Prior to the arrival of white homesteaders, the Indian police and the tribal courts had exclusive responsibility for law and order on the reservation. Policemen patrolled the entire preserve, keeping intruders and unauthorized cattle out and enforcing the superintendent's orders in Indian communities. The court met monthly in each of the four districts and heard cases involving violations of regulations (drunkenness, adultery) and disputes between individuals (conflicting claims to property, settlement of estates, and so forth). Once the homesteaders began arriving in 1909 and 1910, many people believed that the tribe would come under the jurisdiction of the new counties that would be organized on the opened lands. Some even expected the reservation institutions to disappear. The *Pierre Daily Capital-Journal* promised that with the new law "another district is unfolding to civilization. . . . No doubt good towns will spring up in this valley which is not so famed, but much larger than the renowned valley of the Mohawk."[39] These predictions proved incorrect. Drought and dust storms accompanied the homesteaders to their claims. Instead of prosperous new farms and bustling boom towns, the open lands produced stunted crops and shattered dreams. In the summer of 1913, Farming Superintendent Charles Davis reported that "the reservation is the worst burned I have about ever seen. . . . At present there is no market for agricultural lands."[40]

Because of their many hardships the white settlers had no interest in policing Indian communities. As a result few reservation residents were prosecuted in the state courts.[41] In addition the scattered non-Indian communities made law enforcement more difficult. As Superintendent King wrote in 1912, "the opening of the . . . reservation . . . created . . . a community without law . . . this was quickly taken advantage of by bootleggers, gamblers, horse thieves, cattle rustlers and soldiers of fortune generally."[42] Because the state did not act in the face of this rising crime rate, the duties of the Indian police and the tribal courts did not disappear but became even more important. While obviously an arm of the superintendent and not always popular, the reservation's law enforcement officers were respected in the community. Elderly members of the Cheyenne River Tribe still recall the effectiveness of the Indian courts during these years. For example, a man from Cherry Creek remembers, "They had a tribal court (when I was young). . . . That judge he didn't go to school, he have no education, but just a little. . . . and they'll have a court there. And a real court too, them days. . . . and there's a policeman, didn't go to school, he stands there. . . . That's the kind of law and order we had, them days, they were pretty strict. . . . But that's a real court they have."[43]

A similar point can be made about the government schools on the reservation. Here again many people felt that the new county governments would accept Indian children into their schools and, as a consequence, that the BIA schools would disappear. The agency superintendent reported in 1914, for example, that he expected three day schools to "likely be abandoned for the next year, and the public schools organized in their place." This idea was killed in 1915, when South Dakota repealed a law that had opened its schools to Indians.[44] From that time forward, only children whose tuition was paid by the government would be allowed to attend local white schools. As a result, most Indian children continued to be educated together, either in their own communities or in boarding schools. As in the area of law enforcement, rejection by white society caused tribal members to maintain their ties with each other.

Finally, the presence of boss farmers in each of the four districts helped hold the communities together. The farmers lived at the subagencies and were primarily responsible for supervising individual farms and acting as ombudsmen for all BIA business. Boss farmers were involved in arranging leases, distributing rations, assisting the tribal courts, and hearing complaints. Once the white homesteaders arrived, a new duty was added to this list: keeping settlers off tribal land and away from Indian cattle. Disputes arose almost as soon as the reservation was opened. The boss farmer was in a unique position. He was a white man, but he was a *federal* official. He knew the Indians well and was responsible for their government-issue property. Cheyenne River may have been unusual, but most of its farmers seem to have been honest and willing to challenge local whites if they felt there was a reason. They did this, for example, in 1915, when Dewey County tried to tax the assets of allottees and when the South Dakota herd law was being used to capture and steal Indian cattle.[45]

Through all of their activities, the boss farmers were living reminders to the native people on the reservation that they were a distinct community that could expect certain kinds of help and protection. Some of the favor of the strict life that focused around a boss farmer is conveyed by an elderly resident who remembers Cherry Creek in the years before World War I: "Cherry Creek used to be something like a town. They had a restaurant, a warehouse, . . . and a police headquarters, court house, and doctor's office, and carpenter shop and blacksmith shop—[they had] everything."[46] "Everything" was at the subagency. It was where people went for their ration and lease money; it was where court was held; it was a place for visiting and keeping in touch with each other.

These patterns, established in the years prior to World War I, persisted through the 1920s. The tribal council continued to block congressional attempts to open more land or reduce their power. The Indian police and the tribal courts both functioned despite the influx of white settlers. County and state officials still had little interest in extending their jurisdiction to tribal members, and the Cheyenne River courts continued to be respected (this situation was not affected by the 1924 citizenship act[47]). Reservation day schools and the boss farmer system remained important measures of the tribe's separation from the state government. In all these areas, it was clear that the new reservation culture that had emerged at Cheyenne River would continue into the future.

Why did the Great Sioux Agreement, designed to "absorb" the

four Lakota bands at Cheyenne River, fail? Why did this reservation—which was supposed to be a focus of government efforts to assimilate native people—remain an Indian preserve? The preceding discussion of events of the early twentieth century on the reservation has suggested some answers. The reservation became the setting for a new kind of culture, one that adopted certain non-Indian institutions but which used these to defend traditional  values and goals. The reservation was a new environment for the people of Cheyenne River. It placed new restrictions on their activities and made new demands on them, and pressure from the outside world forced them back on themselves. As a result, they used many of the new reservation institutions as vehicles for self-defense and cultural survival. The tribal council, which the government had thought would be useful only when there was property to be sold or leases to be signed, became an effective force in the struggle to hold on to unallotted tribal lands. The courts and police system emerged as the only protection available against lawless homesteaders or errant fellow tribesmen. The schools—while bleak and often cruel—gave native children an alternative once they had been rejected by the white community. And the boss farmers, with all of their duties, created a focus for life in each district and served as a reminder of the kind of protection federal power could provide. All of these institutions—even though they were inventions of the government—were used to serve the interests of tribal members.

It would be incorrect to interpret this narrative as a simple defense of the Indian police or the tribal council or the BIA schools, for it is important to remember that each of these institutions was forced on the tribe. What is more, they benefited the tribe only because the people at Cheyenne River had rich traditions and a continuing loyalty to their culture. Those feelings of identity and strength, which overrode the horrors of the past, shaped the activities of those who were drawn to the new reservation institutions. The council opposed land openings, the policemen chased off cattle rustlers, and the people gathered at the subagencies because they never stopped feeling that they belonged to a special group and that they had an obligation to each other that was greater than the sum total of outside pressure. Thinking back to these early years, one of the tribe's oldest members recently recalled, ''In 1912 they had a fair in Dupree [a town on the opened portion of the reservation] and I remember one white man, Congressman Henry L. Gandy, he said forty years from now there won't be no Indians. . . . He come near make it. . . . But we Indians will be Indians all our lives, we never will be white men. We can talk and work and go to school like the white people but we're still Indians.''[48] Beginning with that feeling, many of the people who participated in government-sponsored institutions worked to make those institutions serve the interests of the group. Without a sense of identity within the tribe, these institutions might have served their original purpose. And the reverse is true: if the traditions had remained without the new institutions, they alone might not have succeeded in keeping the tribal culture alive. The Gamble bill would have passed, law and order would have vanished, and reservation life would have had no focus.

Every culture is constantly changing. Values and traditions may persist, but ways of life are never static. The creation of the Cheyenne River Reservation caused dramatic changes in the lives of the people who were forced to live there. But despite these upheavals, the culture of those people survived. Thus we should view the early twentieth century not as a period of assimilation but as a time of rapid cultural change. The councilmen, the tribal judges, the policemen, and the rest were caught up in this process. They faced great pressures, but all through the crisis they worked to maintain their culture rather than to surrender it. For this reason, the early history of the Cheyenne River Reservation should be understood not as a time of defeat and hopelessness but as a crucial period of adaptation and survival. Forced into a strange new world, these people used the tools available to them to protect and preserve the place they now call their homeland.

# Notes

1. Henry L. Dawes to Secretary of the Interior Teller, quoted in Loring B. Priest, *Uncle Sam's Stepchildren: The Reformation of United States Indian Policy, 1865–1887* (New Brunswick, N.J: Rutgers University Press, 1942), pp. 194–95.

2. See Howard R. Lamar, *Dakota Territory, 1861–1889: A Study of Frontier Politics* (New Haven, Conn.: Yale University Press, 1956), chaps. 8–9; Everett Dick, *Sodhouse Frontier, 1854–1890: A Social History of the Northern Plains from the Creation of Kansas & Nebraska to the Admission of the Dakotas* (New York: D. Appleton-Century Co., 1937).

3. See 25 *U.S. Stat.* 888–99.

4. John Noble, quoted in Francis Paul Prucha, *American Indian Policy in Crisis: Christian Reformers and the Indian, 1865–1900* (Norman: University of Oklahoma Press, 1976), pp. 186–87.

5. See Prucha, *American Indian Policy*, pp. 169–87. Congress authorized the first version of this agreement in 1882.

6. See U.S. Department of the Interior, Office of Indian Affairs, *Annual Report of the Commissioner of Indian Affairs to the Secretary of the Interior, 1890* (Washington, D.C.: U.S. Government Printing Office, 1890), p. 42.

7. U.S. Public Health Service, Public Health Indian Hospital, Eagle Butte, South Dakota, *History of the Cheyenne River Reservation*, pp. 1–5.

8. *Annual Report of the Commissioner of Indian Affairs, 1890*, p. 42.

9. *Annual Report of the Commissioner of Indian Affairs, 1890*, p. 323.

10. *Annual Report of the Commissioner of Indian Affairs, 1890*, p. 45; *Annual Report of the Commissioner of Indian Affairs, 1896*, p. 284; *Annual Report of the Commissioner of Indian Affairs, 1899*, pt. 1, p. 328.

11. *Annual Report of the Commissioner of Indian Affairs, 1895*, p. 282; *Annual Report of the Commissioner of Indian Affairs, 1897*, p. 263; Thomas Downs to Commissioner of Indian Affairs, August 26, 1907, General Correspondence, Cheyenne River, File 031, Records of the Bureau of Indian Affairs, Record Group 75, National Archives (hereafter RG, NA); *Annual Report of the Commissioner of Indian Affairs, 1899*, pt. 1, p. 328.

12. Tabulation based on unpublished allotment schedule, Cheyenne River Agency Realty Office, Eagle Butte, South Dakota. See Frederick E. Hoxie, "Jurisdiction on the Cheyenne River Reservation: An Analysis of the Cause and Consequences of the Act of May 29, 1908," a report prepared for presentation in *U.S. v. Dupris*, No. CR77-30056-01, U.S. District Court, District of South Dakota, app. 2.

13. Hoxie, "Jurisdiction on the Cheyenne River Reservation," app. 2.

14. *Annual Report of the Commissioner of Indian Affairs, 1897*, p. 262.

15. See Ira A. Hatch to Commissioner of Indian Affairs, February 11, 1903, Letters Received #10772, 1903, RG 75, NA.

16. See U.S. Department of Commerce, Bureau of the Census, *Historical Statistics of the United States, 1789–1945* (Washington, D.C.: U.S. Government Printing Office, 1949), 106.

17. *Lone Wolf* v. *Hitchcock*, 187 U.S. 565 (1903).

18. For a detailed description of the effects of the *Lone Wolf* decision on land openings at Rosebud and elsewhere, see Frederick E. Hoxie, "Beyond Savagery:

The Campaign to Assimilate the American Indians, 1880–1920'' (Ph.D. diss., Brandeis University, 1977), pp. 380–92.

19. *Pierre Daily Capital-Journal*, April 13, 1908.

20. Gamble's bill was S. 1385, and Hall's was H.R. 10527; both were presented in 60th Cong., 1st sess.

21. Acting Secretary of the Interior Frank Pierce to James McLaughlin, December 26, 1907, General Correspondence, Cheyenne River, File 308.1, RG 75, NA.

22. ''Proceedings of the General Council of the Cheyenne River Sioux Tribe, 6, 7, and 8 January 1908, at Whitehorse, South Dakota,'' enclosed in Superintendent to Commissioner of Indian Affairs, January 23, 1908, General Correspondence, Cheyenne River, File 054, RG 75, NA.

23. Ibid.

24. U.S. Senate, Committee on Indian Affairs, *Sale of Portion of Surplus Lands on Cheyenne River and Standing Rock Reservations*, 60th Cong., 1st sess., S. Rept. 439, April 15, 1908, pt. 2:19.

25. Ibid., 2:18.

26. James Crow Feather to Commissioner of Indian Affairs, April 25, 1908, General Correspondence, Cheyenne River, File 308.1, RG 75, NA.

27. 35 *U.S. Stat.* 460. The area was opened by a presidential proclamation dated August 19, 1909. See 36 *U.S. Stat.* 2500.

28. ''Proceedings of the General Council of the Cheyenne River Sioux Indians, 3 June 1909,'' Folder 63023-09, General Correspondence, Cheyenne River, File 054, RG 75, NA.

29. L. F. Michael to Commissioner of Indian Affairs, August 2, 1909, General Correspondence, Cheyenne River, File 054, RG 75, NA.

30. Robert Gamble to Richard A. Ballinger, December 14, 1909. General Correspondence, Cheyenne River, File 308.1 (No. 99923-09), RG 75, NA.

31. *Annual Report of the Commissioner of Indian Affairs, 1911*, p. 113.

32. James McLaughlin to Secretary of the Interior, February 10, 1910, General Correspondence, Cheyenne River, File 308.1 (no. 99923-09), RG 75, NA.

33. ''Minutes of Council Held by James McLaughlin, Inspector—Department of the Interior, with the Indians of the Cheyenne River Agency, South Dakota, Relative to the Sale and Disposition of the Surplus Lands of Their Reservation as Contemplated by Senate Bill 108, 62nd Congress, 1st session,'' p. 6, attached to James McLaughlin to the Secretary of the Interior, November 23, 1911, Legislation, File 5-1: Cheyenne River—Opening (pt. 1: 62d Cong.), Records of the Office of the Secretary of the Interior, RG 48, NA.

34. Ibid., p. 7.

35. Ibid., p. 8.

36. Ibid., p. 10.

37. Superintendent of Cheyenne River Agency School, quoted in Secretary of the Interior to R. J. Gamble, n.d., Legislation, File 5-1, RG 48, NA. The agency superintendent's views were expressed in Thomas J. King to Commissioner of Indian Affairs, February 27, 1912, General Correspondence, Cheyenne River, File 308.1 (No. 99923-09), RG 75, NA.

38. Edward Swan to Hon. William H. Taft, April 1, 1912, Legislation, File 5-1, RG 48, NA.

39. *Pierre Daily Capital-Journal*, June 4, 1908.

40. Charles Davis to Superintendent, August 14, 1913, General Corespondence, Cheyenne River, File 916, RG 75, NA.

41. A search of the criminal court records of Dewey and Ziebach counties for

1910–20 revealed that only four tribal members were prosecuted for violations of state law during that period. One of the four was an adopted white man. For details, see Hoxie, "Jurisdiction on the Cheyenne River Indian Reservation," pp. 117–28 and apps. 97–114.

42. Thomas J. King to Commissioner of Indian Affairs, March 25, 1912, Response to Circular #612, Special Series A, Box 1, RG 75, NA.

43. Hoxie, "Jurisdiction on the Cheyenne River Indian Reservation," app. 75.

44. "Superintendents' Annual Narrative and Statistical Report from Field Jurisdictions of the Bureau of Indian Affairs, Cheyenne River, 1914," Sec. 3: Schools, pt. 2, RG 75, NA; South Dakota, *Session Laws* (1915), chap. 168.

45. See *U.S.* v. *Pearson*, 231 F. 270 (8 U.S. Cir., 1916), and Thomas J. King to Commissioner of Indian Affairs, March 25, 1912.

46. Hoxie, "Jurisdiction on the Cheyenne River Indian Reservation," app. 12.

47. See Charles Burke to Charles D. Munro, March 2, 1923, General Correspondence, Cheyenne River, File 173, RG 75, NA; and J. Henry Scattergood to W. F. Dickens, February 11, 1932, General Correspondence, Cheyenne River, File 175, RG 75, NA.

48. Interview with Olney Runs After, Cherry Creek, South Dakota, August 25, 1977.

# CHAPTER 4

# The *Winters* Decision and Indian Water Rights: A Mystery Reexamined

## BY NORRIS HUNDLEY, JR.

*Water rights must be considered one of the most important questions facing Plains Indians today. Indeed, in this century water rights have always been important, but recently, given the demands of the modern American economy and the acquisition of tribal legal assistance, Indians have been more likely to press for their full share. Considering the marginal utility of much Plains Indian land and the water shortage in much of the region, it is not surprising that Plains Indian people have had to contend with all of the other residents for their portion of this precious resource.*

*Thus the judicial system of the United States has had to consider the water rights of American Indians in the postfrontier era. The most important decision by the Supreme Court was handed down early in the century in a case involving the Gros Ventres and Assiniboines of the Fort Belknap Reservation, in northern Montana. By an eight to one vote, the Court reaffirmed Indian treaty rights, including the right to water. In 1908,* Winters v. U.S. *yielded the "Winters doctrine."*

*In the following selection Norris Hundley, a leading student of water rights in the American West, provides background information about the* Winters *decision and attempts to clarify what the justices meant to say. Hundley suggests that the decision "represented a major advance for Indians at a time when reversals for them were the usual order of the day" but quickly adds that "the advance proved to be more symbolic than real," for it did not*

From *Western Historical Quarterly* (January, 1982): 17–42. Reprinted by permission.

*assure reservation Indians a "clear and unquestioned right to water."*

*Nonetheless, one can only imagine how limited Indian water rights would be in the Plains without the* Winters *decision. In a time when Indians were expected to vanish along with their reservations,* Winters *gave vital additional evidence that Indians would continue to be Indians and that reservations would remain as their homes.*

*Hundley's article also indicates the degree to which Indian and non-Indian fates were intertwined by the early 1900s; other articles in this anthology will demonstrate how conflict, dependence, and interdependence have characterized Indian-white relations in the Plains from that time since. By a careful review of the history of the* Winters *case we may learn much about Plains Indian rights in twentieth-century America.*

WATER is the natural resource of greatest concern in western America, an area of few rivers, sparse rainfall, and monumental struggles over the precious commodity. Joining increasingly in the struggles have been Native Americans, most of whose reservations (55 percent of them) and reservation population (75 percent of it) are found in the driest portions of the region and whose hopes to lessen their poverty—the severest in the nation—rest on the ongoing disputes and negotiations over water. No less concerned are non-Indians, whose cities, industries, and farms area are already using most of the West's water and who have asserted rights to nearly all the rest. At the heart of these controversies both past and in the making are differences over a 1908 decision rendered by the Uniteds States Supreme Court in *Winters* v. *United States.*[1] That decision announced for the first time the existence of an Indian water right, but the meaning of the Court's action has become clouded in a debate that has exacerbated conflicts between Indians and non-Indians and created a crisis of national significance.

In its eight-to-one decision of January 6, 1908, the *Winters* Court held that the creation of an Indian reservation carried with it the setting aside of water as well as land.[2] This so-called "reserved" water right constitutes a special right that differs significantly from all other kinds of water rights. Unlike a riparian right, which resides only in owners of land bordering a stream, it can be invoked to divert a stream onto nonriparian lands. Unlike the doctrine of prior appropriation, which has been adopted in some form by all western states, the reserved right exists whether or not Indians are actually using the water, and it continues unimpaired even if the Indians should subsequently cease their uses. About these characteristics of the Indian right there is essential agreement, but because of apparent ambiguities in the *Winters* decision that agreement extends to little else. For more than a half a century, attorneys, legal scholars, and historians have quarreled over the meaning of the decision with three questions in particular dominating their differences: the quantum of volume of the Indian right, the legitimate uses to which the water guaranteed by the right can be put, and the priority of the right in relation to the rights of non-Indians desirous of the same water sources.[3] The vital importance of water has fired the imagination of disputants and inspired them to fashion a multiplicity of answers to these questions and to erect on those answers contradictory theories about the fundamental nature and extent of the Indian right. Additional by-products have been bitter court battles and others now in the planning stage, an Indian right that exists more in theory than in practice, the frustration of atempts to implement public and private water plans, and the inability of both Indians and non-Indians to make informed investment decisions.[4]

Encouraging the disagreement over the *Winters* case has been a tendency to treat the decision as an isolated incident—to view it out of context and unrelated to what preceded it and what contemporaries thought it represented and accomplished. The purpose of this essay is to correct that one-dimensional approach and, on the basis of heretofore overlooked manuscript materials and a reexamination of published documents, to attempt to clarify the Court's intentions, especially concerning the quantum, legitimate uses, and priority of the Indian right. These questions are closely interrelated and take their meaning fron understanding of the law as it was applied at the district, appellate and U.S.Supreme Court levels as well as from an understanding of the events and attitudes that precipitated and accompanied the legal action.

The issues that precipitated the *Winters* decision first emerged in the late spring of 1905 on the Fort Belknap Reservation in northern Montana, the home at the time of 1,300 Gros Ventre and Assiniboine Indians. "So far this Spring," wrote William R. Logan, the reservation superintendent, to the commissioner of Indian affairs on June 3, 1905, "we have had no water in our ditch whatever. Our meadows are now rapidly parching up. The Indians have planted large crops and a great deal of grain. All this will be lost unless some radical action is taken at once to make the settlers above the Reservation respect our rights. To the Indians it either means good crops this fall, or starvation this winter."[5]

The situation described by Logan had been in the making ever since the late 1880s, when the vast Indian territory originally set aside in 1855 as the Great Blackfeet Reservation was reduced to three smaller reservations—Fort Peck, Blackfeet, and Fort Belknap. In separate agreements with several different tribal groups, U.S. commissioners negotiated for the surrender of over 17,500,000 acres. They were candid about the reasons that had brought them west. "The time has come when Indians can not hold vast bodies of land as heretofore," stated Charles F. Larrabee in late 1886 to the natives gathered at Fort Peck Agency in Montana. "White people are coming to America from all parts of the world. Emigrants are flocking over the plains and the prairies; the demand for land increased from day to day; the cry is, "More land! more land!" The Government must take care of and provide land for her white children, as well as the Indians."[6]

Negotiations with the Gros Ventres and Assiniboines took place at the Fort Belknap Agency in January, 1887, during "a period of extremely cold weather" and lasted for three days.[7] Despite temperatures so low that it proved impossible to take minutes of the proceedings, most adult Indian males attended the talks and on January 21 accepted the terms presented to them, "reserving to themselves" some 600,000 acres. This represented only a small fraction of their original holdings, but the promise of houses, stoves, livestock, clothing, medical care, and farming and mechanical implements proved compelling to a people on the verge of starvation.

Technically the agreement opened to the Fort Belknap Indians an almost unlimited range of opportunities, for they were assured the means "to educate their children in the paths of civilization . . . and in any other respect to promote their civilization, comfort, and improvement." As a practical matter, though, their future was sharply circumscribed. The funds promised for supplies were limited—the equivalent of about seventy-three dollars per person a year for ten years—and the agreement required that preference in the distribution of goods go "especially to those who in good faith undertake the cultivation of the soil, or engage in pastoral pursuits." Other language, in conformity with the practice of the day, described the Indians as being "desirous" of becoming "a pastoral and agricultural people."[8] Even more explicit about the future of the natives was the report filed with the commissioner of Indian affairs by the U.S. negotiators several weeks after the talks. The Indians "must be encouraged in stock-raising as well as in agricultural pursuits. They can never become self-supporting in any other way," a conclusion reinforced by geographic and climatic considerations. "The land selected for them are as good, if not the best, for agricultural purposes in all that region of country, being well watered and susceptible of irrigation at a small cost. They ware also admirably adapted to stock-raising. . . ."[9] The principal source of water in the area was Milk River, and the center of that stream was established as the northern boundary of the new reservation.

Once endorsed by the Indians, the Fort Belknap agreement was incorporated into a bill containing almost identical agreements with the other northern Montana tribes and sent to Congress, which approved the measure with little discussion in March, 1888.[10] On May 1, President Grover Cleveland signed the bill into law and prepared the way for an influx of settlers onto the former Indian lands. That influx intensified as a result of tracklaying by the Great Northern Railroad, which by 1890 completed its route across Montana. Farmers, ranchers, and merchants moved first into the better watered areas, including the Milk River valley, where they platted such towns as Havre, Harlem, and Chinook and diverted water to their lands and communities. For a while the water supply was adequate, but by 1905 increased diversions combined with a severe drought to deprive Fort Belknap Reservation of water and spark Superintendent Logan's appeal to Washington for "radical action."

The specific course of action recommended by Logan was not as radical as his choice of words indicated. In one sense, of course, it was. That he vigorously sought help for his Indian charges at a time when most Americans still considered the natives an obstacle to progress was unusual and testified to his dedication and willingness to follow what he knew would be an unpopular course. He soon had a reputation in Montana as "the most unpopular 'Indian' in the country," a designation he bore proudly.[11] But the course he urged on his superiors was not novel, for he asked them to invoke the doctrine of prior appropriation, a principle long sanctioned by Montana law and which vested title in the first person to use water. Specifically, he recommended action against those settlers whose water rights dated from 1898, the year when an earlier superintendent at the reservation had filed for a flow rate of 10,000 miner's inches of Milk River water. "If the water were turned loose above us, and only the prior locators to the . . . [1898] appropriation were to take water," he told the commissioner of Indian affairs, "there would be plenty to reach us to give us at least one good irrigation this summer, and from that we could at least raise a crop. If not done, our crops will be a total loss, unless there is a great deal of rainfall."[12]

When Logan's plea reached Washington, Commissioner Francis E. Leupp was away on one of his many absences. Acting in his place was Larrabee, a longtime employee of the Office of Indian Affairs and, as fortune would have it, one of the negotiators of the 1888 agreement creating Fort Belknap. He responded quickly and positively to Logan's appeal, endorsing the superintendent's decision to rely on the 1898 appropriation and urging Secretary of the Interior Ethan A. Hitchcock to petition the Justice Department "to protect the rights of the Indians."[13] Larrabee had no doubt that his recommendation would have the approval of his absent superior, for Leupp shared the widely held view that assimilation was in the best interests of the Indian, and he advocated educational opportunities, especially for younger and "still measurably plastic" natives who could be trained as artisans, ranchers, and farmers. His predecessor had nearly doubled appropriations for irrigation projects, and he wished to extend those advances, not preside over their undoing.[14] So, too, did Secretary of the Interior Hitchcock. Only four days after receiving Larrabee's request, he asked Attorney General William Moody "to take immediate steps to establish and protect the water rights of the Indians."[15] Moody needed no persuading. He approved the request on the same day he received it.

Less than two weeks after Logan had appealed to Washington, the Justice Department sent a telegram to Carl Rasch, U.S. attor-

ney for the district of Montana, ordering him to intervene on behalf
of the Indians: "Take promptly such action as may be necessary to
protect interests of Indians against interference by subsequent
appropriators of water of Milk River."[16] Two weeks later, on June
26, Rasch asked Judge William H. Hunt of the federal district court
in Helena for an injunction against twenty-one defendants, including two irrigation companies and a cattle firm.

Rasch's bill of complaint formalized Logan's request that the
injunction be sought against those whose appropriations were later
than 1898, though the district attorney also asked that the reservation be protected in its use of an additional 1,000 inches diverted by
pump, beginning in 1889. The total rate-of-flow sought was
11,000 miner's inches—10,000 inches diverted by gravity flow
beginning in 1898 and 1,000 inches diverted by pump since 1889.
Use of these waters on the reservation had been "long prior" to the
diversions made by the non-Indians, Rasch told Judge Hunt, and
had been "constantly and uninterruptedly" maintained until the
present crisis.[17]

Though convinced of the correctness of his position, Rasch
lacked solid evidence for his assertions. Neither he nor Logan had
been able to locate documents demonstrating that the reservation
had formally filed for the water claimed. Logan had uncovered a
filing for 10,000 inches in 1898, but that had been made in the
name of Luke C. Hays, the reservation superintendent at the time,
and not in the name of the reservation or by Hays on behalf of the
reservation. Because of his uneasiness, Rasch sought a way to
protect himself "in case the necessity therefor should arise."[18] His
solution was to broaden his legal position by alluding somewhat
ambiguously to "other rights" possessed by the Indians and the
federal government. He singled out riparian law as being especially applicable, since the reservation abutted Milk River; in
addition he believed the Indians and government possessed a right
to sufficient water to accomplish "the ends . . . for which . . . the
reservation was created." These "riparian and other rights," he
concluded, entitled the reservation "to the uninterrupted flow of
*all* of the waters of . . . Milk River."[19]

Rasch's invocation of such "riparian and other rights" did not
harmonize with his argument based on prior appropriation or with
his request for an injunction against only twenty-one defendants
instead of all non-Indians using Milk River water. But the lack of

harmony was calculated rather than inadvertent. To issue an injunction against all the non-Indians—estimated to number between 225 and 250—would, Rasch believed, raise "complicated questions" about the "riparian rights of the Government and the treaty rights of the Indians" and frustrate "the imperative necessity of securing a sufficient amount of water for the . . . reservation with the least-possible delay."[20] Such concern was well taken. Every informed person knew about the ambiguous corner of the law occupied by treaty rights. And as for water law, there were aspects of it that were just as debatable. While many attorneys and legal scholars argued that prior appropriation was the fundamental water law of Montana, others insisted that riparian principles applied there as well. They claimed that the United States, as the owner of federal reservations in Montana (or any state), possessed title as a riparian to the waters required by those reservations.[21] Rasch knew this was an unpopular position in the arid West, and thus he and Logan understandably chose to emphasize the legally less offensive doctrine of appropriation. Still, since Rasch did not want to exclude any principle that might redound to the benefit of the Indians and the government, he carefully fashioned his complaint to give himself as much latitude as possible.

Judge Hunt said nothing about legal theories, but he hesitated not at all in issuing a temporary restraining order against the settlers. He did so on the same day that Rasch filed his complaint. The order he gave was sweeping. He forbade the non-Indians from diverting any water from Milk River or "from in any matter or by any means interfering with or obstructing the free and uninterrupted use and enjoyment of the waters of said Milk River and its tributaries . . . upon the Fort Belknap Indian Reservation."[22]

Rasch was delighted with the order—but only for twelve days. On July 8, Hunt modified the injunction and permitted the non-Indians to make diversions so long as they did "not deprive" the reservation of "the number of inches . . . claimed"—the 11,000 miner's inches specified in the complaint.[23] The settlers had sought this modification on the grounds that a sudden warming trend had melted the snowpack in nearby mountains and increased the flow of the river to a point where the Indians were unable to use it all. Rasch at first opposed the modification but then went along with it when Hunt issued oral instructions that appeared to protect the Indians' interest. The judge directed the settlers to confer with

Superintendent Logan and "only . . . to divert such waters as . . . [the superintendent] did not need on the reservation." "The effect of the order," Rasch explained to Logan on the same day it was issued, "is . . . that none of the defendents are entitled to take and divert any water, if they thereby interfere with the enjoyment of the necessary amount of water required by you on the reservation."[24]

Despite the judge's instructions, Rasch remained uneasy. The injunction was temporary, the settlers had not yet filed their formal response to the order, and here was still the need for hard evidence to support the reservation's claims based on prior appropriation. He urged Logan to continue the search for documents and to supply him "with the name of the witnesses who are familiar with the situation and . . . the use that has been made of the water on the Fort Belknap Reservation from the time the buildings were erected there." His course of action remained essentially unchanged: "I shall rely upon the appropriations made . . . and upon the riparian doctrine, but the principal proposition in the case is the use that was made of the waters for beneficial purposes upon the reservation."[25]

Rasch's worst fears about his evidence was confirmed about a week later, when the settlers formally responded to the injunction. To his chagrin, if not his complete surprise, many of them proved that they, not the Indians, had been the first to divert the waters of Milk River. He also learned that Indian water uses were less than half of what he had been led to believe. Studies recently completed by Logan indicated that the reservation was diverting 5,000 inches, not the 11,000 inches claimed in the complaint. The superintendent estimated the total amount of land susceptible of irrigation at 30,000 acres, six times the area then being cultivated, but he calculated "present necessities" at only 5,000 inches.[26]

These revelations, while jarring to Rasch, who now abandoned the appropriation doctrine in favor of riparian law, buoyed the hopes of the settlers. But this time the settlers' enthusiasm was short-lived. Two weeks later, on August 7, Judge Hunt dealt them a body blow by issuing a general injunction and offering an explanation that took all parties by surprise. "In my judgment," he stated, "when the Indians made the treaty[27] granting rights to the United States, they reserved the right to the use of the waters of Milk River, at least to an extent reasonably necessary to irrigate their lands."[28] Rasch had earlier alluded to such a treaty right, but

he had attached little significance to it, far less than to the appropriation doctrine or even to riparian law, which he now considered his
"strongest point."[29] For Judge Hunt, however, the treaty rights of
the Indians were paramount, and he was not bothered that the 1888
agreement said nothing about water. He based his order primarily
on two points: "the purposes of the treaty"—as revealed in the
provisions providing the Indians with livestock and agricultural
equipment that would enable them "to become 'self-supporting, as
a pastoral and agricultural people, and to educate their children in
the paths of civilization' "—and the climatic conditions of northern Montana, which "tell us that water for irrigation is indispensable in successful farming." To Hunt the fact that the settlers had
begun using the water first was immaterial. The "defendants can
acquire no rights to the exclusion of the reasonable needs of the
Indians." Since those needs were currently 5,000 inches, his
injunction forbade the settlers from interfering with the flow of that
much water to the reservation. When he issued his formal order the
following day, he chose words making clear that his injunction
established a minimum volume fo water for the reservation and not
a ceiling: the reservation "requires . . . not less than five thousand
inches."[30]

News of Hunt's order spread quickly through the communities
of the Milk River valley. Alarmed settlers hurriedly called public
meetings in which they denounced the injunction and petitioned
their congressmen for help. Some urged an appeal of Hunt's order,
others demanded that Congress open to homestead entry the
reservation lands along the Milk River, and still others petitioned
for a reclamation project to bring additional water into the Milk
River Basin.[31] The reclamation project was not a new idea. Settlers
had long recognized that the waters of Milk River, even without
diversions to satisfy Indian needs, were inadequate, and they had
pressed the newly created Reclamation Service for help. As early
as 1903 the service had responded with a plan—the Milk River
Project—to divert the nearby St. Mary River into the headwaters of
the Milk, but little progress had been made because of wrangling
over water rights and complications resulting from the Milk and St.
Mary being Canadian as well as United States streams.[32]

Hunt's order spurred the settlers to renew their demands for the
reclamation project and to redouble their efforts to resolve legal
differences among themselves. It also prompted Montana's U.S.

Senator Thomas Carter to introduce a bill, which was ultimately unsuccessful, to separate the Fort Belknap Indians from their water, and it provoked a powerful demand for an appeal of the injunction to the Ninth Circuit Court of Appeals.[33] Intensifying the pressure for the appeal was settler fear that the award of 5,000 inches gave the Indians all the water available during the irrigation season. No one (including the Reclamation Service) knew the precise volume of the river's flow, but most believed that little, if any, surplus remained for even temporary use by non-Indians. "[W]ith an allowance of 5,000 inches to the Indians of the Belknap reservation," complained the *Havre Plaindealer*, "it would seem that other vested rights carry vastly more wind than water." The *Havre Herald* agreed: "The decision of the court grants them the right and title to . . . more than flows in the river all summer."[34]

This same fear suffused the appeal filed in mid-August by the settlers with the Ninth Circuit Court in San Francisco. They denied that the 1888 agreement had reserved any water "except to the extent perhaps of entitling the agency to the use of waters for domestic purposes at the agency buildings." Certainly, they insisted, there was no intention to reserve the vast amounts of water needed for irrigation. "In fact, it cannot be seriously contended that the Indians at the present time are desirous of irrigating their lands or converting them to the purposes of agriculture." To the settlers, Hunt's injunction would destroy communities already developed by giving the Indians a right they neither possessed nor wanted. "[Y]ou are asked" by Hunt, they told the court, "to read into the treaty an intention to confer upon the Indians a right which they had never exercised, did not then claim, and would not now exercise but for governmental compulsion, and which when exercised would destroy the value of every acre of land ceded by them to the United States, and lay waste thousands and thousands of acres made fertile by the labor and expenditure of settlers, who had gone upon them under express authority from the government."[35]

The appellate court was unmoved. On February 5, 1906, the panel of three judges unanimously upheld the injunction. Their reasons dovetailed with those of Hunt and were grounded in what they insisted was the "true interpretation of the treaty of May 1, 1888." That the agreement said nothing about water rights was beside the point.

We must presume that the government and the Indians, in agreeing to the terms of the treaty, . . . knew that "the soil could not be cultivated" without the use of water to "irrigate the same." Why was the northern boundary of the reservation located "in the middle of Milk River" unless it was the purpose of reserving the right to the Indians to use of said water for irrigation, as well as for other purposes? . . . We are of the opinion that the court below did not err in holding that, "when the Indians made the treaty granting rights to the United States, they reserved the right to use the waters of Milk River, at least to an extent reasonably necessary to irrigate their lands. The right so reserved continues to exist against the United States and its grantees, as well as against the state and it grantees."[36]

The appellate court accepted Hunt's assessment of the current requirements of the Indians but indicated that the reservation's right could be extended to embrace the entire river. "Our former decision . . . ," announced the court in October, 1906, when it rejected a second appeal of the settlers, "construes and gives effect to what we understand to be the obvious meaning and intent of the treaty, and holds that by the expressed terms of that treaty there was reserved to the Indians the waters of Milk river as part and parcel of the reservation set apart to them."[37] The appellate court reaffirmed this principle with greater precision less than two years later in *Conrad* v. *United States*, a case involving the water rights of Montana's Blackfeet Reservation that had been created at the same time as Fort Belknap and as a result of the same series of negotiations. "The present case is in many respects similar to the Winters Case," announced the three justices, two of whom had participated in the earlier decision. "The law of that case . . . determines the paramount right of the Indians . . . to the use of waters . . . to the extent reasonably necessary for the purposes of irrigation and stock raising, and domestic and other useful purposes." Although the future needs of the reservation could not be known with precision, the court did not find this a problem. "Having determined that the Indians on the reservation have a paramount right to the waters . . . . , it follows that . . . the amount of water specified in the decree should be subject to modification, should the conditions on the reservation at any time require such modification." All that need be done is to "apply to the court for a modification of the decree."[38]

Besides affirming the Indian right to water, the appellate court took advantage of its *Winters* decision to probe the legal source for the right to reserve water, a question that later generations of attorneys would vigorously debate. In issuing his injunction, Judge Hunt had observed that it was "the Indians . . . [who] reserved the right to the use of the waters," but he had said little about the source of that right other than to suggest that it was inherent with Indian nations and dated from the period before 1888 when "nearly the whole Northern Montana . . . was recognized as Indian country."[39] The appellate court went significantly beyond Hunt by holding that the United States as well as the Indians possessed the authority to reserve water and that both had done so in the 1888 agreement. All appropriations made by the settlers were "subject to . . . the 'existing rights' of the government and of the Indians on the reservation," stated the court.[40] The United States, as absolute territorial sovereign, possessed title through conquest and purchase to all the country's possessions and title in fee to the public domain, which included the lands inhabited by the Indians. As sovereign and as the owner of the public lands, the U.S. also naturally held rights to the streams on those lands. In support of its position the appellate court cited earlier decisions, including the 1899 U.S. Supreme Court opinion in *United States* v. *Rio Grande Dam and Irrigation Co.*, from which it quoted extensively. "[I]n the absence of specific authority from Congress," the Court had declared on that occasion, "a state cannot by its legislation destroy the right of the United States, as the owner of lands bordering on a stream, to the continued flow of its waters so far at least as may be necessary for the beneficial uses of the government property."[41] The appellate court also found particularly persuasive a 1904 decision of the Montana Supreme Court: "When the government established the reservation [in this case a military reservation], it owned both the land included therein, and all the water running in the various near-by streams to which it had not yielded title. It was therefore unnecessary for the government to 'appropriate' the water. It owned it already. All it had to do was to take it and use it."[42]

For the Indians, the authority to reserve the water derived from their "right of occupancy." The U.S. possessed title in fee to Indian lands, noted the court, but it recognized in the Indians a right to occupy their lands until the U.S. extinguished that right. "It is a right regulated by treaties, not by deeds of conveyance," John Marshall had stated in 1810 in *Fletcher* v. *Peck*. "[T]he Indians . . . have an unquestionable, and . . . unquestioned right to the lands they occupy, until that right shall be extinguished by a voluntary cession to our government,'' affirmed Marshall twenty-one years later in *Cherokee Nation* v. *Georgia*.[43] Though the cession of native lands had often been far from voluntary, the appellate court believed that Marshall's opinion—and the many subsequent court decisions affirming it—was controlling. Especially telling for the appellate court was an 1875 decision of the U.S. Supreme Court in which the rights of both the government and the Indians had been reaffirmed in a single opinion. ''The treaty reserved them [lands] as much to one as to the other of the contracting parties,'' the Court had stated in *Leavenworth* v.*United States*. ''Both were interested therein, and had title thereto. In one sense, they were reserved to the Indians; but, in another and broader sense, to the United States, for the use of the Indians.''[44] Thus both the U.S. and the Indians possessed special rights of their own to reserve land and, in the opinion of the appellate court, the water necessary to make the land valuable.

The appellate court's decision bitterly disappointed the settlers of the Milk River valley, but as before they refused to accept defeat. They again pressed their congressmen for legislation to undo the court action and called mass meetings to express their resentment. ''The contention . . . that the Indians are, by first right, entitled to all the water flowing through their reservations is wrong! wrong!'' shouted the president of the Milk River United Irrigation Association to an angry crowd.[45] Such sentiments had been fanned by the stark headlines of valley newspapers: ''A Serious Situation for Water-Users,'' ''Indians' Rights to Water Upheld,'' ''Indians Will Have Waters,'' ''Indians Have First Claim.''[46] Unlike other newspapers, the *Chinook Opinion* was less worried about the immediate effect of the decision than its long-term impact. The paper's editors believed that in ''an ordinary year'' the Indians' use of 5,000 inches ''would not seriously affect the flow of the stream.'' On the other hand, cautioned the *Opinion*, ''there would be nothing to prevent them from increasing the 5,000 inches to an amount that would irrigate all of the reservation, and that in preference to and regardless of the farmers who have invested their money and time in reclaiming the valley and building a prosperous community of homes.''[47] But whether the threat was perceived as being immediate or in the more distant future, settlers believed that an appeal to the U.S. Supreme Court was imperative.

The Office of Indian Affairs and the Interior Department also favored an appeal. "[T]here is a disposition to question the correctness of the conclusions of the court in this case," observed Acting Commissioner of Indian Affairs Larrabee to Superintendent Logan in March, 1906, "but if the court of last resort were to pass on the matter, the rights of the Indians would be then so clearly defined that like contests would be avoided in the future."[48] Time would prove Larrabee to be overly optimistic, but he and the settlers got their wish when the Supreme Court agreed to hear the case and scheduled arguments for October, 1907.

The settlers for the most part took the opportunity merely to reaffirm their earlier position. They again emphasized the priority of their right and their belief that virtually all the usable waters of the river were at stake. The action of the lower courts, they declared, "deprived [them] of the use of any of the waters of . . . [the] stream during the period of year when the said waters are most needed."[49] They were willing to concede 250 inches to the Indians, but only because they believed that amount had been used in the vicinity of the agency's buildings prior to their own diversions. They also believed there was an additional 2,900 inches that could be reclaimed for the Indians from undeveloped springs and streams on the reservation. (In their second appeal to the Ninth Circuit they had pegged that amount at 1,000 inches less.[50]) Just as before, the issue seemed clear-cut: "If the claim of the United States and the Indians be maintained, the lands of the defendants and the other settlers will be rendered valueless, the said communities will be broken up and the purpose and object of the Government in opening said lands for settlement will be wholly defeated."[51]

Once again the settlers' pleas proved unpersuasive. On January 6, 1908, the Supreme Court in an eight-to-one decision rejected their appeal. Speaking for the majority, Justice Joseph McKenna acknowledged that the settlers who had moved onto the lands ceded by the Indians in the 1888 agreement needed water to establish "civilized communities" of their own, but this admission produced no water for them. "We realize that there is a conflict of implications," admitted McKenna, "but that which makes for the retention of the waters is of greater force than that which makes for their cession."[52]

The Court's reasoning squared in virtually all essentials with that of both Judge Hunt and the Ninth Circuit Court of Appeals. Treaty rights were again held to be paramount: "The case, as we view it, turns on the agreement of May, 1888, resulting in the creation of Fort Belknap Reservation." That agreement, asserted the Court, clearly anticipated that the Indians would embark on an agricultural and pastoral existence for which water was absolutely mandatory. "The reservation was a part of a very much larger tract which the Indians had the right to occupy and use and which was adequate for the habits and wants of a nomadic and uncivilized people," declared the justices. "It was the policy of the Government, it was the desire of the Indians, to change those habits and to become a pastoral and civilized people."[53]

To later generations of attorneys and legal scholars, the Supreme Court seemed unclear about who had actually reserved the waters—the federal government, the Indians, or both—and the constitutional authority for doing so. Where the appellate court had indicated explicitly that both the U.S. and the Indians possessed "rights" to set aside water, the Supreme Court did so only implicitly. In one part of its opinion the Court stated that "the Government did reserve them [the waters]," while elsewhere it observed that the Indians had done so: "It is contended . . . [by the settlers that] the Indians . . . made no reservation of the waters. We realize that there is a conflict of implications, but that which makes for the retention of the waters is of greater force than that which makes for their cession."[54] Because the Court did not indicate specifically at any place in its opinion that both the Indians and the government had reserved the water, later scholars accused the Court of being ambiguous, and most felt free to locate the authority to reserve water in either the U.S. *or* the Indians (but seldom in both) and then to erect elaborate and contradictory legal theories about the nature of the Indian right.[55] Such confusion of voices seems traceable less to the Court than to a desire to read into the decision what one wishes to find there.

The evidence seems clear: the Supreme Court located authority to reserve water in both the Indians and the U.S. It is possible to argue that the Court might have been clearer but unconvincing to insist that it was not clear enough. When the decision is viewed within its larger historical context, its meaning seems unmistakable. The Court, after all, had sustained the judgment of the appellate court, which had provided a comparative assessment of the rights of the Indians and the federal government. Equally telling, the principle that both the government and the Indians possessed the authority to reserve land had not been an aberration of the appellate court but was part of the conventional legal wisdom of the day and had been affirmed by Congress, prominent legal expert like Clesson S. Kinney, and earlier court decisions.[56]

McKenna had fashioned the Supreme Court's opinion as he did to counter particularly troubling arguments of the settlers. When he referred to the reservation of water by the federal government, he did so to deny the settlers' claim that any such reservation would have been automatically repealed with "the admission of Montana into the Union . . . 'upon an equal footing with the original States.' "[57] McKenna had refuted a similar claim three years earlier in *U.S.* v. *Winans* when he had unequivocally upheld "the power of the United States . . . to create rights which would be binding on the States."[58] That case had dealt with a dispute over Indian fishing rights, but McKenna felt the principle involved was the same. As author of the earlier opinion, he had considered the issue settled, and he now chose language reflecting his belief that the matter was definitely closed. "The power of the Government to reserve the water and exempt them from appropriation under the state laws is not denied, and could not be."[59] As evidence, he cited his own earlier opinion as well as *U.S.* v.*Rio Grande Dam and Irrigation Co.*, the decision that had figured prominently in the thinking of the appellate court about the government's authority to reserve water.

Similarly, when McKenna referred elsewhere in his opinion to the reservation of water by the Indians, he did so to counter still another vexing charge of the settlers—their contention that the Indians had never intended to set aside water. In rebuttal he declared:

The Indians had command of the lands and the waters—command of all their beneficial use, whether kept for hunting, 'and grazing roving herds of stock,' or turned to agriculture and the arts of civilization. Did they give up all this? Did they reduce the area of their occupation and give up the waters which made it valuable or adequate? . . . if it were possible to believe affirmative answers, we might also believe that the Indians were awed by the power of the Government or deceived by its negotiators. Neither view is possible. The Government is asserting the rights of the Indians.[60]

Thus the Supreme court, like the appellate court, upheld the authority of both the U.S. and the Indians to reserve water. The government by virtue of its right as absolute territorial sovereign and the Indians by virtue of their right of occupancy could reserve land and the water necessary to make the land habitable. And since the Indians' right extended back to that unrecorded moment when they first occupied the area, their right was necessarily prior to the rights of all later settlers, even those—and in the case of Fort Belknap there were none—who might have begun using water before the reservation was established. By emphatically denying that the Indians had surrendered their "command of the lands and the waters," the Court was acknowledging that they possessed the ultimate priority; they were reserving something that was already theirs.[61]

Just as later generations of attorneys and legal scholars differed over who reserved the waters and the larger meaning of such action, so too have they quarreled about the volume of the Indian right. The quantum as determined by the *Winters* court seems best understood by viewing it within the framework of events of which it was a part. When Judge Hunt issued his injunction in 1905, he based the quantum on two considerations: the "purposes" of the agreement establishing the reservation and the "reasonable needs of the Indians." The temporary restraining order of June 26 held that agriculture was a major purpose and that the irrigation needs of the Indians required all the water in the river. Twelve days later Hunt modified his order, permitting the settlers to make diversions so long as 11,000 inches were allowed to reach the reservation, and even then Hunt issued oral instructions forbidding the settlers from diverting "any water if they thereby interfere[d] with the enjoyment of the necessary amount required by the . . . reservation." Then, on August 7, Hunt issued his general injunction. Relying on the testimony of Superintendent Logan, he pegged the current Indian need at "not less than five thousand inches," though he made that figure subject to a higher principle: "Defendants can acquire no right to the exclusion of the reasonable needs of the Indians."[62]

As a westerner familiar with the critical importance of water in the region, Hunt had readily agreed to modify his earlier orders when he realized they provided the Indians with water in excess of their needs. To do otherwise, he knew, would be to waste water, an unconscionable act. The principle he evolved seems readily apparent: the Indians had a right to all the water they could put to reasonable use, and the non-Indians could use the surplus waters, if any, not required by the reservation. Put another way, Hunt's allocation was open-ended and subject to change as the needs of the Indians changed. Both the appellate court and the Supreme Court affirmed this principle by upholding Hunt's order and by refusing either to place a ceiling on the Indian right or to establish a specific and permanent volume for that right.[63]

So far as most of the settlers were concerned, the award of even enough water to meet the reservation's current needs had the effect of giving the Indians all the water available during the irrigation season. The settlers' reaction to the Supreme Court decision echoed their responses to the earlier court actions. "At least 5,000 inches of water must be allowed to go down Milk river and this is more water than Milk river carries during the irrigation season," announced the *Havre Herald* four days after the Supreme Court had acted. Observed the Harlem *Milk River Valley News* on January 23, 1908: "As the winter has been very dry and the Indians awarded all the waters of the Milk river the settlers will stand a very poor show of making a living the coming summer unless something is done at once."[64] The *Chinook Opinion* held to the view it had expressed following the decision of the Ninth Circuit Court of Appeals. Its editors continued to believe that during an ordinary year there would be enough water for the Indians and settlers—but only if the Indians did not expand their uses beyond 5,000 inches. "The worst feature of the decision," reaffirmed the *Opinion*, is "the possibility that an immense increase in that amount will be demanded after a while in the name of the Indians."[65]

The fear of the *Opinion* was the delight of Superintendent Logan. "[T]he Indians of the Fort Belknap Reservation under my charge have the prior water right to as much of the waters of Milk River as they can put to economical use. In other words," he stated in October, 1908, "under the rulings of the Appellate Court of San Francisco and the Supreme Court of the United States we are not confined to any particular amount of water but are confined to its economical use. It is problematical how much water we will use. Possibly not more than we are using at the present time but we still maintain the right to use more if it becomes necessary as our cultivated area along Milk River becomes larger."[66]

Closely related to the issue of the quantum of the Indian right is the question of the legitimate uses to which the Indian water can be put. Some attorneys and legal scholars have invoked the *Winters* decision to argue that the volume of the Indian right is determined solely by the agricultural needs of the reservation. Put another way, they contend that the Indians are restricted in the ways in which they can use their water. Others have challenged such an interpretation, insisting that the Indians can use the waters for any purpose—fishing, recreation, tourism, manufacturing, mining, the operation of a nuclear power plant, or any other activity, including one requiring more water than irrigation—which promotes their "civilization" and hence conforms to the alleged major reason for reservations.[67]

It is clear that the negotiators of the 1888 agreement, Judge Hunt, the Ninth Circuit Court of Appeals, and the Supreme Court, believed that a fundamental purpose of the reservation was to "civilize" the Indians and that agriculture was to be the principal means to that end. Logan had sought the water for an irrigation project, and the current needs of irrigation agriculture at Fort Belknap had been the measure for the specific volume of water awarded the Indians by Hunt in 1905. Such action conformed to the conventional wisdom of Americans in the late nineteenth and early twentieth centuries who believed that the plow offered the major route to civilization for Native Americans. But there is evidence that federal officials believed reservation Indians in general and Fort Belknap Indians in particular could achieve civilization through means other than agriculture. "Mechanical arts" and "pastoral" activities received major attention in the 1888 agreement (and in scores of treaties with other Indian groups), but no "civilized" pursuit was expressly excluded in that agreement nor in the decision of Judge Hunt, the appellate court, or the Supreme Court. The 1888 agreement acknowledged the desire of the Indians not only "to become self-supporting, as a pastoral and agricultural people" but also "*in any other respect to promote their civilization, comfort, and improvement.*"[68] Judge Hunt and the appellate court called attention to the same language,[69] and the Supreme Court pointedly denied that the Indians had surrendered their "command of the lands and the waters—command of *all* their beneficial use, whether kept for hunting 'and grazing roving herds of stock,' or turned to agriculture and *the arts of civilization.*"[70]

More importantly, the U.S. Supreme Court had determined long prior to either the 1888 agreement of the *Winters* decision that treaties had to be construed broadly when defining Indian rights under those treaties. "The language used in treaties with the Indians," Marshall had stated in 1832 in *Worcester* v.*Georgia*, "should never be construed to their prejudice."[71] This principle was regularly reaffirmed by subsequent Courts, including the *Winters* Court, which invoked it as support for its contention that there had been an implied reservation of water in the 1888 agreement. "By a rule of interpretation of agreements and treaties with the Indians," declared the Court, "ambiguities occurring will be resolved from the standpoint of the Indians."[72]

The evidence seems convincing: when Indians entered into an agreement setting aside lands and waters, they retained the right to sufficient water for any purpose that would promote their "civilization"—in other words, for any reasonable purpose.[73]

The *Winters* case dealt with an issue of unusual significance to America both at the turn of the century and today. In determining the existence of an Indian water right, the Supreme Court delivered a landmark decision, but the meaning of that decision has become the subject of sharp debate. Such controversy was probably inevitable as Indians and non-Indians contended for a limited resource needed desperately by both. Still, a close examination of the developments surrounding the Winters decision seems to dispel much of the subsequent confusion concerning the Court's action. The evidence suggests that the *Winters* Court intended for the Fort Belknap Indians to have all the waters from the Milk River that they could put to reasonable use. In reaching this judgment, the Court appears to have properly construed the 1888 agreement as reserving water as well as land. Some might argue that the Court erred in rendering a decision that seemed to award all the available water to the Indians while denying any to the settlers who had moved onto the newly opened public lands. A major purpose of the 1888 agreement had been to open former Indian lands to white settlement, and for that water was an absolute necessity. But Judge Hunt, the Ninth Circuit Court of Appeals, and the Supreme Court unhesitatingly sided with the Indians. The reserved right, they concluded, was prior to the claims of non-Indian settlers and entitled the Indians—and the federal government, as sovereign, on behalf of the Indians—to sufficient water to fulfill the purposes of the reservation. Those purposes were thought by the courts as well as by the negotiators of the 1888 agreement to be primarily stock

raising and agriculture, but other reasonable uses were not prohibited—and according to the broad construction mandated for
Indian agreements since John Marshall's day, they could not be.

The *Winters* case represented a major advance for Indians at a
time when reversals for them were the usual order of the day. But
the advance proved to be more symbolic than real. The decision has
not assured reservation Indians a clear and unquestioned right to
water. Nowhere has this been more apparent than at Fort Belknap.
Indian water use there has remained at about 5,000 inches, a rate of
flow equivalent to diversions of approximately 25,000 acre-feet
during the irrigation season. The total runoff of Milk River at Fort
Belknap is considerably greater—an average of nearly 250,000
acre-feet, according to latest estimates—but most of this arrives at
the wrong time of the year for agricultural use. In 1910 the
Reclamation Service believed that it was "not practicable to build
flood water reservoirs," but in 1939 technological, and political,
developments enabled construction of Fresno Dam with a storage
capacity of approximately 100,000 acre-feet.[74] But long before
construction of Fresno Dam officials in the Interior Department
were insisting that the maximum flow decreed to the reservation by
Judge Hunt had become the maximum that the Indians could use.
"It is our understanding," announced the manager of the Milk
River Project to the reservation superintendent in June, 1919,
"that the [Fort Belknap] Agency is entitled to divert the entire
natural flow of the Milk River *up to 5,000 inches*. . . ."[75] Any
"excess natural flow," later officials affirmed, "belongs first by
prior appropriations to certain lands of the Chinook division, and
the remainder, if any, is available for the lower [Milk River]
project."[76] The amount available for non-Indians increased significantly as work on the Milk River Project (especially Fresno Dam)
progressed. Such developments testified convincingly to the settlers' success in offsetting the *Winters* decision. As early as 1909,
the year following the Supreme Court's action, the settlers had
helped pressure the federal government into concluding a treaty
with Great Britain over the waters of the Milk and St. Mary rivers,
thereby permitting the Reclamation Service to begin major construction on the Milk River Project.[77] Such success then and during
subsequent decades reflected not just effective lobbying by the
settlers but more especially the dramatic shift in power within the
Interior Department as the ambitious Reclamation Service (after

1923, the Bureau of Reclamation) gained in influence and the Bureau of Indian Affairs declined in prestige. At Fort Belknap, the Indians' attempts to expand their cultivated lands and to develop their extensive mineral resources have met with frustration.[78]

The current situation at Fort Belknap would not surprise Superintendent Logan. He had hoped for the best but feared the worst. "The Indians feel very much elated over the fact that their rights have been protected . . . and are looking foward to a period of prosperity," he told the commissioner of Indian affairs shortly after the Ninth Circuit Court of Appeals had upheld Judge Hunt's injunction. "But O Lord,they don't know the white man with his bulldog tenacity and never give up spirit."[79] If they did not know then, they do now.

This essay by no means resolves the controversies over the Indian water right, for at the heart of those disputes has been (and is) the lack of sufficient water to satisfy the needs of both Indians and non-Indians. Nor does it explain all the legal uncertainties of that right that have developed during the last three-quarters of a century. But the evidence here seems to clarify the *Winters* Court's views concerning the quantum, legitimate uses, and priority of the Indian water right.

# Notes

1. For an overview of the development of these controversies and a discussion of their larger significance see Norris Hundley, Jr., "The Dark and Bloody Ground of Indian Water Rights: Confusion Elevated to Pinciple," *Western Historical Quarterly* 9 (October, 1978): 454–82.

2. *Winters* v.*United States*, 207 U.S. 564 (1908). The name of this important decision contains a clerical error. Henry Winter was only one of many appellants in the case, but his name seems to have been the only one garbled in the official record—Winter was transformed into Winters. See "Twelfth Census of the United States: Population, 1900—Montana," vol. 3: "Choteau County, Chinook township," sheet no. 9, Microfilm T623, roll 910, National Archives; Response of Henry Winter, *United States* v. *Mose Anderson et al.*, 9 U.S. Cir., July 12, 1905, Records of the U.S. Ninth Circuit Court of Appeals, Box 6659, U.S. District Courts Records, Record Group 21, Federal Archives and Records Center, Seattle (hereafter RG).

3. In 1963 in *Arizona* v. *California* the U.S. Supreme Court determined the priority and established the basis for determining the quantum of the water rights of five Indian reservations along the lower Colorado River. In 1979 in a supplemental decree the Court held that the five reservations were not restricted in the uses to which they could put their water. Some legal scholars believe the decision may apply only to the lower Colorado River. In any event the Court gave no reasons for its supplemental decree in 1979, and it based its 1963 decision about quantum on the reasoning of a Special Master. On the priority of the Indian right see the discussion later in this article (including note 61 below). See also 73 below, as well as *Arizona* v. *California et al.*, 373 U.S. 600–601 (1963), 439 U.S. 422 (1979); *Report of the Special Master on Arizona* v. *California* (n.p., December 5, 1960), 262–66; Charles J. Meyers, "The Colorado River," *Stanford Law Review* 19 (1967): 71; Susan Millington Campbell, "A Proposal for the Quantification of Reserved Indian Water Rights," *Columbia Law Review* 74 (November, 1974): 1299–1300; and Rebecca E. Wardlaw, "The Irrigable Acres Doctrine," *Natural Resources Journal* 15 (April, 1975): 375–84.

4. For a sampling of the court decisions and the extensive literature reflecting the confusion and documenting the larger importance of the Indian water rights question for the nation see *Conrad* v. *United States*, 161 F.829 (9 U.S. Cir., 1908); *United States* v. *Walker River Irrigation District*, 104 F.2d 334 (9 U.S. Cir., 1939); *United States* v. *Ahtanum Irrigation District*, 236 F.2d 321 (9 U.S. Cir., 1956); *Arizona* v. *California*, 373 U.S. 340 (1963); Harold A. Ranquist, "The *Winters* Doctrine and How It Grew: Federal Reservation of Rights to the Use of Water," *Brigham Young University Law Review* 3 (1975): 639–724; Michael C. Nelson and Bradley L. Cooke, *The Winters Doctrine: Seventy Years of Application of "Reserved" Water Rights to Indian Reservations, University of Arizona Arid Lands Resource Information Paper No. 9* (Tucson: University of Arizona Press 1977); Edward W. Clyde, "Indian Water Rights," in Robert Emmet Clark, ed., *Waters and Water Rights : A Treatise on the Law of Water and Allied Problems* (Indianapolis: A. Smith Co., 1967–76), 2: 373–99; James L. Merrill, "Aboriginal Water Rights," *Natural Resources Journal* 20 (January, 1980): 45–70; Rupert Costo, "Indian Water Rights: A Survival Issue," *Indian Historian* 5 (Fall, 1972): 4–6; William H. Veeder, "Water Rights: Life or Death for the American Indian,"

*Indian Historian* 5 (Summer, 1972): 4–9; Rosalie Martone, "The United States and the Betrayal of Indian Water Rights," *Indian Historian* 7 (Summer, 1974): 3–11; William H. Veeder, "Indian Prior and Paramount Rights to the Use of Water," *Rocky Mountain Mineral Law Institute Proceedings* 16 (1971): 631–68; Paul Bloom, "Indian 'Paramount' Rights to Water Use," ibid., 669–93; Monroe E. Price, *Law and the American Indian: Readings, Notes and Cases* (Indianapolis: Bobbs-Merrill, 1973), pp. 310–29; Eva H. Morreale, "Federal-State Rights and Relations," in Clark, ed., *Waters and Water Rights*, 2: 59–61; Wardlaw, "Irrigable Acres Doctrine," 375–84; Robert D. Dellwo, "Indian Water Rights—The Winters Docterine Updated," *Gonzaga Law Review* 6 (1971): 215–40; Harry B. Sondheim and John R. Alexander, "Federal Indian Water Rights: A Retrogression to Quasi-Riparianism?" *Southern California Law Review* 34 (1960): 1–61; Peter C. Maxfield, Mary Frances Dieterich, and Frank Trelease, *Natural Resources Law on American Indian Lands* (Boulder, Colo.: 1977) pp. 207–38; John Patterson, "Extent of Indian Water Rights on Reservations in the West," *Rocky Mountain Law Review* 18 (1946): 427–30; John Patterson, "Indian Reserved Water Rights: The *Winters* of Our Discontent," *Yale Law Journal* 88 (1979): 1689–1712; Richard L. Foreman, *Indian Water Rights: A Public Policy and Administrative Mess* (Danville, Ill. Interstate, 1981).

I count myself among those who have misread the Winters decision. In an earlier article that dealt only in part with the case itself, I observed that the decision was "contradictory or, at best, ambiguous"—a position which, as I suggest in the present essay, rests on inadequate attention to the circumstances surrounding the decision. Hundley, "The Dark and Bloody Ground of Indian War Rights," 470.

5. William R. Logan to Francis E. Leupp, June 3, 1905, Fort Belknap Indian Agency Papers, Box 20, Records of the Bureau of Indian Affairs, RG 75, Federal Archives and Records Center, Seattle.

6. John V. Wright, Jared W. Daniels, Charles F. Larrabee to J. D. C. Atkins, February 11, 1887, File 6581–1887, Records of the Office of the Secretary of the Interior, Indian Division, Letters Received, RG 48, National Archives. This letter was reprinted in *Reduction of Indian Reservations*, 50th Congr., 1st sess., H. Exec. Doc. 63, 1888; the quotation appears on p. 26.

7. Ibid.; "Note by Indian Office," n.d., Special Case 144, Records of the Office of Indian Affairs, Letters Received, RG 75, National Archives.

8. 25 *U.S. Stat.* 113–15. At this time the population of the reservation was about 1,700. *Reduction of Indian Reservations, H. Exec. Doc. 63*, p. 7.

9. Wright, Daniels, and Larrabee to Atkins, February 11, 1887, File 6581–1887, Records of the Office of the Secretary of the Interior, Indian Division, Letters Received, RG 48.

10. *Cong. Rec.* 19 (Washington, D.C., 1888), pp. 1842, 2479, 3608.

11. Logan to Leupp, February 17, 1906, Box 20, Fort Belknap; Indian Agency Papers, RG 75.

12. Logan to Leupp, June 3, 1905, Box 20, Fort Belknap Indian Agency Papers, RG 75.

13. Larrabee to Ethan A. Hitchcock, June 9, 1905, File 58730, Records of the Department of Justice, RG 60, National Archives (hereafter NA).

14. Donald L. Parman, "Francis Ellington Leupp, 1905–1909," in Robert M. Kvasnicka and Herman J. Viola, eds., *The Commissioners of Indian Affairs, 1824–1977* (Lincoln, Nebr.: University of Nebraska Press, 1979), p. 224; W. David Baird, "William A. Jones, 1897–1904," in ibid., pp. 217–18.

15. Hitchcock to U.S. Attorney General, June 13, 1905, File 58730, Records of the Department of Justice, RG 60.

16. U.S. Attorney General to Carl Rasch, June 13, 1905, File 58730, Records of the Department of Justice, RG. 60.

17. "*United States* v. *Mose Anderson et al.*: Bill of Complaint" (9 U.S. Cir., June 26, 1905), Box 6659, Records of the U.S. Ninth Circuit Court of Appeals, RG 21.

18. Rasch to U.S. Attorney General, August 28, 1905, File 58730, Records of the Department of Justice, RG 60; memorandum from D.D.C. to U.S. Attorney General, December 18, 1905, ibid.; Logan to Leupp, June 3, 1905, Box 20, Fort Belknap Indian Agency Papers, RG 75.

19. "*United States* v. *Mose Anderson et al.*: Bill of Complaint" (9 U.S. Cir., June 26, 1905), 9, Box 6659, Records of the U.S. Ninth Circuit Court of Appeals, RG 21. Emphasis added.

20. Rasch to U.S. Attorney General, August 28, 1905, File 58730, Records of the Department of Justice, RG 60.

21. The unsettled nature of the law sometimes resulted in the federal government simultaneously pursuing conflicting policies. For criticism of the government on this score in 1905–1906 see File 58730, Records of the Department of Justice, RG 60.

22. "*United States* v. *Mose Anderson et al.*: Temporary Restraining Order" (9 U.S. Cir., June 26, 1905), Box 6659, Records of the U.S. Ninth Circuit Court of Appeals, RG 21; *Chinook Bulletin*, July 6, 1905.

23. "*United States* v. *Mose Anderson et al.*: Order Modifying Restraining Order" (9 U.S. Cir., July 8, 1905), Box 6659, Records of the U.S. Ninth Circuit Court of Appeals, RG 21; *Chinook Bulletin*, July 13, 1905.

24. Rasch to Logan, July 8, 1905, Box 52, Fort Belknap Indian Agency Papers, RG 75.

25. Ibid.; Rasch to Logan, July 13, 1905, Box 52, Fort Belknap Indian Agency Papers, RG 75.

26. Rasch to U.S. Attorney General, August 28, 1905, File 58730, Records of the Department of Justice, RG 60; memorandum from D.D.C. to U.S. Attorney General, December 18, 1905, File 58730, Records of the Department of Justice, RG 60; "*United States* v. *Mose Anderson et al.*: Testimony" (9 U.S. Cir., August 15, 1905), Box 6659, Records of the U.S. Ninth Court of Appeals, RG 21; *Havre Herald*, February 9, 1906.

27. Technically the 1888 agreement was not a treaty, for it had been negotiated after Congress had abandoned the treaty system in 1871. Even so, Judge William H. Hunt (and later the Ninth Circuit Court of Appeals) referred to it as a treaty. The Supreme Court did not employ that term, but it discussed the agreement as if it were a legally binding treaty. The courts have held that similar agreements are "legally binding in much the same way that earlier treaties are still binding." Wilcomb E. Washburn, *The Indian in America* (New York: Harper and Row, 1975), p. 103.

28. "*United States* v. *Mose Anderson et al.*: Memorandum Order" (9 U.S. Cir., August 7, 1905), Box 6659, Records of the U.S. Ninth Circuit Court of Appeals, RG 21.

29. Rasch to U.S. Attorney General, August 28, 1905, File 58730, Records of the Department of Justice, RG 60.

30. "*United States* v. *Mose Anderson et al.*: Memorandum Order" (9 U.S. Cir., August 7, 1905), Box 6659, Records of the U.S. Ninth Circuit Court of Appeals, RG 21; "*United States* v. *Mose Anderson et al.*: Order" (August 8, 1905), ibid.

31. *Havre Herald*, August 11, 1905, January 19, 1906; *Havre Plaindealer*, August 19, 1905; Harlem *Milk River Valley News*, August 30, 1905, January 17, 1906; *Cong. Rec.* 40 (Washington, D.C., 1906), p. 943.

32. George Wharton James, *Reclaiming the Arid West* (New York, 1917), 176–87; U.S. Department of the Interior, Bureau of Reclamation, *Reclamation Project Data* (Washington, D.C.: U.S. Government Printing Office, 1961), pp. 341–43. See also File 548, Milk River Project, Records of the Bureau of Reclamation, RG 115, NA.

33. Harlem *Milk River Valley News*, August 30, 1905, January 17, 1906; *Cong. Rec.* 40, p. 943; *Havre Herald*, January 19, 1906.

34. *Havre Plaindealer*, August 19, 1905; *Havre Herald*, August 11, 1905.

35. *Winters et al.* v. *United States—Ninth Circuit Court of Appeals: Brief for Appellants* (n.p., [1905]), 32, 41–43, copy in File 58730, Records of the Department of Justice, RG 60. The case had begun as *United States* v. *Mose Anderson et al.* with Winter's name following Mose Anderson's in the list of defendants. Because Anderson did not join in the appeal, Winter's name (misspelled as Winters) advanced to the top of the list and the case on appeal became *Winters et al* v. *United States*.

36. *Winters et al.* v. *United States*, 143 F. 743, 749 (9 U.S. Cir., 1906).

37. Ibid., 148 F. 686 (9 U.S. Cir., 1906). Participating in this decision were two of the three judges who had rejected the first appeal. One of the holdovers wrote the opinion.

38. *Conrad* v. *United States*, 161 F. 831, 835 (9 U.S. Cir., 1908).

39. "*United States* v. *Mose Anderson et al.*: Memorandum Order" (9 U.S. Cir., August 7, 1905), Box 6659, Records of the U.S. Ninth Circuit Court of Appeals, RG 21.

40. *Winters et al.* v. *United States*, 143 F. 747 (9 U.S. Cir., 1906).

41. Ibid., 749; *United States, Appt.* v. *Rio Grande Dam and Irrigation Company and the Rio Grande Irrigation & Land Company Limited*, 174 U.S. 703 (1889).

42. *Story* v. *Woolverton*, 78 Pac. 590 (Mont. 1904).

43. *Winters et al.* v. *United States*, 143 F. 748–749 (9 U.S. Cir., 1906); *Fletcher* v. *Peck*, 10 U.S. 121 (1810); *Cherokee Nation* v. *Georgia*, 30 U.S. 16 (1891).

44. *Winters et al.* v. *United States*, 143 F. 748 (9 U.S. Cir., 1906); *Leavenworth* v. *United States*, 92 U.S. 747 (1875).

45. *Havre Herald*, November 23, 1906; *Chinook Opinion*, February 22, March 1, December 13, 1906; *Havre Plaindealer*, March 3, May 19, 26, 1906; Harlem *Milk River Valley News*, November 24, 1906; Logan to Commissioner of Indian Affairs, February 17, 1906, Box 20, Fort Belknap Indian Agency Papers, RG 75; Cyrus C. Babb to Chief Engineer, April 10, 1906, File 548, Milk River Project, Records of the Bureau of Reclamation, RG 115.

46. *Chinook Opinion*, February 8, 15, 1906; *Havre Herald*, February 9, 16, 1906; *Havre Plaindealer*, February 17, 1906.

47. *Chinook Opinion*, February 15, 1906.

48. Larrabee to Logan, March 7, 1906, Box 11, Fort Belknap Indian Agency Papers, RG 75.

49. "*Winters et al.* v. *United States*: Petition of Appellants to U.S. Supreme Court" (January 9, 1907), File 58730, Records of the Department of Justice, RG 60; *Winters* v. *United States*, 207 U.S. 569, 570 (1908).

50. *Winters et al.* v. *United States—Ninth Circuit Court of Appeals: Brief for Appellants* (n.p. [1906]), 19 File 58730, Records of the Department of Justice, RG 60.

51. *Winters* v. *United States*, 207 U.S. 570 (1908).

52. Ibid., p. 576.

53. Ibid., pp. 575, 576.

54. Ibid., pp. 576, 577.

55. See n. 4.

56. Clesson S. Kinney, *A Treatise on the Law of Irrigation* (Washington, D.C., 1894), pp. 201–203; *Leavenworth* v. *United States*, 92 U.S. 747 (1875); *Worcester* v. *Georgia*, 31 U.S. 579–81 (1832); *United States* v. *Cook*, 86 U.S. 592–94 (1874); *Buttz* v. *Northern Pacific Railroad*, 119 U.S. 66–68 (1886); *Missouri* v. *Roberts*, 152 U.S. 116–20 (1894).

57. *Winters* v. *United States*, 207 U.S. 577 (1908).

58. *United States* v. *Winans*, 198 U.S. 383 (1905).

59. *Winters* v. *United States*, 207 U.S. 577 (1908).

60. Ibid., p. 576.

61. In 1963 the U.S. Supreme Court in *Arizona* v. *California* held that the Indian right extended back only to the date when a reservation was created, but in that case the court was dealing with reservations established by executive order or an act of Congress. None of them had been created as Fort Belknap had—by agreement with Indians living on ancestral lands—and thus there was no semblance of a treaty or agreement whereby the Indians could have retained or "reserved" their rights. This distinction, while apparently advantageous to treaty reservations, downgrades the rights of nontreaty peoples who, whether they continue to live on ancestral lands or have been placed on reservations elsewhere, are still descendants of the first inhabitants who held dominion over the continent's land and water for hundreds of years prior to European arrival. It also fails to apply with equality to those Indians, especially in the Southwest, who were practicing irrigation agriculture long before the Spaniards arrived and who live on reservations not set aside by treaty. In fact, some Indians—for example, the Pueblo tribes of New Mexico—live on lands not set aside by treaty, statute, or executive order. See *Arizona* v. *California*, 373 U.S. 600 (1963). For a discussion of the distinctions the law makes in the rights of treaty and nontreaty Indians see Daniel G. Kelly, Jr., "Indian Title: The Rights of American Natives in Lands They Have Occupied since Time Immemorial," *Columbia Law Review* 75 (1975): 665–86. See also Maxfield, Dieterich, and Trelease, *Natural Resources Law on American Indian Lands*, pp. 213–18, 220–21; Merrill, "Aboriginal Water Rights," pp. 45–70.

62. "*United States* v. *Mose Anderson et al.*: Temporary Restraining Order" (9 U.S. Cir., June 26, 1905), Box 6659, Records of the U.S. Ninth Circuit Court of Appeals, RG 21; "*United States* v. *Mose Anderson et al.*: Order Modifying Restraining Order" (9 U.S. Cir., July 8, 1905), ibid.; "*United States* v. *Mose Anderson et al.*: Memorandum Order" (9 U.S. Cir., August 1905), ibid.

63. *Winters et al.* v. *United States*, 143 F. 749 (9 U.S. Cir. 1906); ibid., 148 F. 684 (9 U.S. Cir., 1906); ibid., 207 U.S. 564 (1908).

64. *Havre Herald*, January 10, 1908; Harlem *Milk River Valley News*, January 23, 1908.

65. *Chinook Opinion*, January 9, 1908.

66. Logan to C. F. Ellis & Co., October 4, 1908, Box 59, Fort Belknap Indian Agency Papers, RG 75.

67. See footnote 4.

68. *25 U.S. Stat.* 113, 114. Emphasis added.

69. "*United States* v. *Mose Anderson et al.*: Memorandum Order" (9 U.S. Cir., August 7, 1905), Box 6659, Records of the U.S. Ninth Circuit Court of Appeals, RG 21; *Winters et al.* v. *United States*, 143 F. 744 (9 U.S. Cir. 1906).

70. *Winters* v. *United States*, 207 U.S. 576 (1908), emphasis added. Those who insist that the Indians can use their water only for irrigation invariably cite the following statement in the headnotes of the Supreme Court decision: "This Court holds that there was an implied reservation . . . of a sufficient amount of water from the Milk River for irrigation purposes," ibid., 564. Whatever else might be said about this statement, the Supreme Court has held that the headnotes to its decisions

possess no legal authority. "[T]he headnote is not the work of the Court," declared the Supreme Court two years prior to the Winters case, "nor does it state its decision. . . . It is simply the work of the reporter, gives his understanding of the decision, and is prepared for the convenience of the profession in the examination of the reports." *United States* v. *Detroit Timber & Lumber Compan et al.*, 200 U.S. 337 (1906).

71. *Worcester* v. *Georgia*, 31 U.S. 581 (1832).

72. *Winters* v. *United States*, 207 U.S. 579 (1908).

73. In 1963 the Supreme Court, in *Arizona* v. *California*, held that the quantum of the right of five Indian reservations along the lower Colorado River was to be determined by the "practicably irrigable acreage on the reservations." The Court believed that such a measure conformed to the government's intention in creating the reservations, could be applied with a fair degree of accuracy, and represented a way of resolving the uncertainty of non-Indians about the extent of the Indian right. In a supplemental decree sixteen years later the Court stated that the Indian water right was not restricted "to irrigation or other agricultural application," but the Court offered no reasons for its holding. The five reservations dealt with in this decision had been created by statute of executive order; none had been created in treaty. *Arizona* v. *California*, 373 U.S. 600–601 (1963); *Arizona* v. *California*, 439 U.S. 422 (1979).

74. Milk River Project," December 17, 1910, File 548, Milk River Project, Records of the Bureau of Reclamation, RG 115; interview with Thomas Michael Watson, September 22, 1980, a civil engineer with the firm of Morrison-Maiarle, which recently investigated the water needs and uses at Fort Belknap Reservation; U.S. Department of the Interior, Bureau of Indian Affairs, Missouri River Investigation Project, "The Fort Belknap Reservation Area: Its Resources and Development Potential," *Report No. 198* (Billings, Mont., 1972), p. 97; Department of the Interior, *Reclamation Project Data*, pp. 342–43.

75. Project Manager to A. H. Symons, June 23, 1919, File 548, Milk River Project, Records of the Bureau of Reclamation, RG 115. Emphasis added.

76. H. H. Johnson to Chief Engineer (Denver), December 7, 1932, File 187A, Box 466485, Office of Chief Engineer, Records of the Bureau of Reclamation, RG 115, Federal Archives and Records Service, Denver, Colo. Five years earlier Commissioner of Reclamation Elwood Mead had stated that "5,000 miner's inches marks the amount considered and found by the [district] court to be sufficient, else the injunction would have called for a larger amount. The principle announced in the [Supreme Court] decision may entitle the Indians to the use of whatever quantity of water may be necessary, but I believe it is clear that the decree in this case would protect them in the use of only 5,000 miner's inches." Mead went on to concede that "the Indians are entitled to use whatever water they may require limited to the normal flow of Milk River." Since by "normal flow" he meant the unregulated flow, Mead's concession produced essentially no additional water for the Indians. By 1932, Reclamation officials were again insisting that the Indian right was limited to a specific volume—5,000 inches. This same amount was all that the Justice Department claimed on behalf of the Indians in a suit filed in 1979. Mead to Charles H. Burke, July 9, 1927, ibid.; interview with Watson.

77. James, *Reclaiming the Arid West*, 176–87; Department of the Interior, *Reclamation Project Data*, 343. From the outset of the Milk River Project the Indians have been denied rights to any St. Mary River water brought into the basin. According to an expert who has recently investigated the situation, virtually all the St. Mary Water arrives when the non-Indians can use it. This means that the Fresno reservoir essentially captures only Milk River water, which—except for one-seventh of the reservoir's capacity that is permitted to go to the Indians—is then improperly made available to non-Indians. Interview with Watson.

78. Department of the Interior, ''The Fort Belknap Reservation Area,'' 14–16, 22, 37, 97–99; U.S. Department of Commerce, *Federal and State Indian Reservations and Indian Trust Areas* (Washington, D.C.: U. S. Government Printing Office, 1974), p. 278; U.S. Department of the Interior, Bureau of Indian Affairs, *Estimates of Resident Indian Population and Labor Force Status* [mimeograph] (n.p., 1973), p. 12.

79. Logan to Leupp, April 29, 1906, Box 20, Fort Belknap Indian Agency Papers, RG 75.

# CHAPTER 5

# The Indian New Deal and the Years
# that Followed: Three Interviews

## CONDUCTED BY JOSEPH H. CASH
## AND HERBERT T. HOOVER

*Commissioner of Indian Affairs John Collier encountered some of the
stiffest resistance to his "Indian New Deal" in the Plains. Although
the Depression meant difficult problems for Plains Indians, many
people did not find the solutions in the Collier program. In both the
northern and southern Plains tribal representatives questioned the
nature of the Indian Reorganization Act and other initiatives of the
era.*

*Toward the south Indians in Oklahoma who had been forced to
adapt perhaps more fully than had other Indians to an individualistic
society often wondered aloud whether Collier was trying to turn back
the clock to an earlier, communal era. Fiery spokesmen such as
Joseph Bruner, a Creek, influenced many Plains Indians to be suspicious of the commissioner and his motives.*

*As the following interviews reveal, there was also considerable
disagreement among Indians in the north about the nature of Collier's
program. For many people who had endured half a century of
"Americanization," the commissioner's notions seemed surprising.
Moreover, Collier had learned about Indian life primarily through the
Pueblo peoples of New Mexico, and it was questionable whether that
understanding could be transferred in its entirety to another region. In
any event there could be no doubt that the Indian New Deal would
have both immediate and long-term effects.*

The interviews with Ben Reifel, Antoine Roubideaux, and Alfred DuBray, are
reproduced from archival typescripts in the American Research Project collection
at the Oral History Center on the campus of the University of South Dakota in
Vermillion, S.D. Reproduced with the permission of Herbert T. Hoover, director
of the collection.

*After World War II, however, the Bureau of Indian Affairs changed its course once again. The so-called termination era saw the federal government attempt to withdraw services and abandon trust responsibilities to the Indians. Through programs such as the relocation of Indians in cities the bureau discouraged residence on the reservation. While most Indian tribes were not "terminated," the shock waves from the bureau's turnabout were felt throughout the Plains and the rest of Indian America. Indian activism of the 1960s may be traced directly to the era preceding it, when the need for organization and collective action became clear.*

*Through oral history projects the living memories of the generation between the 1930s and the 1950s have been preserved. One of the most important programs in Indian oral history proved to be the Doris Duke projects. The Duke project in the University of South Dakota allowed hundreds of northern Plains Indians to be interviewed during the late 1960s and the beginning of the 1970s. Joseph H. Cash and Herbert T. Hoover, members of the Department of History in the university, had major responsibility for these efforts.*

*Herbert T. Hoover kindly gave the editor of this volume permission to work from the original transcripts of the following interviews with three men who were important participants in Indian political life. Ben Reifel earned a doctoral degree from Harvard University, worked for the Bureau of Indian Affairs, and served as a United States congressman from South Dakota. Antoine Roubideaux, tribal chairman and secretary, was for decades a vital figure in the politics of the Rosebud Reservation, of South Dakota. Alfred DuBray worked as an administrator for the bureau in many locations, including the Winnebago Reservation, in Nebraska.*

BEN REIFEL, BRULÉ SIOUX. INTERVIEWED BY JOSEPH H. CASH IN THE SUMMER OF 1967 IN WASHINGTON, D.C.

CASH: This is Congressman Ben Reifel of the First District of South Dakota. Congressman, you were very active in the '30's on the Rosebud and Pine Ridge reservations in connection with the Indian Reorganization Act, were you not?

REIFEL: Yes, I was. I was a farm agent at Oglala, South Dakota, on the Pine Ridge reservation in 1933. When the bill was being

considered by the Indians on the reservations in regional conferences, at the same time it was being considered here in the
Congress prior to enactment. And I was impressed by the
possibilities of the bill. The original plan was to set up a well-
coordinated system of government by tribes. One of the primary
benefits that I thought would come from it would be that if they did
go through with their judicial system whereby the tribal courts
would be tied in with a federal system of courts, this would correct
the weakness in Indian courts where there is no appeal for the tribal
organization or for the tribal courts. That, of course, persists to the
present time and is one of the weaknesses in the judicial system of
tribal courts now. Some attempts are being made to correct it.

Well, there were many aspects of the original plan written out in
the bill that was presented to Congress that got changed. I think it
was a plan for communal use of the tribal property and the development of the property on a communal basis. I think in the minds of
some this was identified with communism in some way or another,
when really it was nothing more than enlarging upon present tribal
holdings of especially land in common. That is the case even today
in many of the reservations that aren't allotted, like the Navajos in
large parts. And it was thought to develop these properties on a
communal basis. One of the major defects at least as far as members of Congress were concerned at the time, was that it was
divesting an individual of his property without his consent. Some
of the provisions of the proposal would take land that was allotted
in severalty to an individual and put it back into common ownership. And this was believed to be a violation of personal property
rights without due recourse to the courts. So it all finally came out
in a much modified program known as the Wheeler-Howard Act,
subsequently designated as the Indian Reorganization Act of 1934.

Well, I happened to be on the Pine Ridge reservation, as I said,
as a farm agent. And I was impressed with the whole program, by
the time it finally became a law. I could speak and write the Sioux
language and took one of these old ABC charts that they used to use
in Indian schools on a little stand. And on one side I would write a
little synopsis of each section. I think there were some 18 sections
to the bill, or really to the law. And right alongside of it, I would put
the Indian translation and draw some pictures to illustrate what it
meant. I did this in my farm district. Then, when the tribal leaders
met in a reservation-wide meeting, they were having it explained to

them, but the people from the districts from which I was working attending the meeting seemed to be better informed. The others wanted to know where he got the information. He said, well, I was down there helping with it, so the superintendent of the reservation at that time, James H. McGregor, sent word down for me to come up and put on my chalk talk for the tribal leaders. As a result of this experience, then I went with him from one district on the reservation to another to explain the law.

CASH: Were you hired to do this?

REIFEL: I was a farm agent. Of course, the superintendent had authority to delegate any of his employees to other assignments than their primary assignment for short periods of time. So, I was with the superintendent at the meetings on the reservation. There was considerable agitation against the legislation because the older members of the tribe and some of the younger ones, too, felt that what was going to happen here was that their lands were going to be taken away from them and put into common ownership. And this they were very fearful of and I didn't blame them for this. I think this was a carryover from the original provisions of the bill, or rather, the original bill that was proposed by John Collier, who was then the Commissioner of Indian Affairs. And he had held regional meetings where the tribes would come in and he was trying to develop a receptivity on the part of the Indians for the legislation.

CASH: They had one in Rapid City.

REIFEL: They had one held in Rapid City. I remember I attended that one. Back in those days I was just a young person in the government service. But I became very interested, so I took annual leave and went up there and spent all the time at the conference listening to what was going on. Well, there was this opposition then to the bill itself, or to the act. Now the act was unusual in that unless the Indians turned it down it would go into effect. I would have a referendum on it. So the law was passed by Congress subject to acceptance-rejection by the tribe. So this made it necessary then to go out and explain to the tribes prior to elections to be held, the provisions of the act.

And so with the little experience I had on the reservation, explaining with my charts, there was a person by the name of Joe Jennings who was superintendent of Indian education for South Dakota, and he was designated by the Commissioner of Indian Affairs to take responsibility for explaining the Indian Reorganization Act to tribes throughout South Dakota, and I think in Montana, Nebraska, and North Dakota. So, being aware of what I was doing at Pine Ridge, he asked the superintendent if I could be used to do this explanation with him in the Sioux country because I spoke the Sioux language. So I traveled throughout the state of South Dakota to the various Indian tribes that were scheduled to vote on the legislation and explained its provisions. Then following that, some tribes adopted it and some did not. I remember Crow Creek was one tribe that turned it down. Sisseton was another; I think they turned the legislation down completely. And, I believe, also the Yankton reservation.

By this time, this was in July of 1935, the commissioner then established under the law some field agents to help with the promotion of the legislation on the Indian reservations, and so I was designated as one of the first to be a field agent. In July of 1935, I got the appointment and I came down to Washington in March of that year and was down here a couple of months getting some background information on it. And then I was headquartered in Pierre until 1942 when the war broke out and I was ordered to active duty. But during that seven year period, I worked with Indian tribes to explain the provisions of the law, and when they got that done, then the tribes if they wanted to move ahead, could adopt a constitution and bylaws. Following that, they could establish a corporate charter.

All of these had to be explained, drafted by the tribal members, and then voted upon in open elections. And you got a great deal of opposition and much excitement for it and camps developed, one against the other. In the Dakotas, we had a group called the Old Dealers. You see this emerged out of the Roosevelt New Deal period and so Collier, then commissioner, said that we would have a New Deal also for the Indians. So this was dubbed the New Deal, and anyone who was for it was a New Dealer and the older members, who saw themselves losing control because of an elected council pretty much patterned after our own kind of elections.

Up until then, for instance at Pine Ridge, they had what was considered seven districts on the reservation and the seven districts each had, I think, ten delegates who would come to a tribal council and they'd sit there and carry on for three or four days. This would be 80 or 90 people coming together. And this was a kind of a traditional system where they didn't have much, if any, power at all, but they did have an opportunity to express their views and to give vent to some of their feelings. I think they saw themselves losing this, what little influence it had—at least their participation in the Indian system.

CASH: Do you think it was an old generation of leadership opposing a new?

REIFEL: It was the old generation of leadership who was opposing it, and to this day you have this older group that I think still look upon themselves as the so-called Old Dealers. The term is, the New Dealers were called Oon-tey-cha, meaning the new way of life. And they had the old timers.

CASH: Did you notice in the opposition any difference between the full bloods and the mixed bloods?

REIFEL: Yes. Well, you have of course the old-timers, the older people were largely full bloods. And then you had among them, I think, some opportunists. At least they appeared to me to be that then, and I think I would not change my mind now, who tended to help the older ones and they themselves could not see themselves getting into the new system. Either by lack of education or because of maybe their prior lack of leadership, they were in a position because they could speak English and could identify themselves and provided a means of communication on the part of the so-called Old Dealers against the new program.

Another problem we had with it and still have with Indian administration is that the landed property of the tribe is held in the name of the United States in trust. And then Congress charges the Secretary of the Interior with the responsibility of exercising that trust. Therefore, over the years they have certain rules and regulations that have been established for the protection or the exercise of that trust, every honest effort, I think, designed to protect the Indians in the use of their property. And so the constitution as it was written says in practically every section "with the approval of the Secretary of the Interior," and if he doesn't turn it down within a certain period of time, it becomes effective.

And the Old Dealers, so-called, said, "Well, you see, I told you. The Secretary's still going to have control. He's having control. You got to go to him." The newer ones said, "Well, this is, of course, necessary under the circumstances." But then at some point when they tried to move beyond what the law would permit and the Secretary would step in to prevent its completion of the enactment carried in the force, why then they would begin to get shaken a bit, feeling that they were unnecessarily restrained. There were provisions in the constitution by which after a certain period in some instances the Secretary's authority would expire, and so on. But never was there any authority in the constitution where the Secretary's trust responsibility was completely taken away. And of course it couldn't be, because if the Indians are to keep their land in trust subject to or not subject to local taxation, why then it would have to be considered at least in a sense a kind of federal property, because it would be in the name of the United States, being held in trust.

Well, then, so there was this feeling that the tribal councils did not get enough authority to really do the things they wanted to do in behalf of the people they represented. And they had along with this federal charter of incorporation. Now that again created a lot of difficulty for old-timers, because the corporate charter authorized the tribe to accept gifts and property and also to hypothecate tribal property for any loans that they may get from the federal government.

Well, the older, those who were opposed, said, ''Well, here's a group of people that are governing our people. They're a small group. They weren't representing all the people and the older people didn't think they were being represented adequately. So there was a great deal of feeling about the acceptance of the charter—that this would cause them to lose the land, and if they borrowed the money, the federal government later on, if they won a claim, this would be an offset against the claim. There were many things like that. Every kind of ghost was raised against it that they could imagine and some of it had just enough fact to it to give it a color of truth. And I could understand their apprehensiveness in this regard.

The law was accepted at Pine Ridge, but they didn't take the corporate charter. I guess at Rosebud they took all three. I think that probably was true. Lower Brule accepted all three. Crow Creek didn't accept anything. Standing Rock accepted the law, but never got a constitution or a charter. Cheyenne River accepted all three, as I recall.

CASH: The New Deal did a lot of other things as well as the Indian Reorganization Act. I've heard a lot of people say that it pushed education on the reservation.

REIFEL: Well, the New Deal gave impetus to a lot of things in rural areas. There was a definite feeling, I think, across the whole United States that there was going to be a revival of the cottage industries. The Industrial Revolution had sort of run its course and we're going back out on the land. I think that the leadership of the Indian Bureau, under Mr. Collier had this feeling and I've heard him say that the Indians are in the vanguard of this great world-wide movement back on the land. And they set up little rehabilitation projects and canning kitchens and little cottages around and developed the irrigation plots up on Red Shirt Table at Pine Ridge—local turkey, poultry project, cattle project, and the thing's going, well, seemingly great guns. They established a school there and it was really a community school. The teacher and his wife and the whole family lived and worked with this group. It was quite an exciting sort of thing, if this was really what was happening. But then World War II came along and the Industrial Revolution really came to its own. And in agriculture we were able to produce more than we ever did before, with, I guess, half the young farmers off the land.

CASH: Do you think that those irrigation and cattle co-ops were ended primarily by the war?

REIFEL: Well, I think they were ended by two things. One, they would come to an end because there was a disruption by the war itself, with the young men and women leaving the reservation, going into the army. And then, they were just beginning to reach a point where property was being accumulated visibly. They set up these cooperatives on the one man, one vote basis, so that we have people who have not thought in terms of plowing back their net into increased capital investment. A lot of them see something accumulate, they want to divide it up as soon as they saw, for instance, on the Red Shirt Table, cattle beginning to get accumulated and livestock and other property and a little money in the bank. You could have a free vote, so pretty soon they had enough votes to vote themselves the division of all they had and that just sort of ended the thing.

Superintendent Whitlock organized what they call the Tribal Land Enterprise. It was a real imaginative approach to resolve this terrific problem resulting from the heirship, the parceling of the land which was originally allotted in 80, 160, 320 acres. And the idea at that time was that you could lease grazing land for three or four cents an acre. If you got five and ten cents, this was terrific. And farm lands were low in value. As soon as Secretary Ickes took over, he issued an order that no lands would be sold. He put a complete ban on the sale of Indian lands.

Well, during this period while the lands weren't being sold, of course, the people were dying and their lands were being probated according to state law and heirship provisions were applying and the land was being fractionated, so Mr. Whitlock devised this idea that a piece of farmland was worth two acres of grazing land. On this basis, they appraised the farmland at a certain figure; I believe it was ten dollars an acre and the grazing land at five dollars. And if I had, let's say I had the equivalent of 160 acres of ten different pieces, I could turn all these over to the TLE and get back a TLE certificate that I was entitled to so many acres. Then I could go out and, if by this time the tribe had accumulated, say, 160 acres of farmland, I could take these certificates and turn them in and have this use right to these 160 acres. I thought this was an excellent approach.

The idea was excellent in that it would make it possible for individuals who owned these fractionated interests all over the reservation to consolidate their holdings. Now one of the weaknesses in it was from the standpoint of ownership; the land became tribal land, but the individual had the use right which he could pass on to his heirs and so on, and avoid this horrible situation we're in. But what happened was that during the war, land values began to go up. And here are these folks with these certificates, twelve dollars for fractionated interest, and another one for something else. It was never intended that these shares would be sold to some outsider or to a member of the tribe. But there was enough pressure brought on and pretty soon, they were beginning to pick up these TLE certificates for ten or fifteen cents on the dollar. Then it got out of hand, where an individual might buy through an enterprising member of the tribe. All of this put the thing in something less than acceptable posture. So it created a lot of unhappiness because it did deprive some people of their land holdings. And it also was an ideal means of enterprising people taking advantage of others. I think they finally got it resolved now, so that this is beginning to move along the basis in which it was originally intended.

In education, I think the Meriam Survey in 1928 really set the basis for improvement. Up until then, there wasn't much done in the boarding school. With the Meriam survey, it began to bring in professionally qualified people—more doctors, more nurses, more teachers. The New Deal sort of built right on this.

One of the misfortunes among the Indians, I feel personally as far as education was concerned, was because of this whole national feeling of reversion to the land and the Indians were in the vanguard. The first director of Indian education in the Bureau of Indian Affairs under the New Deal was, I can't think of his name at the moment, but he was the first president from the National Progressive Education Association [Carson Ryan]. He wanted to move on a learning by doing and this was carried further by the second president of the National Progressive Education Association, Mr. Willard Beatty.

There's nothing wrong with the John Dewey approach, if you had enough teachers well-trained and the equipment to follow the John Dewey method, but here we had Dr. Willard Beatty come out, and said, no curricula, throw out the state courses. Study, I don't want to find any books in the classroom. These poor teachers were just going around because they'd never been taught how to handle this situation. A few conferences were held and wonderful speeches were made about the value of the Dewey approach and progressive education. And so he had kids just roaming around trying to find something to do. And through that period, you see, I think that a lot of time was lost.

There was a feeling: well, the Indians went away to boarding schools and they came back to the reservation anyway, so why train them to leave? Let's train them to stay where they are: So you had goats brought in, and little projects where the kids would work with rabbits and chickens and gardens, and they tended to be losing sight of learning to read and to write and to figure. And they said, ''Well, you could learn all these things just as rapidly if you related your arithmetic to the chicken house and to the goats and amount of milk a goat had and all this. But the teachers just weren't prepared for this. And as a consequence, I think they lost lots of time there.

But there was a part of the Meriam survey and the start in the direction of improving the educational system back in 1928. This was carried through so you got some better school buildings, for instance. And then, of course, with the second world war coming along, you had apparently a lot of young people from the reservations going into the armed forces. You have the Navajos, for instance, who had a real awakening for the need of education. And so they were able then to get the Navajos to bring their children to school.

But other than a general revival in bringing additional money for facilities, I think the methods that were implemented as a result of this wave of progressive education sweeping the country, I don't believe did the education system, as far as the Indian children are concerned, much help. There was, of course, out of the Indian Reorganization Act a stepup in the educational loan programs that were being made available to Indians. But this had also started back in 1928. In 1928, I got one of the first loans that was made available under the Indian program as recommended by the Meriam survey, where the Indian could borrow money without having to pay any interest until he got a job when he got out. And over a period of four years, I borrowed $900. This was back in from 1928 to 1932. So whatever was done in education or in anything in Indian affairs, was on really a kind of foundation that was established as a result of the recommendation of the Meriam survey.

CASH: How do you think the law and order system worked under the Wheeler-Howard Act?

REIFEL: Well, up until the time of the Wheeler-Howard Act, of course, you just had the tribal courts. And there really wasn't too much of a necessity for a sophisticated court system. You had one of the old tribal leaders who was respected in the community and he was designated by the superintendent of the reservation as the judge. And then you had some tribal policemen. And then there was a code of tribal offenses set up, a blanket for the United States, I guess, and if the Indian violated this, then he was brought before the judge and the judge was probably one who couldn't read or write in some instances. He issued a sentence to him and this is about all there was.

But there was an effort on the original bill to set up a real sophisticated federal court system that would go all the way from the little tribal Indian community right up to federal court if necessary and have an appeal just like any other. But in the revising and the amending of the bill it finally came out there wasn't any federal court set-up. So all they did then was for the tribal constitution to provide. The law said that whatever laws, whatever rights or powers the Indian tribe had that was not taken away from them by the government the tribe still had. One of these was law and order

jurisdiction over its people. And then on the basis of that, the
constitution provided that the tribal council would establish a law
and order code for the reservation. Then they brought in the state
codes, and in most instances, along with the federal laws and tried
to work out the best compromise to fit the situation on the reservation. So then you actually have then a code of offenses defining
what an offense was and then also laid the limits down as to what
the sentence would be. And then there was a provision in it that the
individual would be informed of his rights and all this sort of thing.

But again, because the courts couldn't pay very much, a person
who would accept the responsibilities of tribal judge usually was
somebody that if he had a high school education, you were fortunate. In most instances, he probably had what might not be much
better than a good eighth grade education. Which was probably not
too bad, I mean, if he had good judgment and a lot of native ability.
But the weakness of the whole system was, and still is, that this
court, once it finds an individual guilty, there is no appeal from it. I
mean, this is it. He can't appeal it and we're still worrying with it.
There was nothing in the Indian Reorganization Act that enables a
case to be carried beyond the tribal; the tribe is the final authority.
And in a small community like Pine Ridge, even though it is 8000
scattered over the land there, you begin to get somebody in court
and you get friends and so on. If there are no personalities involved, the person who is aggrieved always feels that there is some
partiality involved and this sort of thing. So there's lots of painful
experiences as a result. A person gets thrown in jail and there's no
appeal.

But there hasn't been any way to rectify it. Now, as I say, had the
original bill gone through it would have set up a system of district
Indian courts under the federal system, through which you could
appeal right up to the Supreme Court, if it was necessary. But now
on the reservations you have the state law applying in certain
instances, the federal law applying in certain instances, and then
there's this no man's land, so to speak, in which the tribal courts
apply and it's in this area where a tribal member is sometimes
without any recourse to an appeal.

CASH: Do you think that on balance the Indian is better off under the
Reorganization Act than the previous system?

REIFEL: Oh, yes. I think that the educational consequences of the
Indian Reorganization Act in constitutional government, for in-

stance—all the discussions that have gone on as to one's rights with respect to laws, these are the things that had never been discussed to any extent before. Here it brought the people directly into involvement with the federal law being considered by Congress and it was being talked over with them before it was enacted into law. And then it was talked about all the time it was in Congress and they sent delegations down. And then, following that, they had an opportunity to reconsider whether they wanted the law or not. And then, after that, after they accepted the law or go through all the problems of setting up a constitution and by laws and then adopting and formulating resolutions and ordinances and all of this, I think it was helpful for improving their knowledge of government and our society generally.

CASH: Do you think that economically he's better off under the Wheeler-Howard Act?

REIFEL: In many respects. The Wheeler-Howard Act made possible those loans that are still being expanded in amount. Authorizations are increasing that made loans to the individuals at a lower rate of interest than he could get through the Farmers Home Administration. The problem there is, again, that here is a person who gets a loan, and his neighbor may feel that he's just as qualified to get the loan as the fellow who gets the loan. Then you build up some neighborhood jealousy as a result of this, where you can't get enough money to take care of everybody and so you've got to be selective. Well, in being selective you select those who could benefit most rapidly from this.

In many instances, this may be individuals who are just a little above the margin by the guidelines and the standards on which a loan is granted. This makes the other fellow say, "Why can't I?" Or the tribal council or the credit board is helping relatives. Or they find all kinds of reasons. So, you disappoint more people than you help. I think it's true today with our efforts to try to help the poor, when we really get into some pretty massive problems. And you touch a little here and a little there and you actually sometimes raise hopes of people beyond possibilities of meeting them. And with these programs, I think this is what's happened on Indian reservations. But on balance, they've gotten more loans and helped more people from this standpoint. They have improved, I think, the law and order system, so that the individual, in spite of all this, has a better chance. The law enforcement programs are a little more sophisticated in recognizing the rights of the individuals. The land program that is being worked out at Rosebud through all the trials and tribulations it's gone through is a move for improvement in the right direction. The educational loan programs of the Indian Reorganization Act are continuing to be increased; these were, I think, a forerunner of what we have for the nation as a whole now.

ANTOINE ROUBIDEAUX, BRULÉ SIOUX. INTERVIEWED BY JOSEPH H. CASH IN THE SUMMER OF 1967 ON ROSEBUD RESERVATION, SOUTH DAKOTA.

CASH: This is Antoine Roubideaux, secretary of the Rosebud Sioux, former tribal chairman. Could you tell me about the Indian Reorganization Act?

ROUBIDEAUX: Well, Congress passed this 1934 Act. And the only way it would go into effect would be to have the tribe ratify it. The government, under Mr. John Collier, who was Commissioner of Indian Affairs at that time, called me into Washington. I was just a young farmer and rancher at that time. I went to Washington and they gave me an orientation on this law. I came back and then I started in with my people. I talked to people all over the reservation about it.

John Collier was the guy that really was behind this 1934 Act. He wanted to get the people organized and so the Indian tribes will be self-governing people, and handling their own affairs, controlling their own money, controlling their own land. Before that, the BIA was handling everything.

The tribe had money deposited here, but they couldn't spend it the way they wanted. If the old council passed a resolution wanting to use that money for a certain thing, why the superintendent said no and, well, that was it. They take the money and they use it as they saw fit. So I met with the constitutional committee and I asked them that we request legal help from the Interior Department. Which we did, and the superintendent wrote the request for us. And the constitutional committee signed it, and they sent it to Washington. About two weeks later, two lawyers came out here. Felix Cohen came out and Fred Diker came out. We met for about a week straight with the committee, and they worked on this new constitution. The constitution that we operate under now, they worked on it. They got it all set up and I had to get out with the committee into every community of the reservation to explain it. They had to vote on it it, yes or no. So we explained it to them, and they voted on it. I think it was in November they voted on it. And they carried it. They adopted the new constitution.

CASH: I noticed that all these votes were fairly close.

ROUBIDEAUX: Yes, it was.

CASH: Who was opposing you on that?

ROUBIDEAUX: Well, Eugene Little, who was one of the long hair Indians. He was chairman of this old council. And he opposed ratifying, going under this 1934 Act. And he had great followers; they call themselves Old Dealers. They're the ones that opposed everything: the referendum on the '34 Act, the constitution, and the charter. Well, they ratified the constitution. And the old council had faith in me and that's why they elected me as the first president.

. . . The main thing, Felix Cohen says, let the people put their wishes together. Don't force them to it. And that's what we did.

CASH: How was the first government?

ROUBIDEAUX: Well, at that time, it was a new thing. You had to deal with laws and some were a little bit skeptical. They were afraid to move. But I finally moved them around and I got them started and I got this charter ratified. And at that time, you know, the depression was on. Everybody was hard up. And that's what I told my people. You're all hard up. I hate to see you walking out on the road. I said, "Many times I pick some of you up on the road. You get these things done. You, your tribe, could borrow money and you could go into cattle business. You could farm your own land, develop your own resources." And that's what they did; and it's been going ever since then. The revolving loan fund is working.

They set up, I think over a period of two years, about 14 livestock associations. And at that time, the Rosebud Sioux tribe had a break. During that time they were borrowing all these ERA cattle, you know? The government bought up all these cattle. They had a bunch of them there in Old Mexico. So, John Collier writes to me, and he says, "If you want some cows, we'll give you some cows on repayment." In kind repayment, see? Instead of paying cash back, if they give you ten head, you pay back ten head, say in two or three years. So I accepted that, and I think they shipped us about three hundred head. And that's when we start putting out these cattle to the Indian people. And in addition to that, we gave them a cash loan.

On irrigation, that was the government's responsibility. They came out here with a lot of sums of money and they started developing these community irrigation gardens. And then they showed how to run these things. And in addition, they built about 18 or 19 canning kitchens.

Then they got the Indians to get together and grow wheat. And then the government would go out there and thresh it for them. They bring the wheat in here, and they make flour, and they make pancake flour and take it back out to them. Then the Indians had flour for the winter. That was a good program. It was operating smoothly until the war, World War II, broke out. Then they just jerked the program out.

At that time they had an extension woman here who went out. About every community had a canning kitchen. And then they brought them these pressure cookers, and sealers, and cans, and everything they use to can their food. Showed them how to do it. And they had vegetables they wanted to can. Well, they bring it to this canning kitchen and they can their own food. And that was a good program. But the government furnished the money, see, and then they supervised it. And that's how the thing was a success. Of course, when World War II broke out, why they just jerked out their money. And at that time, we had that CCC program, you know, where they were going around building dams and reforestation work. And today, if you see any dams on the reservation, they built them, the government did.

Unemployment was so bad. They must have put 300 to work. If you had a team of horses that will pull a scraper, why they put you to work. They had them in groups, all over, building dams. At the same time, they had a lot of rodent control work. You know, like the prairie dogs were overtaking the rangeland. They had a group working, going around poisoning them.

CASH: Did that older element that went around the old treaty council continue to buck you during the '30's?

ROUBIDEAUX: Yes. What they call the Old Deal Council. Most of the active leaders at that time backed away from it and went under this new one. But that old element kept up the old council. They tried to convince the people to vote no on this 1934 Act. Same way with the constitution, same way with the charter. And you could realize what I put up with. When they'd meet, there's be about two or three hundred of them. And they'd call me out there and tear me apart. They give me hell. But I stayed with them, for educational purposes. I kept telling them, ''Your conditions and situations are bad.'' Now, I said, ''Let's get organized and get some help to your people, because you're old, you can't farm, you can't ranch, and you can't go on to college, and there's no economic advantages to you. But your children, your grandchildren, need that help. Why do you try to block them from making progress?'' Well, I convinced some. They stepped out. But that group kept agoing, kept agoing, kept agoing. They went up until World War II and then these old fellows started dying off. Finally, they just went out.

CASH: How does that Tribal Land Enterprise work?

ROUBIDEAUX: Well, now yesterday we met. The fractionation of heirship interests has got real bad. Before the 1934 Act, when the allottee dies, the Secretary of the Interior comes out here and just puts it up for sale. Takes that money and deposits it to an account, and the heirs will get the money. When we adopted this 1934 Act, they stopped the sale. When the Rosebud reservation was set up, we started out with a little over three million acres. And in 37 years, we lost two-thirds of that land holding. It all went into the ownership of the whites. So that was one of the things that the Commissioner really hit hard: we got to stop this. You got to stop this. You got to have a land to make a living on. Your land base is needed. Where are you going to go it you continue to sell your land? The White man comes in and says, ''I'll buy your land, put in an application.'' So he does. And the Indian sells it. This '34 Act stopped that.

CASH: It stopped that, but it also made it so that this land went into multiple heirship. That is a kind of a mess, too, isn't it?

ROUBIDEAUX: Yes. That's when the multiple heirship starts to build up. So that's why we set up this Tribal Land Enterprise. If one of the heirs want to sell your interest, you can come in here and you sell your land to this Tribal Land Enterprise. When this started out, they had no money. We had to borrow money from the government to start operating. And we started buying. At the same time, the people were poor. They had to have something. So they sell their heirship interests to the tribe. Of course, every time we buy land, it becomes tribal land. So we're building up again what we lost over a period of 37 years.

CASH:  Can you tell me one more thing? I've heard that the Catholic Church opposed the Indian Reorganization Act. Is there anything to that?

ROUBIDEAUX: Yes. Not only the Catholic, but the other denominations, because they were in with the Bureau of Indian Affairs, you know? They controlled the lives of the Indian people. And they couldn't worship their own way or exercise their ceremonies. That was one reason why Mr. Collier said they were denying their freedom of worship. And that's how the Native American Church, where it involved this peyote, started organizing.

The Bureau in conjunction with these various denominations, they set up regulations. Like stopping Indians from growing long hair, stopping the Sun Dance or other ceremonial dances, and by making sweat baths their own way. And they couldn't exercise any of their own culture. Mr. Collier threw everything out of the window. They had regulations set up so they could only dance Indian just once a month and they had to get permission from the superintendent. These things were all set up in conjunction with these various denominations of churches. Mr. Collier came along and said, ''No, you're denying the freedom of worship. Let the Indians exercise these traditions, cultural, any ceremony he wants like he used to. Leave him go.'' That was the reason that they knew if the Indian people went under this '34 Act, they would lose control of the Indian, you know.

CASH:  Did they get out and really actively work against this Act?

ROUBIDEAUX: Yes. They worked against it. I heard one fellow talk to these Old Deal Council people out here. That that was a socialistic form of government that John Collier was trying to set up on this reservation. These Indian missionary workers don't want the Indians to go back to the old ways, like the way they worship, to exercise their cultural heritage and ceremonies or whatever you call it. That was the reason why. They knew that if the Indian people went under this '34 Act all this stuff will be thrown out the window. Which they did.

Today the Indian exercises his worship the way he wants. They could dance every day and every night if they want to. They put on Sun Dances here and what they [call] Yuwipi. It's a ceremony where they bound them up with a string and they talk to little spirits. They could do that now.

ALFRED DUBRAY, BRULÉ SIOUX. INTERVIEWED BY HERBERT T.
HOOVER ON JULY 28, 1970, ON WINNEBAGO RESERVATION, NE-
BRASKA

HOOVER: This is Alfred DuBray, superintendent of the Winnebago Agency. Where were you born and raised and educated? How
did you get here?

DUBRAY: Well, I'm originally from South Dakota—was born on
the Rosebud reservation and grew up there on the reservation until,
I guess, twenty years of age. And I went to high school in Winner
and of course this was in the depression days. Going to college was
a rather difficult thing, but I did manage to go to finish a course in
business administration at Mitchell—two years, a year and a half.
This was the extent of that.

I started working in the Bureau of Indian Affairs in 1938, and
have been around the Bureau for 30 some years now. Starting from
Rosebud agency for a short period of time, then I moved to
Washington, transferred to Washington central office in Washington, D.C. I spent about 10 years there, then to various places at
various levels. I moved back to Turtle Mountain and was administrative officer for about two years, and then Pine Ridge for about
two years or so, and then from there I moved into the area office
level down in Oklahoma, at Anadarko. I was there for about three
years and moved over to Muskogee, Oklahoma in another area
office and was there about nine years. Then from there up here.
I've been here about seven years.

HOOVER: You were around when the Indian Reorganization Act
was applied at Rosebud.

DUBRAY: Right. I never had too much contact, of course, with the
agency before. We always lived way out in the country and our
contacts with the Bureau were at that time with what you would call
farm agents or boss farmers. These were a few abandoned districts
out in the outlying areas of the reservations. So they would come
around and keep us informed and deal with leases and things of this
type.

We lived in a community where there was quite a number of
Indian families and many of them were my relatives. I remember
them talking about this New Deal that was coming out at that time.
Of course, this was in the administration of Franklin D. Roosevelt
and his new commissioner was John Collier, who immediately
proposed to Congress a new era for the American Indian people.

He proposed this legislation and, of course, the Indian people referred to it as the New Deal. Nobody really understood it too well. They knew that they were going to have to vote on something whether they wanted to or not. And, of course, among the Indian people, it is very difficult many times to get things accurately to them. It is a matter of communication. That is very difficult, because they will interpret it so many ways. Well, they had all kinds of stories going about this new program. Many were against and many were for it, for what they understood of it; it was very difficult because it was such a radical change from their way of life, really—their customs and practice. Up to that point, most all of their governing procedures in the tribe were handled through tribal leaders designated by the chiefs, who handed down leaders from one generation to another. They looked to these tribal chiefs or leaders to guide them in their procedure. They had no formal government of any kind, while they were fairly well organized. Anyway, they didn't lack for that, but this was quite a radical change to vote on something and have a structured tribal government. I think many of them looked at this as another way for government to take over more control. So, through all this, controversy was going back and forth within the tribal groups.

Finally, the Bureau got going on this and organized themselves fairly well and established some positions as to the responsibilities of these employees; people in these positions would go around to explain the Reorganization Act to the people from all the reservations, as best they could. Well, as I remember, the one on Rosebud, the reorganization man they called him, was Mr. Ben Reifel. It was a man who had been in Washington worked for the Bureau and was very capable and he was selected as one of these men to go out in the Rosebud area—and explain this, sell it in other words. So he did and he spent quite a lot of time there. Then finally they were given deadlines or dates to vote. I don't remember all the details on that, but they had a rather close vote, as I recall, on this on the Reorganization Act on the Rosebud reservation.

And, of course, the point of interest to many of them was it had a lot of advantages in it that many people didn't see—such as making loan funds available, huge amounts of that, farm programs were developed through this, cattle raising programs were initiated. Educational loans were beginning to be made available for the Indian youngsters who had never had any opportunity before to attend any higher institutions, unless somebody sponsored them. So there was a new feeling there in education.

Mainly the tribal governing body section got busy there and they established this governing body and voted their representatives and their council members. It was, I think, difficult for the people to really recognize what they were doing for probably several years after that, until they got into the change.

HOOVER: I gather from what you say that Ben Reifel was a fairly effective salesman, then?

DUBRAY: Well, I would say that from my own personal opinion, probably if it wasn't for him, if he didn't represent the Bureau that it would have been very unlikely that this would have been in effect. Because he could speak the language and he knew the people and had many relatives and friends on the reservation. It made it easier for him to get this program across and I think that this had a lot to do with it.

HOOVER: How has the Reorganization Act worked out here in Winnebago?

DUBRAY: Well, of course, I've been here less than seven years, but from what I can determine they have the same advantages in their constitution and bylaws as most all other tribes had under the Reorganization Act. I don't believe that this particular reservation did too much in the area of utilizing their resources as they should have. They had some very valuable land here on this reservation— farm land. This is an intensified farm area and they have very good land. Well, maybe they did in those days—that is 30–40 years ago. Farming wasn't as productive and great as it is today probably, but 40 years ago they were just beginning a complete change. As what happened on the Rosebud reservation, the people took several years even to realize that they were in a new type of situation.

I am sure that on this reservation maybe to many people it may not look [as if] there has been much progress, but there really has been when you look and compare. Even if it isn't a natural change, if nothing else it [is] just progress whether you want it or not in many ways, especially with the materialistic things, but in many other ways they haven't progressed. In the human resource side, probably much of that is natural, because they have resisted that. They wanted to retain their status as tribal people, Winnebagos, on this reservation, for example. I think this is probably true across the nation as far as American Indians are concerned. Much of the progress people make comparisons with the dominant society or the non-Indian and say, gee, there is no progress here. They are worse off than they were 40 years ago. Well, it depends on what you are trying to compare. The way I see it, it has been the policy of the Bureau of Indian Affairs for a great many, many years to make them more like the non-Indian. And there has been great resistance in most tribes, in the Plains area anyway; they have resisted this attempt, in many cases, vigorously. You take the next reservation south of here; the Omahas have really resisted this and it's very evident in their tribe today. You can compare them with the Winnebago and probably on the surface it appears that they are not quite as far advanced, because there has been a resistance to being like the dominant society.

And it is going on today. They are attempting to resist, especially the older generation. The younger people, the youngsters in elementary and secondary schools that are living here on the reservation, are kind of being caught in between. Their middle aged parents many times are still resisting very strong against the efforts of teaching of the dominant society, but they still believe in education, and this kind of confuses things, too.

HOOVER: How do most of the people here make a living?

DUBRAY: They all pretty much fall in the category of being poverty stricken people. They place the poverty line at, I believe, around $3000 a year income. Well, the income average on this reservation is between $1000 and $1500 a year. Their income is primarily from lease rentals here on the reservation land that they may own. This applies to those people who are generally in the elderly group or in the middle aged group and have income from land, because the younger people have no land unless they inherited it. So it's income from land, income from a spot job or part-time work, generally unskilled work, agricultural work to a great extent. And even that is fading out now, even in the years that I have been here. There has been a tremendous reduction in that because of the great increase in single ownership of farms. Going to mechanization of farms has greatly reduced this hand labor they were accustomed to doing here. Some work in the industry in Sioux City or near by areas.

But I think the significant thing about this, the entire Winnebago population, is that we have about 2000 members on the Nebraska Winnebago rolls. There are approximately 700 people living on the reservation here in Nebraska. So you can see almost two-thirds of these people, or 60 some percent of these people, are gone. They have to a great extent on their own initiative left here for better opportunities and they are living in all parts of the country.

So what we are talking about here locally are these approximately 700 people and you analyze these and you find that a great percentage of them, oh, over fifty percent of these, are elderly people. And these people, of course, are living in some kind of dole—welfare, old age, social security, veterans benefits, and some other kinds of income—a small income. These people are living on this type of income because of their age and being unskilled, besides uneducated, many times. So a great percentage of these are going to be in this category of low income, regardless, from now on until they pass on.

Then you have another maybe 25 percent of this group that is left that are children, the school age children, that are living with parents or grandparents or relatives, and kids from broken homes. Then we have another maybe ten percent more of a people who are disabled and unable to work and if they are able to work, they are unskilled. So they have to do spot work. Then you have another, say ten percent, who are handicapped in other ways.

Just a final thing about the work force here. We are out making the effort, of course, like they are on most reservations, to get industry located on or near the reservation to provide employment. I would say if [we] were fortunate, we could find 100 people as workers for an industry here. Now many of these people on the Winnebago reservation that are employable men and women work in the nearby communities.

There is one possibility of an increase in the population by bringing back some of these people who have gone. They are not all successful. Many of these people are living in urban centers and are probably far worse off than people here in the worst conditions. They may not have the best housing here and their income may not be as great, but they do have a lot of freedom here as far as open spaces, clean air, and sanitary facilities in their homes. Many of these people living in the urban centers are finding real difficulties, because they are handicapped, leaving here many times with a very limited education. They obtained some kind of a skill when they went away, training, but maybe that skill is more or less depleted. I know I have heard from many on the West Coast. Technology changes; the skill more or less becomes obsolete and they are immediately out of a job and living in pretty bad circumstances in certain cases.

Now many of these people would come back to the reservation if there was any kind of hope or possibility of them being able to find some kind of permanent employment. If the tribe were fortunate enough to establish and develop resources and with our assistance were able to locate some kind of permanent industry here, for example, that would employ men and women, it would be a good possibility that they would bring quite a few back to the reservation. And I think the tribe is looking in this direction. They're presently developing an industrial park here on tribal land south of the village in Winnebago. This will be an excellent spot for industry and there have been several contacts already for locating industries there.

Locating industries on the reservation is not the answer to all the problems; it is one of the things that helps. As people get older, even among Indian people that are living away from their homeland, they consider this their home regardless of where they are and how long a time they are away. We have people coming back here periodically to retire, independent people, coming back home after many years of being away to live among and with relatives and be here in their later years. But this kind of offsets itself with the leaving and the coming up to this point. There hasn't been any great loss in the past several years.

HOOVER: I wanted to ask you about relocation. Was relocation voluntary or was this part of relocation sponsored by the government?

DUBRAY: Well, to a great extent, most of these are voluntary. In the early stages of this program in the early 50's there was a lot of pressure placed on the people. It was always considered a voluntary program, but there was a lot of promotion of the program in the early stages. I know from my own experience that this program was initiated as the adult vocational training program, but what was known as the relocation program was started in the early 50's when I was at Pine Ridge. We were one of the first to have a relocation officer and in order to get the thing going, and it was kind of a crash program, we just went out and rounded them up in trucks. You know, you want to go to California or somewhere and get a job . . . sure, everybody was jumping on the bandwagon. They wanted the trip or something, so a lot of it was confusion to begin with. This is true with a lot of new programs, to get a crash thing going. Congress gives you money. They want results right away and by the time you go back next year for your funding you better have some results to show, or it's: why did you . . . we gave you money for this and how come all of this didn't happen? To get a new program going you have to hire specialized people to do it. There are a thousand different things you have to get going. Well, the first year or two is just more or less chaos, to get a program off the ground of that magnitude.

It had real problems. A lot of the people were pushed into this program to begin with. This is the reason the returnee rate was so high to begin with, probably 50 percent or more, and it still today runs in the one-third range, even if it is a voluntary program going on today.

HOOVER: Is that because of individuals or maybe the change in job needs?

DUBRAY: Well, I think that it is a little naturally of both, but I think the greatest determinant is the fact that the individual is just not able to assimilate himself into the community, these urban centers. The reason why they return is because they just can't make it from a standpoint of being able to accustom themselves to urban living. That, of course, is a basic reason, in addition, generally it is just because they just can't make it economically. Their skill is just not great enough to provide an average standard of living and they would just have to slip back down into a lower class of living. They have a program where they won't let them get down into the ghetto area to live in order to have a little extra money. But after they once get on their own, they can't control them and then they go back down in there or they give up and get back to the reservation.

To me, I would far rather live on the reservation than some of those ghetto areas that they are forced into many times, so I certainly don't condemn anyone for coming back to the reservation from relocation programs or adult vocational training. I've lived in urban centers myself and I know quite a bit about city areas. I think that many of these people that are being sent out are just not going to make it, because first of all, their educational level is pretty low in many instances, even with the best training. They will have a real tough time in this day and age making it in many of these urban centers with the competition and all that is going on.

I have talked to and I have seen many people from each of the reservations that are living in urban centers, like on the west coast—Los Angeles, San Francisco, and those areas. I know of one young couple, they are probably in their 40's, they are Omahas and they have been out in Los Angeles for 12 to 13 years now. They were sent out on the relocation program and he also received training out there as a welder. He is a master welder now and he makes real good money where he works. He has worked for several companies. He isn't working at all right now. He injured himself. He was working for some steel company and he fell off a high building or something. He hasn't worked for a couple years and he gets compensation and he received some kind of insurance settlement.

I know several others that are just barely making it and that is all. They are moving from one pay day to another, so to speak. They have thousands of problems—educational problems with the children, community problems moving in to certain areas, restricted areas, and all this. This is another confusing thing to many Indian people, is being unable to live in areas that they would like to live in and can afford to live in, but in many places they are unable to do this. On the reservation they just don't get into this too much except that they are living on their own home land and they can live where they want to and they don't have this restriction.

The boarding school played an important role in federal Indian policy at the turn of the century. Pictured are students and faculty of the boarding school on the Cheyenne River Agency, South Dakota, 1890. Elaine Goodale Eastman Collection, South Dakota State Historical Society.

Major James McLaughlin engineered many agreements between Plains tribes and the federal government in the late nineteenth and early twentieth centuries. McLaughlin is shown en route to a meeting. Photography by H. B. Perry. South Dakota State Historical Society (n.d.)

Quanah Parker, Comanche (far left), and his council illustrate changing patterns of attire. Parker was an important tribal leader and affiliated with ritual peyote religion. Hargett Collection, Western History Collections, University of Oklahoma (n.d.)

Cattle ranching became a vital part of Plains Indian reservation economies in the early twentieth century. This roundup took place on the Cheyenne River Reservation on October 2, 1911. Cundill photograph, South Dakota State Historical Society.

Housing saw some changes in the early twentieth century along with the increasingly important status of farming and ranching. This photograph was taken shortly after 1900 by Richard Throssel, a Wasco (and adopted Crow) photographer. Throssel Collection, Archives, American Heritage Center, University of Wyoming.

The new century brought questions of law and authority in changing times. Police forces, such as this one on the Crow reservation, were formed to deal with a variety of issues. Throssel Collection.

Given the rapidity of social and economic change, community and extended family support was a valuable resource for Plains Indian peoples. People gathered to share both grief and joy. The group pictured is from the Crow reservation. Throssel Collection.

Farming continued during the hard years of the Depression. Imogene Lincoln Mosqueda, Southern Arapaho, farms tribal land at Cantonment, probably in the late 1930s or early 40s. Western History Collections, University of Oklahoma.

The Indian New Deal included frequent meetings throughout the Plains. Comanche, Kiowa, and Kiowa-Apache tribesmen participate in such a gathering at the Riverside Indian School, Anadarko, Oklahoma in 1940. The photograph by Sekaer, is from the National Archives, Washington, D.C., 75-N-K10-92.

Plains Indian men volunteered in large numbers for service in the armed forces during World War II. Twenty-two members of the Crow Creek Reservation apply for enlistment at the Sioux Falls, South Dakota, recruiting station. National Archives, 75-N-CCR-1.

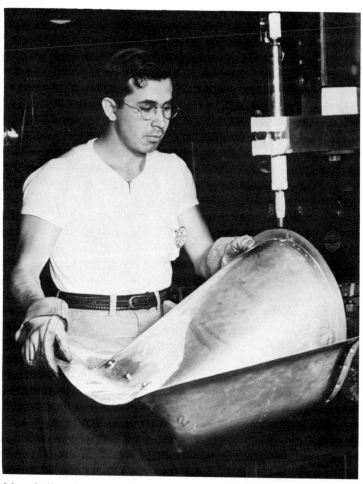

Many Indians found employment in war-related industries in the 1940s. Clifford Martinez, Comanche, worked as a machinist for Douglas Aircraft Company in Santa Monica, California. National Archives, 75-N-IWT-23.

The construction of the Garrison Dam on the Missouri River following World War II forced representatives of the Three Affiliated Tribes on the Fort Berthold Reservation in North Dakota to cede 152,000 acres of their land. The loss is plainly revealed in the faces of these men assembled in 1948. National Archives, 75-N-Fort Berthold-C.

The relocation programs of the Bureau of Indian Affairs encouraged migration to the cities in the 1950s. This family from North Dakota has arrived in San Jose, California in 1957. National Archives, 75-N-REL-H.

Arnold Headley, Northern Arapahoe, participated in a powwow in the summer of 1984 on the Wind River Reservation in Wyoming. Photograph by Dianna Troyer, *Wind River News*.

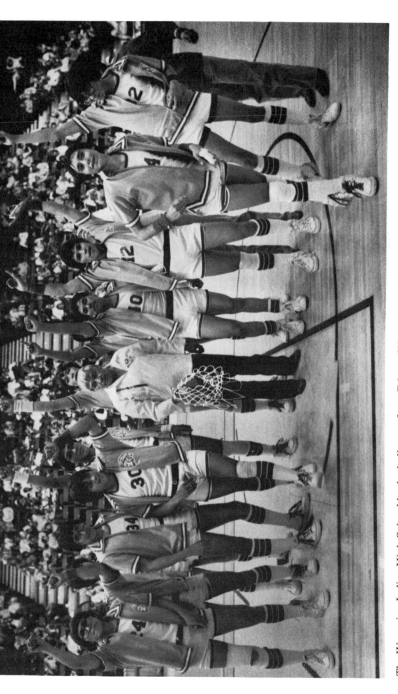

The Wyoming Indian High School basketball team from Ethete, Wyoming, celebrates its victory over Lovell in the Class 2A state championship game in 1984. The team is coached by Alfred Redman, who holds the net. Photograph by Tom Stromme, *Wind River News*. The team was again state champion in 1985.

Nowah'wus (Bear Butte) in western South Dakota remains a holy place for the Cheyenne people. This photograph was taken by Don

CHAPTER 6

# Fighting a White Man's War:
# The Extent and Legacy of American
# Indian Participation in World War II

## BY TOM HOLM

*World War II definitely marked a significant turning point in modern American Indian life. For many Americans from throughout the country service with the armed forces or work in war-related industries off the reservation provided their first intensive contact with the larger American society. In many instances the war altered how Indians saw themselves and how other Americans saw them. It often changed the expectations the Indians had for themselves, but the war also changed what other Americans could demand from Indians or from the federal government's policies regarding Indians.*

*Tom Holm's article reprinted below mentions some tribes outside the Plains, but Indians from the region are really the primary subjects of this analysis. Members of the Sioux, Omaha, Osage, Cheyenne, Kiowa, and Blackfoot tribes are featured in this selection. As Holm makes clear, the contributions of Plains Indian people were vital to America's war effort; in turn, their contributions often improved their sense of self-esteem. The war even revived the warrior tradition in some Plains Indian communities. Many non-Indians began to perceive Indians in a more positive light because of wartime experiences.*

*Yet World War II was not exclusively advantageous for Indians. In addition to the lives lost in battle, other costs had to be borne. The termination era, in which the federal government attempted to withdraw from Indians peoples all federal assistance and protection, was ushered in by the war. The policy of reaffirmation of tribal cultures*

From the *Journal of Ethnic Studies* (Summer, 1981): 69–81. Reprinted by permission.

*that characterized the Indian New Deal reverted to the policy of assimilation.*

*Holm asserts that to blame termination solely upon a conservative resurgence within national politics would be inaccurate. Rather, a combination of conservative and liberal forces encouraged the "emancipation" of American Indians. He concludes that "fighting the white man's war gained sympathy for American Indians, but it also fueled a fire that they did not want and eventually found difficult to extinguish."*

IN 1942, the *Saturday Evening Post* informed its many readers that a Nazi propaganda broadcast had "predicted an Indian uprising in the United States," should American Indians be "asked to fight against the Axis."[1] If quoted correctly, these German statements were not made without a degree of elementary logic. In the name of American progress, Indians had been slaughtered, dispossessed of lands, forcibly stripped of many aspects of their tribal cultures, and left the poorest of the nation's poor. "How could," Radio Berlin was reported to have asked, "the American Indians think of bearing arms for their exploiters?"[2]

But in defiance of German logic and much to the satisfaction of white Americans, the *Post* also reported that Indians were flocking to join the armed forces in order to fight and possibly shed blood for the United States. American Indians flung themselves into the war effort. Indeed, Indian participation in World War II was so great that it later became part of American folklore and popular culture. It was a magnificent gesture worthy of a great people, yet one that would eventually provide little consolation. That the disastrous policy of termination followed so closely the Indian commitment to America's war effort was not a mere historical coincidence. Whites, who made Indian policies at the time, came out of the war with new, or at least different, images of Indian people. These changed views created an atmosphere in which men of varying motives and goals could institute the termination policy under the cloak of liberal rhetoric.

During World War II and the first time ever, all American Indian males between the ages of twenty-one and forty-four were eligible to be drafted. That they were subject to military conscription developed, ironically enough, out of the American Indian experience in World War I. Prior to 1917 not all Indians living in the country were citizens of the United States. Some Indians had obtained citizenship by taking allotments under the Dawes Act of 1887. At the same time others had been denied citizens' rights on the grounds that they had been judged by whites to be incompetent in the legal sense. A few refused to even request citizenship because they believed that it would deny tribal sovereignty and destroy the basis on which treaties could be recognized. Those persons not holding citizenship were exempted from selective service laws. When the United States plunged itself into the war during 1917, thousands of American Indians entered the armed services regardless of their individual legal positions at the time. Many took the military oath to defend the Constitution of the United States without possessing any rights under it, refusing to take advantage of their draft exemptions. By 1918 there were over 10,000 American Indians in the Army, Navy, and Marine Corps, eighty-five percent of whom, according to the Indian policy reform newsletter *Indian's Friend*, entered voluntarily. As the periodical reported, "Indians—men and women alike—are doing their bit to help make the world safe for democracy."[3]

In that era, most government policies toward American Indians were based on the idea that Indians were wards of the government. To the average white American, wardship and citizenship—semi-bondage and freedom—were not compatible. One could not, through government, regulate citizens without infringing upon the individual liberties of the nation's citizenry. Most Americans in the early part of this century were steadfastly against many forms of government interference in the private lives of voting Americans. Indians, according to this line of thought, would have to remain wards, and therefore noncitizens, in order to carry out policies of acculturation, allotment of reservation lands, and education. It was not until after the government, or at least the country's lawmakers, became fully imbued with the idea that individual liberty could be subordinate to the public welfare or to national security and able to place controls on the white population, that American Indian citizenship became justifiable to most whites.

The First World War was met with a tremendous outburst of patriotism—patriotism which called for unswerving loyalty and devotion to the nation. As a result, the war also created a mindset within which the government could increasingly regulate individuals with only slight opposition. Congress, through sedition, espionage, and subversion acts, could essentially remove the guarantees of the Bill of Rights. Regulation, and with it a kind of wardship, became less incompatible with freedom in the American mind. The government, in providing for the general welfare, could, indeed should, curb individual liberties if the rest of society were threatened. Given this notion, it was not difficult for many whites to ease their qualms about conferring citizenship on those Indian people who had fought so willingly and bravely in France. They could remain wards without apparent constitutional conflict.

Subsequently, Indian soldiers and sailors received citizenship in 1919, and in 1924 the United States offered certificates of citizenship to all American Indians not already holding them.[4] Thus Indians, as a result of wartime ideologies, received very few of the actual freedoms of citizenship, but were expected to accept any and all of the responsibilities that went with it. Although many American Indians were denied the right to vote or even to wear tribal clothing or conduct religious ceremonies, they were not excluded from certain duties; when World War II broke out, they became subject to military conscription.

When World War II broke out, American Indians readily accepted these duties. They registered at selective service centers in the cities and at their agencies. There was little protest against the draft, and very few attempted to avoid service on grounds that it was a white man's war. In fact, many Indians refused to wait the prescribed time to enter the military and either requested early conscription or contacted a recruiter and volunteered. The Indian people, just as they had done in 1917, accepted their share of the burden of the war.

According to the then Commissioner of Indian Affairs, John Collier, there were over 7,500 American Indians in the armed forces as of June 1942, less than six months after the attack on Pearl Harbor.[5] By October another observer reported that the number of American Indians in the military had swollen to well over 10,000.[6] By 1944 almost 22,000 American Indians, not counting those who had become officers, were part of the United States armed forces.[7] At the war's end there were over 25,000 Indians in the Army, Navy, Marine Corps, and Coast Guard.[8] "While this seems a relatively small number," wrote Commissioner Collier, "it represents a larger proportion than any other element of our population.''[9]

Not only did Indians fight ''in greater proportionate numbers than any other race'' but they also seemed to draw some of the worst wartime assignments.[10] Again, this experience matched that of the First World War. During World War I whites, as well as most Indians, had argued persuasively that American Indians should be integrated in all of the white regiments and treated like any other soldier. Yet, the *Indian's Friend* proudly reported that ''Indians in the regiments are being used for scouting and patrol duty because of the natural instinct which fits them for this kind of work.'' This kind of racial stereotype, following as it did an attempt to argue against racism in the military, would have been laughable had it not forced Native Americans into precarious assignments.[11]

For the most part these stereotypes were carried over to the Second World War. Indians were natural ''scouts'' and ''warriors.'' Stanley Vestal, a leading authority on the tribes of the Plains, added to this image of American Indians. ''The Indian, whose wars never ended, was a realistic soldier,'' Vestal wrote. ''He never gave quarter nor expected it. His warfare was always offensive warfare.''[12] American Indians were never segregated into separate units as were blacks and Japanese-Americans; yet, they were always mentioned in the press as being quite different from whites. Secretary of the Interior Harold Ickes wrote about the ''inherited talents'' of American Indians that made them ''uniquely valuable'' to the war effort. According to Ickes, the Native American fighting man had

endurance, rhythm, a feeling for timing, co-ordination, sense perception, an uncanny ability to get over any sort of terrain at night, and, better than all else, an enthusiasm for fighting. He takes a rough job and makes a game of it. Rigors of combat hold no terrors for him; severe discipline and hard duties do not deter him.[13]

American Indians for the most part accepted these attitudes toward them and often did their best to conform to such views. A month after the war began, the *New York Times* reported that Chief Kiutus Tecumseh, of Cashmere, Washington, was attempting to organize an Indian ''Scouting force.''[14] One Sioux man, Kenneth Scission, of South Dakota, volunteered for a British-trained American commando unit and quickly managed to become the group's leading German-killer. On a single patrol, Scission was reported to have added "ten notches on his Gerand rifle."[15] Another man, Robert Stabler, a member of the Omaha tribe, landed "alone under heavy fire" to mark the beaches for the infantry in advance of the assault at Licata, Sicily, in 1943. During the Normandy invasion of 1944 a group of thirteen American Indians were in the first wave of paratroops dropped with demolitions in advance of the Allied landings in France. Given these exploits, little wonder that American Indian servicemen garnered several Silver Stars, the Distinguished Service Cross, the Navy Cross, and numerous Purple Hearts, signs that one had not only engaged the enemy but had shed his own blood for the United States.[16]

In 1944, Lieutenant Ernest Childers, a Creek tribal member from Broken Arrow, Oklahoma, was awarded the nation's highest decoration for bravery in battle—the Medal of Honor. He had earlier distinguished himself in the fighting in Sicily with the famed 45th "Thunderbird" Division. Indeed, it was in Sicily that Childers received his battlefield commission. In September, 1943, near Oliveto, Italy, Childers, singlehandedly and in spite of severe wounds, destroyed three German machinegun emplacements, thus opening "the way for the advance of his battalion which had been in danger of annihilation." Childers's exploits implanted the "warrior" image in the American mind.[17]

Perhaps the First American Indian to gain fame in the war was General Clarence L. Tinker. Tinker, on the Osage tribal rolls, had been the first person of Indian descent since the Civil War to become a general officer in the United States Army. After the attack on Pearl Harbor, Tinker was placed in charge of the all-but-destroyed air forces in Hawaii. One of America's pioneer bomber pilots, Tinker reorganized the remaining forces and before the battle of Midway was fought in June 1942 had turned them into a well-trained, highly disciplined unit. Tinker was killed at the battle of Midway. "Ignoring the dangers and refusing to assign anyone else the task," Tinker "personally led the squadrons of bombers which supplied the American spearhead of the attack." Cited for bravery, he was posthumously awarded the Distinguished Service Medal. In the words of John Collier, the Osage general "exemplified the modern Indian soldier."[18]

Tinker was not the only high-ranking officer in the military service of Indian descent. Listed on the Dawes Commission rolls as one-eighth Cherokee, Joseph J. "Jocko" Clark was the first American Indian to have received an appointment to Annapolis. Clark became a rear admiral and was active in many parts of the Pacific during World War II.[19]

But the deepest impressions on the American public were made by an American Indian unit and a single Pima man, "the outsider," Ira Hamilton Hayes. Hayes became a national hero in 1945 when he and some fellow marines were photographed raising the American flag on Mount Suribachi during the battle of Iwo Jima. The photograph seemed to capture the imagination of the public. It exemplified the courage, strength, and tenacity of America's struggle against the enemy. Hayes was returned to the United States to help promote the sale of war bonds and to bolster morale. He became an alcoholic and later died, a relatively young man, on the reservation of his birth. To many Americans, Hayes's life came to symbolize the American Indian participation in the war. He was a hero who fought to preserve the United States but was never given the opportunity to share in America's wealth or society. Although he survived the war, he was doomed to a life of poverty and prejudice. In the American mind he became, along with the hundreds of other Indian veterans, an "outsider." When a very poor motion picture was made in 1955 based on the life of Ira Hayes, its title, "The Outsider," aptly expressed white images of American Indians. America had used them and then had cast them aside.[20]

If Ira Hayes's life came to symbolize to whites what had happened to Indian veterans after the war, a group known as the Navajo code-talkers became the symbol of the great contribution Indians had made during the war. Early in 1942 the Marine Corps recruited an all-Indian platoon.[21] When basic training ended in July of that year, the men were assigned to units overseas. In battle the Navajos acquitted themselves with much glory and later attracted widespread coverage in the national press.[22] During the war their mission had been kept secret. Trained in communications, they had adopted the Navajo language as a code which helped in large part to foil the Japanese attempts to break the advance of American marines in the Pacific. In 1945, when it was revealed that the Navajo language had done so much to help the United States win the war against Japan, the "code-talkers" instantly became national heroes and part of American folklore.[23] In the postwar years nearly every motion picture made about the fighting in the Pacific

contained scenes of usually anonymous Indians speaking their
native languages into field radios and leaving the enemy hopelessly
confused and ready to be soundly defeated.[24]

American Indians gave the United States more than heroes to
glory in or to sympathize with. Indian people also contributed food
and money to the war effort. The Crows of Montana offered their
reservation's resources and tribal funds to the government for the
duration of the war.[25] The Navajo, Shoshone, and several other
tribal governments authorized the secretary of the interior to purchase war bonds from tribal funds.[26] In this manner alone the tribes
contributed millions of dollars to the war effort. In 1944, Harold
Ickes reported that at least $2 million worth of bonds had been
purchased by Indians in one year.[27] In that same year Indian
Commissioner Collier estimated that the total Indian commitment
to the war effort in monetary terms amounted to some $50 mil-
lion.[28]

Throughout the war Indian men and women not already in the
armed forces left the reservations to find work in the cities. The war
had, of course, expanded industry, and the war economy was
booming. Jobs became easy to obtain and easy to keep. It was
estimated that between the years 1941 and 1945 approximately
40,000 American Indians left their home areas to work in the
factories of a wartime nation. John Collier called this movement
"the greatest exodus of Indians" that had ever taken place. More
important, it was looked upon as an inspiring commitment to the
United States by people who previously had not been welcomed
outside of their homelands.[29]

On the reservations, which by 1944 were critically short of a
male workforce, Indian women accounted for much of the production of food. They drove heavy equipment, repaired tractors, and
herded cattle. Principally because of Native American women, the
production of Indian livestock doubled in the ten years between
1933 and 1943. Agricultural output greatly increased as well,
accounting for a significant rise in the standard of living on many
reservations compared to the truly terrible conditions of the Depression years. By 1945 it was estimated that nearly 150,000
American Indians directly participated in the industrial, agricultural, and military aspects of the American war effort.[30]

One reservation was even called upon to participate in the
government's internment of Japanese-Americans. In 1942 the War

Relocation Authority gave "the Indian Bureau the care of 20,000 unhappy Japanese." These people, forced from their homes on the Pacific Coast, were sent to the Colorado River Reservation's "20,000 acres of desert." According to one writer, the internment of the Japanese-Americans on an Indian reservation could become a "valuable piece of social experimentation."[31]

There were a great number of other Indian contributions. In the press American Indians were used to boost morale. Newspapers and magazines projected images of Indians as being loyal, brave, trustworthy fighters, dedicated to the American cause. To most Americans the war was a duel to the death between democracy and fascist injustice. It was a war to free the people of the world from the clutches of Nazi totalitarianism. American Indians, in throwing themselves so unflinchingly and wholeheartedly into the war effort, seemed to validate the American sense of mission. Indians, after all, had been treated miserably; however, even they were totally committed to the crusade against the Axis. According to one young Columbia River tribal member who was quoted in a national magazine, even though his people had been treated badly by the United States, Hitler would be much worse: "We know that under Nazism we should have no rights at all; we should be used as slaves." If oppressed peoples sided with the United States, then logically the American crusade was a just cause.[32]

The media's outlook on American Indians during the war years was decidedly ambiguous. The press generally viewed the Indian war effort as a great boost to the nation's morale. During the first years of the war, groups of American Indians adopted and made "chiefs" of Franklin D. Roosevelt, General Douglas MacArthur, Wendell Willkie, and even Joseph Stalin.[33] Tribes, in efforts to maintain a semblance of autonomy, individually declared war on the Axis. The League of the Iroquois in New York had never ceased hostilities with Germany. The Grand Council of the League simply renewed their declaration of war made in 1917 and included Italy and Japan. Many tribal dancers and singers aided war-bond rallies, and elders posed in their warbonnets for pictures with young men in their new, crisp uniforms. The entire press coverage of American Indians in war was geared to give the impression that Indian people were not only aiding white Americans in the war effort but fervently hoping to share in the victory over fascism and become part of the American democratic way of life.

At the same time, the motion picture industry, perhaps the most powerful image-maker, continued to portray American Indians as savage barriers to the spread of American progress. Most "horse operas" tended to glorify the American past—a past which included western expansion and the theft of American Indian lands. In a few westerns, however, there appeared more and more the "Indian companion" character who, just as in the war, aided the white American in his crusade against injustice.[34] In the war movies an American Indian was usually part of the beleaguered infantry platoon which, because it was made up of members of nearly every ethnic group in the United States, with the exception of blacks, projected a microcosm of America. The American Indian member was presented as loyal, fearless, and capable of sacrifice in defense of the group.

Whites accepted these images with satisfaction. Not only did Indian contributions during the war years tend to endorse the greatness of America's crusade but they were also interpreted to mean that Indians were desperately trying to prove themselves worthy of the rest of society. Actual American Indians' motives for willingly going to war, however, remained far less clear than media coverage led the whites to believe. Among some Indian people there was a strong urge to become accepted by the general population. Taking part in the war could possibly work favorably toward this end. "We want to win the war," an Indian rancher was reported to have said, "because victory will mean new hope for men and women who have no hope."[35]

In their renewed declaration of war against the rulers of Germany, Japan, and Italy, the Six Nations of the Iroquois League not only demonstrated that Indian and white Americans shared a common belief in democracy but made a pronounced statement against the racist policies of Nazi Germany without mentioning the racism practiced at home. "It is the unanimous sentiment among the Indian people that the atrocities of the Axis nations," the League councilman wrote, "are violently repulsive to all sense of righteousness of our people." Moreover, "this merciless slaughter of mankind upon the part of these enemies of free peoples can no longer be tolerated."

Other Indian people saw the Axis as a threat to liberty. The Cheyennes condemned the German, Japanese, and Italian alliance as an "unholy triangle whose purpose is to conquer and enslave the bodies, minds and souls of all free people."[36] A number of California Indians representing some thirty reservations simply thought of themselves as loyal American citizens ready to aid the country. This same group was, at the time, engaged in several lawsuits and claims against the United States government. When war came, they telegraphed President Roosevelt indicating their "readiness to serve our great Nation."[37] In the same vein, the Navajo tribal council delcared that "any un-American movement among our people will be resented and dealt with severely."[38]

Among some tribes a strong warrior tradition actually still existed. The ideologies of most tribal groups, and nearly all of the tribes with the strongest war traditions, were based on ideals of continuity and order. In traditional societies there was a common belief that the Creator had placed the group on earth for specific reasons. Tradition and religion were intermixed so as to be inseparable. Tribal social, economic, and ecological order must be maintained or the entire system would be thrown out of balance and the "good life" destroyed. Although tribal societies were not static—there were adaptations and changes as in every other social group—certain obligations to tradition still had to be maintained. Much of Native American ceremonialism came out of the effort to preserve the social continuity of the tribe and to observe certain obligations to the retention of the traditional view of world order.

Within tribes with strong warrior traditions, such as the Sioux of the northern Plains and the Kiowa of western Oklahoma, the keepers of social philosophy and tribal ceremony were most often males who had *counted coup* on an enemy of the tribe and therefore on an enemy of tribal conceptions of order. After the wars with the whites and the time when the tribes were forced to leave off battling with traditional enemies, the numbers of these prestigious people who had performed acts of honor began to dwindle. The soldier societies to which many of these men belonged were rapidly becoming devoid of members. Because there were no wars, the younger men could hardly *count coup* and thus become part of these groups. The ceremonies that were part of the warrior societies also began to die out.

The First and Second World Wars offered to many Indian people the opportunity of becoming not just American servicemen but soldiers in the tribal meaning of the term. World War II, because it lasted longer and because more men became involved, gave some

Indian men the chance to gain prestige among whites and, most important, obtain status within their own tribes. Kiowa veterans of World War II, for instance, were able to revive the Tia-piah Gourd Dance society, where previously only a handful of men had status as a result of war to participate in the ceremonies of the group. The revival of the society, which has since splintered, meant that a ceremonial obligation to the cultural viability of the tribe could be retained, and with it the Kiowa ideals of order and social continuity would be carried forward. Victory dances were held after the war by several tribes. One, a Hunkpapa Sioux ceremony held at Little Eagle, South Dakota, gave a great deal of prestige to the returning veterans of the Second World War because they were then able to take part in the dance with Takes-his-gun, an elder, a veteran of the tribal wars, and a symbol of the continuity of Hunkpapa society.[39]

Whites vaguely understood the meaning of a warrior tradition within tribal societies. It became, however, a focus and an explanation for all Indian participation in the war. John Collier reported that many Indian men, young and old alike, came to the agencies, rifles in hand, to sign up for the army and "proceed immediately to the scene of the fighting."[40] A Blackfoot contemptuous of the selective service system was said to have stated: "Since when has it been necessary for Blackfeet to draw lots to fight?"[41] Thousands of these kinds of quotes littered the nation's press. In many cases, Indians were made to appear ignorant of modern methods of war, yet they were willing to die for the United States. In all cases their effort demonstrated the "Indian people's faith in their country and their devotion to the cause of Democracy."[42]

The upshot of Indian devotion to the country was a white movement to "amalgamate" Indians into American society. In 1944, Oswald Garrison Villard, writing for *Christian Century*, reaffirmed the American Indian contribution to the war effort and assured readers that the thousands of American Indians fighting overseas and working in war industries were striving to become part of the American mainstream. "Their sole request is that they be awarded citizenship like other Americans," he wrote, "a citizenship unhampered by restrictions which do not apply to everybody." Reservations and federal guardianship, according to Villard, were restrictive and un-American. He was totally convinced that most Indian men and women no longer wanted "to stay at home and be confined within the reservations."[43]

Although Villard sought ''to break up no reservation,'' his entire discourse was directed toward that very goal. According to him, tribal cultures, arts, and ceremonies were unique and worthy of perpetuating but doomed to extinction. American Indians will, Villard asserted, ''tire of being considered circus exhibits.'' Harking back to the arguments of the whites who in the 1880s sought to allot Indian lands and destroy tribal lifestyles in the name of assimilation, Villard thought, along with a pamphlet entitled *Indian Wardship*, that ''imprisoning'' the Indian ''in his yesterday's culture is futility itself.'' It would mean, he said, ''halting his modern adaptation.'' Ominously, Villard quoted and obviously felt kinship with a California Indian agent whose own personal goal in Indian policy was ''to liquidate the U.S. Indian Service.''[44]

Perhaps the strongest statement favoring ''amalgamation'' and the ultimate destruction of the Bureau of Indian Affairs was made by O. K. Armstrong in a 1945 article for *Reader's Digest*. Armstrong claimed to have interviewed American Indians from the entire country and had found them with an ''unmistakable determination'' to ''demand full rights of citizenship.'' Younger Indian people were going, he predicted, to lead a movement in the United States that would eventually set American Indians on their own or at least free them from the entanglements of government bureaucracy. Those Indians, he assured his readers, ''who return from the service will seek a greater share in American freedom.'' Others, who had labored in factories and ''tasted economic opportunity for the first time,'' would not be satisfied, as Armstrong put it, ''to live in a shack and loaf around in a blanket.''[45]

Armstrong saved his heaviest ammunition for an attack on the Bureau of Indian Affairs. In the twelve years since John Collier had taken office as Commissioner of Indian Affairs, Indian policy and the bureau had undergone great change. Since the passage of the Indian Reorganization Act in 1934 tribes could form governments, allotment of Indian lands had ceased, a revolving loan system had been set up to aid in the establishment of tribal businesses, and, in general, the policy of trying to destroy tribal cultures had been curbed. In Armstrong's eyes the Indian Reorganization Act marked a serious setback to the goal of Indian assimilation. According to him, the Indian New Deal had forced ''a collectivist system upon the Indians, with bigger doses of paternalism and regimentation.'' Under it, also, bureaucracy had grown tremendously and with it "red tape" and a greater burden on the taxpayer. After attacking the Indian New Deal in conservative terms as befitting the period, Armstrong continued the assault in a more liberal tone. Since 1934, according to Armstrong, the Bureau of Indian Affairs had allowed the perpetuation of the reservation system and thus had maintained a policy of "racial segregation."[46]

Villard's and Armstrong's statements and the sentiments expressed represented a striking paradox in American thought. Their ideas were well within the boundaries of both conservative and liberal American traditions. They were certainly conservative in that they advocated a policy of less government regulation and interference. At the same time they could wax very liberal. Liberalism in the United States had been, for the most part, nationalistic as well as elitist. It assumed that everyone was in the process of progressing toward the kind of democratic ideals, standard of living, and governmental system that had been developed in the United States. To welcome and promote acceptance of American philosophies and systems among outsiders became the ultimate in philanthropy. If American Indians accepted these ideals, they would "free" themselves and also free whites of long-held responsibilities.

Unlike Villard, however, Armstrong offered extensive solutions to the "Indian problem." He urged Congress to remove Bureau of Indian Affairs restrictions from Indian people. The move, according to Armstrong, would serve to "emancipate" American Indians as well as assist "all Indians to be self-supporting." He argued that the individual ownership of real and personal property would "furnish the same incentive for thrift and good management that are enjoyed by the Indians' white neighbors." Although Armstrong did not openly say that the reservations should be completely done away with, his statements about "segregation" and "emancipation" were to be extremely convincing arguments in favor of the termination policy of the 1950s.[47]

Following the publication of Armstrong's article, the *American Indian* magazine, which was the editorial arm of the American Association on Indian Affairs, printed a series of rebuttals to his arguments. Haven Emerson, the president of the organization, led the attack. According to Emerson, Armstrong's article was "an ill-informed rehash of old fallacies and sentiments" and a "potential danger to the very freedoms which it demands." Emerson's remarks asserted that Armstrong sounded a great deal like the people who, in the previous century, had advocated the policy of allotment in severalty—a policy which proved itself to have been a disastrous mistake.[48]

The remainder of the Fall edition of the *American Indian* similarly attacked the Armstrong article. Both Emerson and historian Randolph C. Downes believed that Armstrong based his arguments on unsupported data. Downes insisted that the Indian New Deal under John Collier had actually promoted self-support and that Armstrong's remarks concerning this aspect of American Indian policy were completely unfounded.[49] Emerson pointed out that a reservation was hardly an "outdoor prison," as Armstrong had suggested. Rather, reservations were land bases on which American Indians could work for economic freedom.[50] Along the same lines another article, written by Walter C. Eells, simply stated that Indian veterans had virtually unlimited opportunities in education and thus were not trapped within the reservations.[51]

Two years later Oliver La Farge recognized the ominous quality of Armstrong's solutions to Indian problems and attempted to refute some of them. La Farge, a Pulitzer prize-winning novelist, anthropologist, and proponent of the Indian New Deal, argued that reservations should be kept intact. He concentrated his arguments on the Navajo reservation and firmly asserted that as an economic base the possession of land was absolutely necessary to American Indian survival. But in the article La Farge described deplorable conditions on reservations and told of a young Navajo war veteran who felt "boxed in" by the system. Even though he did not intend to do so, La Farge actually made a strong case for Armstrong's "reforms."[52]

But views such as Armstrong's were far more compelling to white Americans fresh from a crusade against Nazi tyranny than the arguments presented in the *American Indian* or by La Farge. Indians had "fought for freedom" shoulder to shoulder with the white man yet returned to the grinding poverty of the reservations "segregated" from the society they helped to protect from Hitler. Not only that, but a government bureaucracy supported with public taxes was actively "restricting" the entrance of Indians into that society. Although most of these assumptions were somewhat fallacious, they provided the rhetoric of morality needed to dismantle New Deal institutions, especially the Bureau of Indian Affairs.

The process of "emancipating" American Indians and relieving the federal government of some very old responsibilities began almost immediately following the war. In 1946, Congress created the Indian Claims Commission in order to adjudicate various claims made by Indian tribes against the United States. In large part the establishment of the Commission was a genuine attempt to do justice to American Indians who had suffered at the hands of the government. On the other hand, the Commission was designed also to take care of the suits in order to clear the way for an eventual withdrawal of the government from the "Indian business."[53]

A year later lawmakers in Washington established the "Commission on the Organization of the Executive Branch of Government" and appointed as its head former President Herbert Hoover. Within the Commission's jurisdiction, Hoover set up an "Indian Task Force" in order to investigate and make recommendations on American Indian policies.[54] In 1948, less than a year after its formation, the Hoover Commission issued a rather bland analysis of then-current programs directed by the Bureau of Indian Affairs. Although it condemned the policy of breaking up the reservations into individually-held plots of land and urged caution in effecting rapid changes in policies, it nevertheless asserted that "assimilation must be the dominant goal of public policy" toward American Indians.[55]

Nothing, it seemed, could alter the course that American Indian policy took in the ten years following World War II. Despite protests from the newly organized National Congress of American Indians and some objections from a few government officials, the government moved inexorably toward a policy of termination. Using the argument that the federal government was merely trying to grant the rights and freedoms of citizenship that American Indians had fought so hard for in the war, Congress reduced appropriations of the Bureau of Indian Affairs, urged the agency to promote "assimilation" programs such as relocating American Indians from the reservations to the cities, and pressed for the complete abolishment of federal responsibilities to American Indian tribes. By 1953, Congress, armed with the rhetoric of morality and democracy, was able to pass House Concurrent Resolution 108—a document that provided the power to terminate federal relations with individual tribes.[56]

In 1954 the House and Senate Committees on Indian Affairs held hearings in consideration of the implementation of H.R.C. 108. During the deliberations, which eventually led to bills terminating several tribes in Utah, the Klamaths of Oregon, some Kansas tribes, and the Menominees of Wisconsin, Senator Arthur V. Watkins became the resolution's most active supporter. Watkins at once declared that termination was in keeping with democratic principles and would be "the Indian freedom program." Only incidently would it be a means by which the government could disregard its treaties with American Indians and still maintain its outward moral integrity.[57]

Termination was made fact because it came shrouded in liberalism and morality. American Indians marched off to war for various reasons; yet, whites took the tribes' participation as an unquestionable act of loyalty to the United States. Whites looked upon it as an American Indian effort to prove themselves worthy of "mainstream society." The fact that oppressed people could remain loyal to the United States served to illustrate the justice of America's cause. It tended, in the minds of Americans, to prove America's greatness every bit as much as winning the war had done. In this kind of intellectual climate, termination, no matter what its underlying motives, was easily passed as a liberal, democratic method of solving Indian problems. In the end, fighting the white man's war gained sympathy for American Indians, but it also fueled a fire that they did not want and eventually found difficult to extinguish.

# NOTES

1. Richard L. Neuberger, "On the Warpath," *Saturday Evening Post*, October 24, 1942, p. 79.

2. Richard L. Neuberger, "The American Indian Enlists," *Asia and the Americas* 42 (November, 1942): 628.

3. *The Indian's Friend*, January, 1918. See also *Annual Report of the Commissioner of Indian Affairs, 1920* (Washington, D.C.: U.S. Government Printing Office, 1920), pp. 8–10.

4. 41 *U.S. Stat.* 350; 43 *U.S. Stat.* 253.

5. John Collier, "The Indian in a Wartime Nation," *Annals of the American Academy of Political and Social Science* 223 (September, 1942): 29.

6. Elizabeth S. Sergeant, "The Indian Goes to War," *New Republic*, November 30, 1942, p. 708.

7. Report of John Collier, Commissioner of Indian Affairs, *Annual Report of the Secretary of the Interior, 1944* (Washington, D.C.: U.S. Government Printing Office, 1944), p. 235.

8. Because of the difficulties in identifying American Indians, there has been no accurate count of the people of Indian heritage in this country. The 25,000 in the armed forces during the war is a conservative estimate. See Edward Everett Dale, *The Indians of the Southwest* (Norman: University of Oklahoma Press, 1949), p. 230; and Leonard Dinnerstein, Roger L. Nichols, and David M. Reimers, *Natives and Strangers: Ethnic Groups and the Building of America* (New York: Oxford University Press, 1979), p. 266. A count of 29,000 was made by Gerald D. Nash, *The Great Depression and World War II* (New York: St. Martin's Press, 1979), p. 152. The two best-known studies of the war years in America, Richard Polenberg, *War and Society, the United States 1941–1945* (Philadelphia: J. B. Lippincott, 1972) and John Morton Blum, *V Was for Victory: Politics and American Culture During World War II* (New York: Harcourt Brace Jovanovich, 1976) fail to mention American Indians at all in connection with the war.

9. Collier, "Indian in a Wartime Nation," p. 29.

10. Neuberger, "American Indian Enlists," p. 629.

11. *The Indian's Friend*, July, 1918.

12. Stanley Vestal, "The Plains Indian and the War," *Saturday Review of Literature*, May 16, 1942, p. 9.

13. Harold L. Ickes, "Indians Have a Name for Hitler," *Collier's*, January 15, 1940, p. 58.

14. *New York Times*, January 26, 1942.

15. Ickes, "Indians Have a Name for Hitler," p. 58.

16. *Annual Report of the Secretary of the Interior, 1944* (Washington, D.C.: U.S. Government Printing Office, 1944), pp. 235–36.

17. Ibid., p. 236; *New York Times*, April 13 and 24, 1944.

18. Collier, "Indian in a Wartime Nation," p. 30; See also Virgil J. Vogel, *This Country Was Ours* (New York: Harper & Row, 1974), p. 334; Ickes, "Indians Have a Name for Hitler," p. 58.

19. Vogel, *The Country Was Ours*, p. 335; *New York Times*, January 30, 1944.

20. Vogel, *The Country Was Ours*, p. 329, for a biographical sketch. For analysis of Hayes as a symbol see Ralph and Natasha Friar, *The Only Good Indian: The Hollywood Gospel* (New York: Drama Book Specialists, 1972), pp. 216–218;

and Wilcomb E. Washburn, *Red Man's Land—White Man's Law* (New York: Scribner's, 1971), p. 80.

21. Sergeant, "Indian Goes to War," p. 709.
22. *New York Times*, July 5, 1952.
23. *New York Times*, September 19, 1945.
24. For a comprehensive study of the over 400 Navajos who fought with the Marine Corps during World War II, see Doris A. Paul, *The Navajo Code Talkers* (New York: Dorrance & Co., 1973).
25. *New York Times*, January 8, 1942.
26. *New York Times*, January 30, April 22, 1945.
27. Ickes, "Indians Have a Name for Hitler," p. 58.
28. *Annual Report of the Secretary of the Interior, 1944*, p. 238.
29. Ibid., p. 237; Dale, *Indians of the Southwest*, p. 230.
30. *Annual Report of the Secretary of the Interior, 1944*, p. 237; Ickes, "Indians Have a Name for Hitler," p. 58. For a look at a single reservation see Robert Ritzenthaler, "The Impact of the War on an Indian Community," *American Anthropologist* 45 (April–June, 1943): 325–26.
31. Sergeant, "Indian Goes to War," p. 709. See also *Annual Report of the Secretary of the Interior, 1945*, p. 238.
32. Neuberger, "American Indian Enlists," p. 628.
33. *New York Times*, February 21, June 9, 1943; February 17, 1944.
34. Friar, *The Only Good Indian*, pp. 194, 196–97.
35. Neuberger, "American Indian Enlists," p. 630.
36. Ibid., p. 629.
37. Collier, "Indian in a Wartime Nation," p. 30.
38. Ickes, "Indians Have a Name for Hitler," p. 58.
39. James Howard, "The Dakota Indian Victory Dance, World War II," *North Dakota History* 18 (January, 1951): 36.
40. Collier, "Indian in a Wartime Nation," p. 29; Neuberger, "On the Warpath," p. 79.
41. Neuberger, "American Indian Enlists," p. 630.
42. *Annual Report of the Secretary of the Interior, 1944*, p. 238.
43. Oswald Garrison Villard, "Wardship and the Indian," *Christian Century* 61 (March 29, 1944): 397.
44. Ibid., p. 398.
45. O. K. Armstrong, "Set the American Indians Free!" *Reader's Digest*, August, 1945, pp. 47–48.
46. Ibid., pp. 47, 49.
47. Ibid., p. 52.
48. Haven Emerson, "Freedom or Exploitation! Is Mr. O. J. K. Armstrong's Recent Solution of the American Indian Problem Sound?" *American Indian* 2 (Fall, 1945): 3.
49. Randolph C. Downes, "The American Indian Can Be Free," *American Indian* 2 (Fall, 1945): 8.
50. Emerson, "Freedom or Exploitation!" pp. 5–6.
51. Walter C. Eells, "Educational Opportunities for the Indian Veteran," *American Indian* 2 (Fall, 1945): 17–21.
52. Oliver La Farge, "They Were Good Enough for the Army," *Harper's Magazine* November, 1947, pp. 444–49.
53. See editor's note, Richard N. Ellis, ed., *The Western American Indian* (Lincoln: University of Nebraska Press, 1972), p. 174; Washburn, *Red Man's Land*, pp. 101–108.
54. Angie Debo, *A History of the Indians of the United States* (Norman: University of Oklahoma Press, 1970), p. 283.

55. Lyman Tyler, *A History of Indian Policy* (Washington, D.C.: U.S. Government Printing Office), p. 166.

56. Washburn, *Red Man's Land*, p. 87.

57. Ibid., p. 91; Ellis, *Western American Indian*, p. 188.

# CHAPTER 7

# Federal Water Projects and Indian Lands: The Pick-Sloan Plan, a Case Study

## BY MICHAEL L. LAWSON

*While the federal government is charged with the role of trustee and guardian of Indian well-being, conflicts of interest frequently occur. As Michael Lawson asserts in the following article, flood control and reclamation projects promoted by the Army Corps of Engineers and the Bureau of Reclamation represent classic cases in point of such conflicts. Lawson examines in detail the impact of the Pick-Sloan Plan upon the Sioux people of North and South Dakota.*

*Indians in the Plains have had to confront increasing pressure upon their lands and ways of life in the years since World War II. Once seemingly rather isolated from the needs and demands of the region, save the inroads achieved by their immediate white neighbors, Indian land and water have progressively become more influenced by multi-state development planning. The tremendous growth of urban centers and the burgeoning expectations of contemporary farmers and ranchers have helped foster the building of massive dams such as those at Fort Randall, Oahe, and Big Bend.*

*While such edifices have provided certain benefits for the general public in the Missouri Basin, they have caused many hardships for the Sioux. Lawson's case study should raise larger questions for rural residents of the Plains. He examines here a process of decision making that ignored the interests and wishes of Indian people. Conclusions were drawn by individuals who apparently knew little and cared less about the Indians' welfare compared with the more impor-*

From *American Indian Culture and Research Journal* 7, No. 1 (1983): 23–40. Reprinted by permission.

*tant benefits they saw accruing to a greater number of people through the Pick-Sloan Plan.*

*As rural residents grow steadily more disenfranchised politically, and as the Plains develops urban centers whose people are less familiar with rural values and traditions, priorities emerge that favor suburb and city, industry and region, over the older values and traditions. While the Sioux were the losers in the struggle delineated here, non-Indians have also lost battles of that kind in the years that followed World War II.*

*Lawson's full-scale work* Dammed Indians: The Pick-Sloan Plan and the Missouri River Sioux, 1944–1980 *(Norman: University of Oklahoma Press, 1982) takes a provocative and searching look at the overall effect on the Sioux within the Missouri River Basin. It, too, speaks to how Indian rights may be subsumed by the demands of American society.*

THE history of the application of the European doctrines of discovery and conquest to American Indian tribes in the eighteenth and nineteenth centuries, and the evolution of policies which recognized them as "domestic dependent nations" under federal trusteeship, is well known. The subsequent saga of massacres, depredations, and broken treaties which resulted from the exercise of territorial imperatives on both sides has likewise occupied the pens of many historians. What is less familiar is the fact that the struggle for land and sovereignty did not end in the bloody snow banks of Wounded Knee in 1890, but has continued, for even greater stakes, into the present century.

Preoccupied with the dramatic military confrontations of the nineteenth century, historians of federal Indian policy until recently have paid too little attention to the fact that the erosion of native land and water rights has persisted to the present day. Because of the marginal nature of much of the Indians' remaining land and resources, this neglectful situation has become even more detrimental to tribal interests. Since land has long provided the very essence of tribal existence, and since the future of many of today's tribes depends on their ability to utilize and control their own resources, those issues have become far too grave to be ignored further.

Increasingly in the twentieth century the United States has used its powers of eminent domain to seize large parcels of Indian land for the construction of flood control and reclamation projects. While federal water agencies claim that these dams provide multiple benefits for the general public, Native Americans seem always to be the last to receive these advantages.

In the Missouri River Basin, the Pick-Sloan Plan, the joint water development program designed by the Army Corps of Engineers and the Bureau of Reclamation in 1944, caused more damage to Indian land than any other public works project in America. Whether or not these federal agencies deliberately chose Indian over non-Indian land for their project sites, as some tribal leaders have charged, their plans ultimately affected twenty-three different reservations.

Three of the dams constructed under Pick-Sloan (Fort Randall, Oahe, and Big Bend) flooded over 202,000 acres of Sioux land on the Standing Rock, Cheyenne River, Lower Brulé, Crow Creek, and Yankton reservations in North and South Dakota. These five reservations provide material for an especially appropriate case study of both the federal acquisition of Indian trust land and the application of recent Indian policies.

The development of the Pick-Sloan Plan represented a compromise between the separate water resources programs designed by Colonel Lewis A. Pick of the Corps of Engineers and William Glenn Sloan of the Bureau of Reclamation. The Pick Plan was primarily concerned with the development of flood control measures to protect the lower Missouri Valley, while the Sloan Plan was preoccupied with the construction of irrigation projects in the upper Missouri Basin. Although these seemingly conflicting programs were proposed by two powerful agencies traditionally at odds, a remarkable conciliation of the two plans was very quickly achieved and rather hastily approved by Congress as part of the Flood Control Act of 1944. This modern ''Missouri Compromise'' was accomplished partly as a result of the urgent demand for federal action which followed the disastrous Missouri River floods of 1942 and 1943. It also represented an attempt to head off support that was growing for an alternative plan to develop a Missouri Valley Authority (MVA)—an independent public corporation patterned after the successful Tennessee Valley Authority (TVA).[1]

Officially labeled the Missouri River Basin Development Program, Pick-Sloan was gradually expanded to include the construction of 150 multiple-purpose reservoir projects. In addition to flood control and irrigation, these dams were designed to provide the benefits of hydroelectric power, navigation, recreation, and improve water supplies.[2]

The backbone of the Pick-Sloan Plan was provided by the six massive dams constructed by the Corps of Engineers on the main stem of the Missouri—two of which (Fort Peck and Oahe) rank among the largest earth dams in the world. Together these six projects destroyed over 550 square miles of tribal land and displaced more than 900 Indian families. Most of this damage was sustained by the five Sioux reservations with which this study is primarily concerned: Standing Rock and Cheyenne River, which lost 160,000 acres to the Oahe project; Yankton, which was reduced by 3,300 acres by the Fort Randall Dam; and Crow Creek and Lower Brulé, which gave up a total of 38,000 acres to the Fort Randall and Big Bend projects.[3] In addition, the construction of the Garrison Dam on the Fort Berthold Reservation in western North Dakota resulted in the destruction of 152,000 acres of land belonging to the Three Affiliated Tribes of Mandan, Arikara, and Hidatsa Indians.[4]

Approximately 600 Sioux families were uprooted by these projects. The natural advantages of their former homes could not be replaced on the marginal lands that remained after inundation. The shaded bottomlands had provided a pleasant living environment with plenty of wood, game, water, and natural food resources. Livestock could graze on abundant grasses and take shelter under the trees. The barren upland regions to which these tribal members were forced to move proved less hospitable, more rigorous, and presented far greater challenges to their survival.[5]

The Pick-Sloan projects destroyed 90 percent of the reservations' timberland and 75 percent of the wild-game and plant supply. Trees along the Missouri had provided the tribes with their primary source of fuel and lumber and had protected both man and beast from the ravages of winter blizzards and scorching summer heat. The gathering and preserving of wild fruits and vegetables was a traditional part of Sioux culture. The numerous types of herbs, roots, berries, and beans that grew in the bottomlands added bulk and variety to the Indian diet, and were also used for medicinal and ceremonial purposes. The wooded bottomlands also served as a shelter and feeding ground for a variety of wildlife. The hunting and trapping of this game had provided the tribes with an important source of food, income, and recreation. The loss of bottomland grazing areas seriously crippled tribal livestock operations, which had been the primary industry on most of the reservations. Artificial shelters had to be built to replace the natural woodland shelter belts. Substantial amounts of new fencing had to be erected, and new feed and water sources developed to replace the natural resources of the old habitat. Stockraising thus proved far more difficult, expensive, and risky.[6]

Damages caused by the Pick-Sloan projects touched every aspect of Sioux life. Abruptly the tribes were transformed from a subsistence to a cash economy and forced to develop new ways of making a living. The relocation of the agency headquarters on Cheyenne River, Crow Creek, and Lower Brulé disrupted federal services; disorganized the social, economic, political, and religious life of well-integrated tribal groups; and had a serious effect on the entire reservation population. It was an onerous imposition for tribal members to have to relocate their community halls, churches, and religious shrines. It was even harder for them to disturb the graves of their ancestors and to excavate their cemeteries and private burial grounds.[7]

Physical losses inflicted by Pick-Sloan are more easily quantified than psychological and aesthetic damages. Like any people forced to relinquish their homes, the Sioux hated to give up their land and seek unfamiliar places to live. But their particular circumstances made the situation even more difficult. Unlike others affected by public works projects, they were not able to duplicate their old way of life by moving to a similar environment. After inundation, no Indian land like the old existed. Leaving the reservation was not a viable alternative, because it meant the loss of federal services and close kinship ties.[8]

Much of the Indians' suffering came as a result of the federal government's failure to provide an adequate administrative structure for the Pick-Sloan Plan. In response to the apparently overwhelming opposition to the creation of a Missouri Valley Authority, the Truman administration placed the program under the rather loose-knit coordination of the Missouri Basin Inter-Agency Committee, a nonstatutory body which quickly fell under the domination of the Corps of Engineers.[9]

The Inter-Agency Committee's piecemeal approach to Missouri Basin problems and its preoccupation with engineering methods did not allow for adequate consideration of such important human factors as the condemnation of farms and ranches and the relocation of families. The Army Engineers had nothing in their training or background that prepared them to deal fairly or knowledgeably with Indians, and the federal agency usually charged with that responsibility, the Bureau of Indian Affairs, was hampered during this period by a severely reduced budget and under threat of being abolished altogether by those in Congress who supported the so-called "termination movement."[10]

While a centralized and regionally located Missouri Valley Authority would have received an annual block appropriation for all of its work, the numerous agencies involved with Pick-Sloan had to deal with several separate committees in Congress for their particular part of the overall program. Thus the army often received generous amounts for dam construction during years when the Sioux tribes were not able to receive compensation for their resulting damages. Because of this lack of coordination, tribal members were systematically denied most of the important benefits of Pick-Sloan, their efforts at reconstruction fell far short of their needs, and their reserved water rights were completely ignored.[11]

The Sioux knew little of the Pick-Sloan Plan until long after it was approved. Despite the fact that treaty rights provided that reservation land could not be taken without their consent, none of the tribes were consulted prior to the program's enactment. So confident was the Corps of Engineers that it could acquire the Indian land it needed through condemnation that it began construction on its dams, including those actually on reservation property, even before opening formal negotiations with respective tribal leaders.[12]

Pick-Sloan was thus presented to the tribes as a fait accompli. The Federal government was determined to move the Sioux out of the way, and there was simply nothing they could do about it. Though angry and bitter that the United States would again break the faith of its treaty obligations and sacrifice their interests in order to satisfy white demands for progress, the Indians realized that resistance was futile. Intertribal cooperation was then virtually nonexistent, and the individual tribes were too politically fragmented to permit organized opposition. Access to influential legislators and competent legal counselors was extremely limited, and tribal members were not then inclined to take radical action. Federal officials ignored the protests that did emerge, and the Sioux were eventually forced to accept the inevitable consequences of Pick-Sloan. Gradually, they resigned themselves to making the most of whatever alms might be offered in compensation, but their bitterness did not subside.[13]

Realizing they were powerless to stop the dams, tribal leaders were determined, nevertheless, to negotiate for payments and benefits which would allow them to utilize fully their remaining resources. In light of the congressional debate over termination, they also sought compensation which might permit them to make a giant step toward self-sufficiency, a goal previously established and facilitated by the so-called "Indian New Deal" administration of Commissioner John Collier between 1933 and 1945. Thus Sioux negotiators reasoned that a generous settlement might include the development of new programs and facilities for health, education, housing, community growth, and employment. They also hoped for such direct benefits from the reservoir projects as low-cost electrical power, irrigation, and improved water supplies.[14]

Recognizing its obligation to see that the Sioux received just compensation, Congress in 1950 authorized the Department of the Interior and the Army Corps of Engineers to negotiate separate settlement contracts with respective tribal representatives. In addition to providing payment for all damages, these agencies were also directed to cover the costs of relocating tribal members "so that their economic, social, and religious life can be reestablished and protected." Each of these agencies was required to prepare a detailed analysis of damages, and in the event that they could not reach a satisfactory agreement in the field, Congress was to arbitrate a final settlement.[15]

Negotiations with the separate Sioux tribes, carried on over a period of fourteen years (1948–62), followed a similar pattern. Inevitably army, Indian Bureau, and tribal officials arrived at different estimates of damage. The BIA was often willing to compromise with the Indians. But the Corps of Engineers refused to acknowledge its obligation to provide for relocation and reconstruction and ultimately failed to reach a satisfactory agreement with any of the tribes. Negotiations dragged far beyond established time limits, and Congress was extremely tardy in considering contract provisions. The Yankton, Crow Creek, and Lower Brulé tribes were actually forced to move before agreeing to a settlement, and the Standing Rock Sioux received funds only at the last possible moment. On all of the reservations except Cheyenne River, the Corps of Engineers was able to obtain the immediate Indian land it needed for its projects through condemnation proceedings in the U.S. District Court, despite a 1920 Supreme Court decision which held that a federal agency must have the specific authorization of Congress to do so without tribal consent.[16]

In contract negotiations, tribal representatives, such as Frank Ducheneaux of Cheyenne River and Josephine Kelly of Standing Rock, were simply outgunned. Unversed and unwary, they were forced to do battle with experienced federal experts. Settlement demands drawn up by the Indians were very often circumvented or ignored, and in every case the army resorted to strong-arm tactics by posing the threat of its illegally assumed powers of eminent domain. Local congressmen, such as Representative E. Y. Berry of South Dakota, generally did what they could for their Sioux constituents but too often fell victim to split allegiances and shifting loyalties. The result was a half-a-loaf settlement for each tribe. Although each in turn gained more money and better terms, none of the Sioux tribes came close to receiving what they considered just compensation.[17]

Although the Indians eventually received a total of more than $34 million in compensation, this was less than half the amount they had requested. Because of the arbitrary fashion in which terms were arrived at, settlements provided the five individual tribes differed considerably. Thus, although the Cheyenne River Sioux sustained the most damages, the Standing Rock Sioux received the best overall settlement, and the Crow Creek and Lower Brulé tribes the most generous reconstruction provisions. In addition, all of the tribes were denied requests for benefits such as unlimited shoreline access, the retention of all mineral rights, and the right to have a block of hydroelectric power reserved for their exclusive use.[18]

As long and arduous as was the process of negotiating final settlements, it represented only the first stage of the Pick-Sloan ordeal for these tribal groups. Once compensation was determined, plans had to be implemented for the relocation of tribal members and their property, the reconstruction and restoration of reservation facilities, and the rehabilitation of entire Indian communities. The disruption, chaos, and uncertainty generated by this experience made it a most painful one for all tribal members involved. So shortsighted was Corps of Engineers planning in regard to its projects on the Crow Creek reservation, for example, that families forced to move by the Fort Randall project were relocated within the projected site of the Big Bend reservoir area. Consequently, when time came to open the second dam, these unfortunate tribal members were compelled to move once again.[19]

Over \$20 million of the compensation received by the Sioux tribes was allocated by Congress to establish social and economic programs which would help move them towards the goal of self-sufficiency, so that federal services and supervision might eventually be withdrawn. Because of this intent, the Indians were given far greater responsibility for the administration and use of this so-called "rehabilitation money" than had been permitted with any previous federal programs. In this respect, rehabilitation proved a valuable educational experience, a praiseworthy experiment in self-determination, and altogether the most worthwhile aspect of the Pick-Sloan compensation; although it was absurd, of course, to expect that the tribes could make giant strides toward solving their many social and economic problems with the limited funds made available to them.[20]

The Corps of Engineers completed the construction of its five main-stem dams on the Missouri in 1966. If the benefits which the Sioux have received from these projects are to be gauged, they should first be measured in terms of the purpose for which these dams were originally constructed. Assuming that the \$30 billion Pick-Sloan Plan was truly designed to be beneficial to the people of the Missouri River Basin, then it should be equally of benefit to those people, both Indian and non-Indian, who have suffered the most as a result of its implementation. But such is not the case.

The Bureau of Reclamation and the Corps of Engineers designed their integrated Missouri Basin development program to provide improved flood control, hydroelectric power, irrigation, navigation, recreation, and other important benefits. On balance, however, an evaluation of their efforts at this juncture reveals that Pick-Sloan has not measurably improved the lives of the Sioux people in regard to any of these provisions.

To its credit, the army has succeeded in making long stretches of the Missouri safe from the catastrophe of high floods. This is particularly true in the populous region between Kansas City and Sioux City. But the fact that the dams have improved flood control does not particularly impress the Sioux, since, as one woman on Cheyenne River pointed out, it is quite natural to assume that "if you flood the bottomlands you will then have flood control."[21] Floods on the reservations were never as serious or as frequent as those in the lower basin, and the Corps of Engineers' efforts have still not prevented the continuation of tributary inundations. What the Indians are concerned with is that the army, in most cases, took far more reservation land than was necessary to maintain the reservoirs at their maximum pool level. Yet, in some areas the waters have infringed on Sioux land never purchased by the federal government, and all along the banks, the fluctuation of these undulating waters has created a far greater hazard to tribal livestock and resources than any of the infrequent floods of the past.[22]

Although the Pick-Sloan power plants have definitely increased the availability of electrical power in the Missouri Basin, affordability continues to be the most important factor as far as the Sioux are concerned. For lack of money vast areas of the reservation are still without electrical service, and the Federal government has done nothing to make lower power rates available to the tribes, although the Department of Energy has acknowledged that they qualify as preferential low-cost customers under Section 5 of the Flood Control Act of 1944. The catch is that all of this power has already been committed to non-Indian municipalities and rural cooperatives.[23]

The long and heated debate over the suitability and practicality of reclamation in the upper Missouri Basin has caused frustrating delays, serious cutbacks, and drastic revisions in the original Pick-Sloan irrigation plans. Consequently, the Bureau of Reclamation's two major projects in the Dakotas, the Garrison and Oahe diversion units, have been effectively halted by environmentalists and others who have shifted their support to alternative water development programs. Neither is the outlook particularly bright for the Pick-Sloan irrigation projects proposed for Sioux lands, since most were deauthorized by Congress in 1964. Because of the heavy shale deposits on many of the reservations, it thus remains to be seen whether the Indians' marginal land holdings are truly irrigable and if irrigation farming can ever be financially feasible.[24]

Many of the tribes have experimented with irrigation, but only the Lower Brulé Sioux have come close to success. With the help of a generous grant from the Economic Development Administration (EDA), the tribe constructed the Grass Rope Unit in 1976 and developed irrigation for some 1,500 acres, raising corn, milo, and pinto beans. Plans are presently underway to expand this project to 5,000 acres at an estimated cost of $4.9 million, and a bill presently before Congress would permit the tribe to obtain Pick-Sloan hydropower for its pumping units at a cost of only 2.5 mills per kilowatt hour.[25]

Due to the nature of the clearing operations conducted by the Corps of Engineers, navigation on many of the Missouri River reservoirs is presently obstructed by the large number of trees left standing above the water surface. These obstacles also interfere with recreational activities on the lakes, another of the purposes for which the dams were created.[26]

Of all the benefits promised by Pick-Sloan, the most immediate and successful results in the Dakotas have been realized in the areas of outdoor recreation and tourism. Although some of the Sioux tribes have attempted to capitalize on the sudden recreation boom, none has successfully been able to share in this new prosperity. Since traditional tribal members seldom engaged in fishing, boating, and swimming, the dam projects, by causing the destruction of wildlife and a subsequent decline in hunting, have actually reduced the Indians' favored recreational activity on the reservations.[27] Furthermore, a U.S. District Court has held that the tribes no longer have authority to regulate hunting and fishing on that portion of the reservations which are within the taking area of the reservoirs.[28]

While another of the promised Pick-Sloan benefits was the development of an adequate reservoir water supply for domestic, municipal, and industrial use, most areas of the Sioux reservations are still dependent on ground water sources, which in many cases exceed federal standards for maximum impurities and are generally unfit for human use.[29]

The Missouri River Sioux have received, therefore, almost none of the benefits which were supposed to be provided by Pick-Sloan, although they have suffered a great deal as a result of its implementation. Although many observers feel that the $20 million appropriated by Congress for the rehabilitation of the tribes should rightfully be considered a direct benefit of the water development program, it is clear that these five Sioux tribes could have received money for this purpose independent of the dam project settlements, as did the Navajo, Hopi, Pine Ridge Sioux, and numerous other tribes during this period. These federal funds could certainly have been more effective, in fact, had not the economic life of the reservations been so thoroughly disrupted by the army's dam projects.

What then has been learned from the Pick-Sloan experience? The lessons for the Missouri River Sioux tribes have been bitter and many. But for the federal government they appear to be few. In terms of recognizing Native Americans as human beings with legitimate property rights, it has continued to demonstrate how little has been learned from the mistakes of the previous two centuries.

In regard to the critical issue of Indian water rights, the United States has also maintained the tradition of failing to abide by its own rules as far as the Sioux are concerned. The federal agencies involved in the Pick-Sloan program have never acknowledged the legal doctrine propounded by the Supreme Court in the 1908 case of *Winters* v. *United States*, which held that Indians have a reserved right for the purpose of irrigation to waters that flow either through or along their reservations.[30] In their interpretations of the complex body of law that has developed from the *Winters* decision, some legal experts have claimed that the Indian right also includes the preferential use of water for all existing and potential beneficial uses, a view to which the Sioux tribes have enthusiastically clung.[31]

Granted, neither the Supreme Court nor Congress has ever adequately specified the full nature and extent of Indian water rights. But even the unambiguous provisions of the *Winters* decision would seem to dictate that Congress should have given statutory recognition of the Indians' reserved rights in the Flood Control Act of 1944, and that the Corps of Engineers and Bureau of Reclamation should have made an effort to quantify tribal irrigation water needs, at the very least, and guarantee that they would be met before committing any Missouri Basin water to Pick-Sloan uses.

Since the possession of preferential water rights is absolutely essential for the future economic development of reservation lands, the Sioux should have challenged the federal government on this issue. They did not do so, largely because they have been led to assume that the *Winters* doctrine, in its broadest and most liberal interpretation, is legally concrete; in other words, that they have a paramount right, based on their prior occupancy of the land, to use as much of the Missouri water as they can. Thus they have tended to view any discussion of quantification as an attempt to limit rather than protect their water rights.

In the meantime, the federal government has found new ways to exploit Missouri Basin water resources. In 1975 the Corps of Engineers and Reclamation Bureau launched a program to market an additional 1,000,000 acre-feet of reservoir water each year to private industrial users.[32] The latest benefactor of this federal marketing program was Energy Transportation Systems Inc. (ETSI), a San Francisco-based consortium of heavyweight energy and construction investors. This firm has purchased the right to divert 50,000 acre-feet per year from the Oahe Reservoir in South Dakota for the purpose of supplying water for what will be the nation's largest coal slurry pipeline, to be constructed from the coal fields of Wyoming to power plants in Oklahoma, Arkansas, and Louisiana.[33]

The ETSI water sale has made it evident that judicial decisions or legislative statutes are crucially needed in order to settle the points of ambiguity and disagreement which continue not only to shroud the Indians' water rights but also those of the individual states within the Missouri Basin. If these legal questions can be clarified, federal and state governments might be compelled to quantify the future water needs of the Sioux and other tribes before committing any more of the Missouri's precious water resources to non-Indian users.

A quantification of the water rights of seven of the Sioux tribes might be the positive result of a suit which the State of South Dakota brought to court in 1980. This litigation, docketed as *South Dakota* v. *Rippling Water Ranch, et al.*, has been filed against approximately 60,000 defendants, including the tribes and their individual members, to determine all private and public rights to the use of the Missouri River water system within the state boundaries. But it has taken more than two years just to determine a competent court of jurisdiction, and the recent decision of a federal judge to remand the suit from U.S. District Court to a state tribunal which has traditionally been hostile to Indian interests has served to justify the trepidations of those tribal leaders who have always feared having their water rights adjudicated.[34]

The saga of the Pick-Sloan Plan and its effects on the Sioux tribes of the Missouri River will thus continue well into the future. While it will always be impossible to ignore the abuse of Indian rights which has characterized this program up to now, it is sincerely hoped that a more optimistic conclusion to the episode can someday be written.

# Notes

1. U.S. Congress, Senate, *Review of Plans of Engineer Corps, Army, and Reclamation Bureau for Development of the Missouri River Basin*, 78th Cong., 2d sess., 1944, S. Exec. Doc. 247; Richard G. Baumhoff, *The Dammed Missouri Valley* (New York: Alfred A. Knopf, 1951), pp. 184–95; Bruce Nelson, *Land of the Dacotahs* (Minneapolis: University of Minnesota Press, 1946), pp. 318–28.

2. John W. Ball, "Midwest Flood Also Burst a Political Dike," *Washington Post*, July 25, 1951; Otto G. Hoiberg, *Its Your Business and Mine: Missouri River Basin Development Program; A Study Guide*, University of Nebraska, Extension Division, Booklet No. 175 (May, 1950), pp. 39, 60; Marvin Meade, *The Missouri River Proposals for Development*, Citizens Pamphlet II (Lawrence: University of Kansas, Bureau of Government Research, 1952), p. 22.

3. U.S. Department of the Interior, Bureau of Indian Affairs, Missouri River Basin Investigations Project, *Damages to Indians of Five Reservations from Three Missouri River Reservoirs in North and South Dakota*, Report 138 (Billings, Mont., 1954), pp. 1, 18–19, 47; "Summary and Evaluation of Experiences of Six Indian Reservations Affected by Large Dam and Reservoir Projects on the Missouri River," File 1766–074.1 (General Programs, Missouri River Basin), Record Group 75, Bureau of Indian Affairs (hereafter RG, BIA), Washington National Records Center, Suitland, Md.

4. For a detailed account of the effects of the Garrison Dam on the Fort Berthold Indians, see Roy W. Meyer, "Fort Berthold and the Garrison Dam," *North Dakota History* 35 (Summer and Fall, 1968): 220–355. See also his *The Village Indians of the Upper Missouri: The Mandans, Hidatsas, and the Arikaras* (Lincoln: University of Nebraska Press, 1977).

5. *Damages to Indians of Five Reservations*, pp. 1, 18–19, 47; "Summary and Evaluation of Experiences of Six Indian Reservations."

6. "Summary and Evaluation of Experiences of Six Indian Reservations."

7. Ibid.

8. Ibid.

9. Missouri River Inter-Agency Committee, *The Missouri River Basin Development Plan* (Washington, D.C.: U.S. Government Printing Office, 1952), p. 11; Marian E. Ridgeway, *The Pick-Sloan Plan* (Urbana: University of Illinois Press, 1955), pp. 15–21; Rufus Terral, *The Missouri Valley: Land of Flood, Drouth, and Promise* (New Haven, Conn.: Yale University Press, 1947), pp. 208–10; Baumhoff, *Dammed Missouri Valley*, pp. 169–79; Nelson, *Land of the Decotahs*, pp. 325–28.

10. Nelson, *Land of the Dacotahs*.

11. Ibid.

12. U.S. Department of the Interior, BIA, Missouri River Basin Investigations Project, *Annual Report, Fiscal Year 1948* (Billings, Mont., 1948), pp. 6–8; "Programs and Accomplishments of Interior Agencies Using Missouri Basin Project Transfer Funds," Department of the Interior Report, January 7, 1958, File 50745–44–074 (Missouri Basin Project), RG 75 (BIA), National Archives, "Statement of Responsibilities and Relationships for the Administration of the Oahe–Cheyenne River Act, P.L. 776, 83d Cong.," File 16822–074.1 (Missouri River Basin, Oahe Dam), RG 75 (BIA), Washington National Records Center.

13. Aljoe Agard, former Standing Rock Tribal Chairman, interview conducted

at Fort Yates, N. Dak., August 8, 1972; Frank Ducheneaux, former Cheyenne River Tribal Chairman, interview conducted on Cheyenne River Sioux Indian Reservation, S. Dak., July 30–31, 1972; Richard LaRoche, former Lower Brulé Tribal Chairman, interview conducted at Lower Brulé, S. Dak., August 25, 1971, by American Indian Research Project, South Dakota Oral History Center, University of South Dakota, tapes 784, 789.

14. See n. 13. For a good description of the "Indian New Deal" see Graham D. Taylor, *The New Deal and American Indian Tribalism: The Administration of the Indian Reorganization Act, 1934–1945* (Lincoln: University of Nebraska Press, 1980).

15. *Act of September 30, 1950*, 64 *U.S. Stat.* 1093.

16. "Minutes of Negotiations for Federal Government and Sioux Indians, Missouri River Contract Negotiations," File 17889–074.1 (Missouri Basin), RG 75 (BIA), Washington National Records Center; "Brief in Justification of Appropriation for Certain Yankton Sioux Families," February 28, 1948, File 5491–48–308 (Fort Randall Legislation), RG 75 (BIA), National Archives; U.S. District Court, District of South Dakota: *U.S.* v. *2005 Acres of land, et al, and Standing Rock Sioux Tribe of Indians*, Civil No. 722, March 10, 1958; *U.S.* v. *867 Acres of Land, et al., and the Crow Creek and Lower Brulé Tribes of Sioux Indians*, Civil No. 335, March 9, 1960; *U.S.* v. *9148 Acres of Land, et al., and the Crow Creek Tribe of Sioux Indians*, Civil No. 184, August 4, 1953; *U.S.* v. *7996 Acres of Land, et al., and the Lower Brulé Tribe of Sioux Indians*, Civil No. 186, August 4, 1953. *U.S.* v. *North American Trading and Transportation Company*, 253 U.S. 330 (1920).

17. Agard, Ducheneaux, LaRoche, interviews.

18. *Act of September 3, 1954*, 68 *U.S. Stat.* 1191; *Acts of September 2, 1958*, 72 *U.S. Stat.* 1762–66 (Standing Rock), 1766–68 (Crow Creek), 1773–75 (Lower Brulé); *Acts of October 3, 1962*, 76 *U.S. Stat.* 698–703 (Lower Brulé), 704–10 (Crow Creek).

19. U.S. Department of the Interior, Bureau of Indian Affairs, Missouri River Basin Investigations Project, *Damages to Indians on Crow Creek and Lower Brulé Reservations from Big Bend Dam and Reservoir Project, South Dakota*, Report 165 (Billings, Mont., 1960), pp. 1–10; "Big Bend Relocation Program," Box 6, Decimal File 060 (Pierre Indian Agency), RG 75 (BIA), Federal Records Center, Kansas City, Mo.

20. "Special Report on the Use of Missouri River Dam and Reservoir Project Funds, December 16, 1963," Files 74A390, 223836 (Missouri Basin), RG 75 (BIA), Federal Records Center, Denver, Colo.; "Report Prepared for the Commissioner of Indian Affair's Trip to North and South Dakota, April, 1962," Papers of Philleo Nash, Harry S. Truman Presidential Library, Independence, Mo.

21. Ellen Ducheneaux, former Cheyenne River Tribal Negotiator, interview conducted at Eagle Butte, South Dakota, July 31, and August 1, 1972.

22. Frank Ducheneaux, Agard, and LaRoche interviews; Lloyd LeBeau, former Cheyenne River Tribal Negotiator, interview held at Eagle Butte, S. Dak., July 31, 1972; Kermeth S. Engle, BIA Realty Officer, interview conducted at Fort Yates, N. Dak., August 2, 1972.

23. *Kansas City Star*, May 6, 1972; William E. Warne, *The Bureau of Reclamation* (New York: Praeger 1973), pp. 167–68; Herbert S. Schell, *History of South Dakota* (Lincoln: University of Nebraska Press, 1975), pp. 308–309; Missouri Basin Inter-Agency Committee, *The Missouri River Basin Comprehensive Framework Study* (Washington, D.C.: U.S. Government Printing Office, 1971), 1:165, 5:4.

24. Warne, *Bureau of Reclamation*; Schell, *History of South Dakota*, p. 361;

Elwyn B. Robinson, *History of North Dakota* (Lincoln: University of Nebraska
Press, 1966), pp. 463, 465–66; U.S. Department of the Interior, BIA, Missouri
River Basin Investigations Project, *Potential Irrigation Development, Missouri
River Basin Reservations*, Report 185 (Billings, Mont., 1967), pp. 1–3, app. 10,
pp. 2, 20.

25. U.S. Department of the Interior, BIA, Aberdeen Area Office, *Breakdown
of Appropriations for Phase I, Grass Rope Irrigation Unit, Lower Brule Sioux
Reservation, South Dakota* (1981); *Rapid City Journal*, March 17, 1982: May 1,
1982; U.S. Congress, House, *A Bill to Authorize the Secretary of the Interior to
Proceed with Development of the WEB Pipeline, to Provide for the Study of South
Dakota Water Projects, and to Make Available Missouri Basin Pumping Power to
Projects Authorized by the Flood Control Act of 1944 to Receive such Power*, 97th
Cong., 2d sess., 1982, H.R. 4347.

26. Frank Ducheneaux, Agard, and LeBeau, interviews; Arthur E. Morgan,
*Dams and Other Disasters: A Century of the Army Corps of Engineers in Civil
Works* (Boston: Porter Sargeant, 1971), p. 57.

27. Frank Ducheneaux, Agard, and LeBeau, interviews; Dudley Rehder, Mis-
souri River Division Office, U.S. Army, Corps of Engineers, interview conducted
in Omaha, Neb., May 24, 1972; Kenneth Krabbenhoft, National Park Service,
Department of the Interior, interview conducted at Omaha, Neb., May 22, 1972;
U.S. Department of the Interior, Bureau of Outdoor Recreation, *The Middle
Missouri, A Rediscovery: A Study of Potential Outdoor Recreation* (Washington,
D.C.: U.S. Government Printing Office, 1970), pp. 1, 28–30.

28. U.S. District Court of the District of South Dakota, Central Division,
*Lower Brulé Sioux Tribe* v. *State of South Dakota*, Civil No. 80–3046, April 30,
1982.

29. Frank Ducheneaux, Agard, and LeBeau, interviews.

30. *Winters* v. *United States*, 207 U.S. 546 (1908). For a good historical
analysis of the *Winters* case see Norris Hundley, Jr., "The *Winters* Decision and
Indian Water Rights: A Mystery Reexamined," *Western Historical Quarterly* 13
(January, 1982): 17–42.

31. For an overview of the decisions and interpretations that have evolved since
*Winters* see Norris Hundley, Jr., "The Dark and Bloody Ground of Indian Water
Rights: Confusion Elevated to Principle," *Western Historical Quarterly* 9 (October, 1978): 454–82. For an example of the more liberal interpretations of *Winters*
water rights as they pertain to tribes of the Missouri Basin see William H. Veeder,
"Indian Water Rights in the Upper Missouri Basin," *North Dakota Law Review*
48 (Summer, 1972): 617–37.

32. William H. Veeder, "Confiscation of Indian *Winters* Rights in the Upper
Missouri Basin," *South Dakota Law Review* 21 (Spring, 1976): 283–308.

33. U.S. Department of the Interior, BIA, Aberdeen Area Office, *Facts on
ETSI*, by Michael L. Lawson (1982).

34. U.S. District Court of the District of South Dakota, Central Division, *State
of South Dakota* v. *Rippling Water Ranch Inc., et al.*, Civil No. 30–3031, January
19, 1982.

# CHAPTER 8

# ''What They Issue You'':
# Political Economy at Wind River

## BY LORETTA FOWLER

*The role of tribal government in the modern era has been frequently characterized by debate, dispute, and denigration. Observers have variously regarded the tribal council as an arm of the federal government, as an institution that promotes factionalism, or as an agency that does not represent the traditional tribal members or some element within the tribal populace. On the Pine Ridge Reservation in South Dakota and elsewhere in the region, tribal councils have been beset by conflict and even violence. Journalists and other ''instant experts'' have found in tribal government an easy target and a ready explanation for some of the ills they claim to have just discovered in contemporary Indian existence.*

*'' 'What They Issue You': Political Economy at Wind River'' is valuable in many ways. For one, it offers an alternative perspective on the potentiality and utility of tribal government in a Plains Indian setting. Loretta Fowler's depiction of the workings of the Northern Arapahoe Business Council demonstrates many of the purposes that tribal government may fulfill. The councilmen are perceived by their constituents as individuals who work for them and who intercede on their behalf with Bureau of Indian Affairs officials, non-Indian neighbors, the Shoshones with whom they share the Wind River Reservation, and other people.*

*Fowler's chapter does more than merely describe modern tribal government. She is concerned with the composition of a contemporary Plains Indian community, particularly with the economy of that*

Reprinted from *Arapahoe Politics, 1851–1978,* by Loretta Fowler, pp. 227–55, with permission. Copyright © 1982 by the University of Nebraska Press.

187

*community. For reservations to be homelands for Plains Indians, they must succeed as places where people can do more than eke out a marginal existence. Some of the Araphoes' problems are unique to their particular location, but most are common to Indians generally within the Plains.*

*Fowler also addressed the relationships between the Arapahoes and their Indian and non-Indian counterparts on and near the Wind River Reservation. How the Arapahoes perceive themselves affects, of course, how they see other people. Also, their frequently troubled relations with the bordertowns of Riverton and Lander illustrate larger dimensions of white-Indian contact in the region.*

*This chapter is from Fowler's prizewinning ethnohistorical mono-graph* Arapahoe Politics, 1851–1978: Symbols in Crises of Authority, *a fascinating study of authority and identity through time.*

DESPITE the monthly issue of per capita payments and the greater degree of independence possible for the Arapahoes since the Collier era, economic life is precarious and self-government is still limited. In 1934, one of the Arapahoes who spoke during the meetings about the IRA portrayed the tribe as being circled by a predatory wolf. He expressed in metaphor fears that make Arapahoes rely on tribal leaders for protection from external, hostile forces. These anxieties and fears still persist. In the words of one leader, unless the legal and economic status of the reservation community is preserved, ''there's nothing else but the alleys and trash cans of Lander''—nothing but social discrimination and poverty. Arapahoe political culture and the organizational forms of tribal government are conditioned by the fact that both individually and as a group the Arapahoes must rely on oil and gas royalties and bonuses, that on many levels Indian self-determination is threatened by whites, and that Arapahoe-Shoshone relations are strained. Now, as in the earlier eras, the Arapahoe Business Council is depended on as protector and provider.[1]

The Arapahoe Business Council still manages tribal funds and represents and defends Arapahoe interest in relation to federal, state, and local governments, as well as white interest groups in general. Operating without a constitution and by-laws, the Business Council is authorized by the tribe to represent the Northern

Arapahoes vis-à-vis the federal government and to make decisions in areas that by custom include economic development; the leasing, purchase, and sale of land; conservation of natural resources; and some aspects of health, education, and welfare. Major expenditures of tribal funds and matters of particular significance or controversy are attended to by members of the tribe over the age of eighteen in a general council, which is usally convened by the Business Council. Matters affecting both tribes are dealt with by a joint business council, comprised of the members of the Arapahoe and Shoshone business councils.[2]

Since 1937 members of the Arapahoe Business Council have been elected by popular vote every two years. The Shoshone tribe conducts its election separately but at the same time. All enrolled members of the tribe eighteen years and older are entitled to vote. Before 1972 candidates were nominated in community meetings at each of the Arapahoe residence clusters (Ethete and Lower Arapahoe). In accordance with a decision made by the General Council on August 23, 1972, potential candidates have had to register to participate in a primary; the twelve winners compete in the council election in November. At this time, Arapahoes vote for six candidates at large. The voting is by handwritten ballot and is usually supervised by respected elderly women. When the six newly elected councilmen take office in January, they choose a chairman from their group to preside over meetings. Councilmen receive no salary, but are paid $30 per diem each time they meet. The joint Shoshone and Arapahoe council employs a bookkeeper and clerical workers to staff the Tribal Office.

### THE WIND RIVER RESERVATION TODAY

Wind River Reservation, fifty-five miles from north to south and seventy miles from east to west, lies east of the continental divide at the foothills of the Rockies in west-central Wyoming and encompasses high mountainous terrain in the west, vast areas of range, and some irrigated farmland in the east. The distant mountains form a purple, snow-capped ring around Wind River country. There is a pervasive stillness and, despite the cluster of extended family settlements, a sense of great space. Indian settlement is largely in river valleys to the south.

In April, 1976, there were 3,093 enrolled Northern Arapahoes, approximately three-fourths of whom resided on the southeastern portion of the reservation in two communities, Ethete and Lower Arapahoe, and along the road that connects them.[3] Almost every Arapahoe household included some members who were not enrolled in the tribe, mostly children whose mothers married outside the tribe and children born out of wedlock—543 individuals altogether.[4] Most of the 700 or so Arapahoes who were living off the reservation at that time were married to and living with non-Arapahoes or had temporarily left Wind River for job training or employment.[5]

To the southwest is the residential area of the Eastern Shoshones, who in April, 1976, had 2,202 enrolled members. Approximately 1,454 of these people and 271 nonenrolled individuals were living in a widely dispersed pattern in the vicinity of the BIA headquarters, Tribal Office, and Public Health Clinic at Fort Washakie, and throughout the Burris, Morton, and Crowheart areas. Several hundred of the enrolled Shoshones resided off the reservation, as well.

Along the road from the Ethete community eastward, frame houses, one after the other, sit surrounded by an assortment of items put aside until needed—unused furniture, discarded automobile parts, camping stove, and tipi poles. Clotheslines heavy with freshly laundered clothing thrash against an interminable wind. Horses wander, aimlessly grazing alongside the houses, and dogs of all sizes run about. Groups of young cousins ride horses or run back and forth between the houses.

On the north side of the Ethete road is a small Catholic church, painted in symbolic geometric designs by Arapahoe artists. Here the priest comes from St. Stephen's to say Mass. Where the road turns south, a community center called Blue Sky Hall stands opposite the Arapahoe-decorated St. Michaels Mission, a post office, and an Indian-owned gas station, laundry, and cafe (periodically closed). Farther to the south is an elementary school for Ethete children, and to the east is the Sun Dance Grounds, where the lodge frame of the last ceremony stands, far apart from the houses. Twenty miles farther along the road is Great Plains Hall, the community center for the Lower Arapahoes, and a small public health clinic. Two miles to the south is a post office and small grocery store, opposite an elementary school for Lower Arapahoe children. Here the highway connecting Riverton and Lander is visible, the speed of the cars and trucks noticeably greater than the more leisurely pace on the Ethete-Arapahoe road. Three miles from Riverton at some distance from the highway is St. Stephen's Mission, now the site of an elementary school staffed with St. Stephen's personnel but since 1976 operated as a community-controlled contract school by Arapahoe parents.

During the last decade an extensive federally sponsored home-building program has resulted in far-reaching improvements in living conditions. In 1965 most people were living in small log or frame houses or in trailers, and a few still used canvas tents as extentions to their houses. Not all homes had electricity, plumb-ing, or gas heat. Today most families have larger, remodeled frame houses or prefabricated split-level or ranch-style homes, or live in one of the new housing projects. Jokingly termed Easter-Egg Village by the Arapahoes, the Ethete project stands opposite St. Michael's and has twenty-one prefabricated units brightly painted in blue, pink, green, or yellow. At Arapahoe there is a similar project, of comparable scale although painted in more subdued colors, and several units for elderly Arapahoes, termed in jest Geritol Heights. A new natural-gas line to Ethete and an expanded system of power lines are other recent developments. Television sets are common, telephones less so.

Despite these improvements, the economic situation of the tribespeople is still precarious. The 1970 per capita income on the reservation averaged $1,281, $2,640 below the national average and $2,275 below the per capita income for the state of Wyoming.[6] Shoshone income was higher, so that Arapahoe income averaged even less. Arapahoe families have good reason to depend on councilmen for aid in emergencies. The income to the tribe from mineral royalties allows for considerable flexibility in economic planning, but these resources are limited. To alleviate the econom-ic problems of the Arapahoes, tribal funds must be expended cautiously, new sources of revenue must be sought, and enrollment criteria must be conscientiously enforced lest the tribe's member-ship swell beyond the present capacity of reservation resources.

## The Economics of Reservation Life

Tribal income is derived primarily from deposits of oil and gas. Leases are issued to national corporations, which pay the tribes royalties and bonuses, half to the Arapahoes and half to the Shoshones. Before 1974 this income was deposited in the U.S. Treasury at 4 percent interest. Now the funds are managed by an investment coordinator, who sees that the money earns the highest rate of interest available. In 1976 the Arapahoe share of these funds was about $4.5 million, 85 percent of which was used for per capita distribution. Per capita payments are paid directly to each enrolled Arapahoe on a monthly basis. In 1976 each person received $90 every month. (The Shoshones, with a smaller population, received $136 each.) Fifteen percent of the tribal income is designated for operating expenses (the Arapahoe Business Council budget in 1976 totaled $379,150) and for augmention of capital reserve funds. These funds are allocated by the Arapahoe Business Council (and the Shoshone share by the Shoshone Business Council).[7]

The council seeks to maximize the income from mineral resources by employing an oil consultant, who works with the law firms retained by the Arapahoe and Shoshone business councils to pursue the tribes' interests. The policy of the joint council is to refer applications and bids to these specialists, who have been very effective in increasing the tribes' income.[8]

The joint council is periodically under pressure to invest tribal funds in order to stimulate economic development as well as to augment income. But in the Arapahoe view, after years of victimization by local whites and mismanagement of tribal resources under BIA directives, expenditures should be made only with great caution. The rejection of an effort to use tribal funds to erect a potato-processing factory on the reservation in 1969 was typical of the fate of proposals for economic development. When the BIA representatives and local white businessmen repeatedly argued the feasibility of the project, a member of the joint council offered this evaluation: "On this potato factory, if they want Indians to put money in it there must be something wrong with it." A second Arapahoe councilman concurred, "I'm on that horse, too."[9]

Such cynicism is reinforced by such incidents as the tribes' support of an electronics factory in Riverton. The company, Datel, needed the tribes' endorsement to secure funds from the Economic Development Agency, whose support was contingent on the consent of the "depressed area" (the reservation community). The tribes endorsed the project, and the EDA made a grant of $95,000 plus a sizable loan to match the amount raised by Riverton businessmen. In return for the support of the joint council, Datel promised 150 jobs for Indians by the end of 1967 and 300 jobs eventually. But only thirty Arapahoes and Shoshones were selected for training (out of seventy-five applicants), and only half that number (most of whom were Arapahoe) successfully completed the program. Datel hired only nine of the trainees, and shortly aferward these nine were laid off. A few Indians were hired later. (In late 1969, twenty Indians were employed.) Business councilmen have harbored considerable bitterness over the alleged discrimination and the company's failure to live up to the agreement that the council felt had been made.

The per capita payments are vital to family subsistence, particularly since the rates of unemployment and underployment are high. The Arapahoe Business Council assumes the responsibility of alleviating its constitutents' anxiety about these payments. The amounts fluctuate, and the number of enrolled Arapahoes is increasing. For example, the payment declined from $49 in 1965 to $40 in 1969. The recent rise in the price of oil enabled the tribes to raise more revenue from the renegotiation of mineral leases, but the future rate of production is uncertain.

As an increase in enrollment can produce a decline in the size of the per capita payment, the council carefully checks each enrollment application. In contrast to the situation among many other tribes, such as the Eastern Shoshones and the Northern Cheyennes,[10] decisions about enrollment are not "political." Despite occasional pressure, especially from families with Arapahoe children whose parents did not marry, the Arapahoe councilmen do not deviate from the criteria set in 1956. Cases in dispute always are referred to the tribe's attorney; his decision is accepted by the councilmen.

The concern over keeping the enrollment down was magnified by a suit brought by an Arapahoe woman in an attempt to force the tribe to enroll her children, fathered by a non-Arapahoe.[11] In fighting the suit, councilmen were seen by their constituents as protectors not only of the tribe's solvency but also of the Arapahoes' "sovereign government."[12] An Arapahoe wrote in response to a letter to the editor of the *Riverton Ranger*, "You say the BIA has the last word concerning all our tribal laws; you're right to a certain degree, but we still have a few laws of our own that still hold true and one of them is enrollment, and that's what you women are fighting against."[13] And one man explained the tribe's position in this way: "The suit would do away with tribal law." To the council's relief, the case was dismissed in 1971.

It is also the Arapahoe Business Council's responsibility to ensure that the tribe's income is expended in ways acceptable to its constitutents, that is, in culturally prescribed ways. Allocation takes the form of institutionalized sharing. The process of redistribution serves as a leveling device. This strategy is evident in employment policies, the budgeting of tribal funds for grants and loans, and policies of land management.

High unemployment is a central concern of the council. The per capita payment does not cover living expenses, and unenrolled family members are not entitled to such benefits as tribal loans and grants, tribal scholarships, most reservation jobs, and the right to hunt on the reservation and to fish without a license. A March, 1975, BIA report indicated that of an available labor force of 1,125, 375 men and 210 women were employed, and 292 men and 248 women unemployed. These figures represented a 48 percent unemployment rate, about the same rate of unemployment reported for the same month in 1968.[14]

A recent survey reported that 43 percent of the total jobs held on the reservation in 1974 were in agriculture, 31 percent in government and services (food preparation, aide work, protective service, janitorial work), and 7.7 percent in minerals and mining.[15] Most of the jobs held by Indians are tribally funded (roughly three-fourths), followed by BIA and U.S. Indian Health Service positions. A high job turnover and high incidence of absenteeism are routinely tolerated in the reservation-based jobs. Indians are rarely hired off the reservation except as seasonal agricultural workers. Fremont County is heavily industrialized, with a large percentage of jobs in iron and uranium mines and oil and gas fields; these positions are held primarily by whites. Locally, Indians are hired in the most menial jobs, largely because of discrimination, the disinclination of many Indians to work at the same job for long periods of time without absenteeism,[16] and the reluctance or inability of Indians to commute forty to sixty miles daily to jobs off the reservation.

Educational levels among the Arapahoes lag behind those of Wyoming residents; for Wind River Indians in 1970, the United States Census indicates a medium of 10.3 years of schooling.

Recent federal and tribal incentives, however, have spurred higher educational attainments. In 1968 twelve Shoshones and three Arapahoes had B.A. or M.A. degrees; by 1970 the comparable figures were thirty-eight Shoshones and eighteen Arapahoes.[17] Employment opportunities for most Arapahoes—even those with degrees—are still better on the reservation than off, and employment is most likely in tribal or federal positions. Yet the reservation jobs generally offer low pay, and many are only part-time.

The joint business councilmen budget a sizable portion of the tribes' income for salaries. In addition, they expend great efforts to obtain federal grants and, more recently, state funds with which to hire Shoshones and Arapahoes. Since 1971 the council has pressed successfully for funds from the state office of the Department of Public Assistance and Social Service. Indians were hired to staff the foodstamp program (which replaced commodity distribution in 1974), the meals program for the elderly, Aid to Families with Dependent Children, and the program to insulate the homes of the elderly. The hiring of staff is generally done by the councilmen, all twelve of whom act as an employment committee, and the people they recommend for Indian Health Service or BIA jobs are often hired. Since 1975 the council has used federal grant money (Comprehensive Employment and Training Act funds) to give temporary employment to more than three hundred Indians.[18]

In selecting employees, the Arapahoe Business Council places priority on the financial need of the applicants and on frequency of prior employment—the needy and those who have had little employment are often hired before the less needy, and in fact before the more qualified or experienced. Reputation for participation in the sharing network is also a factor in hiring. People who can be counted on to be generous in helping others in the tribe are considered to be entitled to a job or some other form of aid; people who do not share with other Arapahoes can expect little tribal aid. The councilmen work toward maximum hiring rather than a minimum wage level. For example, in 1974, when the BIA employed fifty-one Indians and paid them $462,800 in wages, approximately the same amount ($476,440) was expended by the Business Council for salaries for five times as many people. A person is usually not penalized for leaving a job; job turnover permits a wider distribution of the funds available for employment. One of the council's main objectives is to allocate jobs impartially; that is, when hiring

is done, jobs are allocated among as many families as possible. If
several brothers apply for jobs in a work crew, only one is selected.
And by custom councilmen abstain from the selection process if a
close relative is an applicant.

Thus the council's aim is to distribute tribal income in some form
or other to as many Arapahoes as possible. Both in employment
policy and in the allocation of grants to clubs, ceremonial groups,
and individuals, councilmen give concrete expression to the Arapahoe view that resources are to be shared throughout the tribal
community and the economic differentials are destructive to the
tribe in both a social and a spiritual sense.

The first of each month Arapahoe families wait in line at the post
office to receive their per capita checks. The entire amount is
usually spent within the week, and families (particularly those with
no employed members) may then resort to pawning property or
asking merchants for credit. But for the most part, Arapahoes count
on a system of institutionalized sharing and petition the councilmen for tribal aid. People with money or food are expected to share
with relatives or friends upon request. Thus the meals program for
the elderly functions to distribute food throughout the community
almost daily,[19] and those with jobs help those without. The sharing
process is institutionalized in the "donation dance": families who
need money to meet an emergency (usually for travel expenses for
a serviceman or a visitor from another tribe) spread a blanket in the
center of the dance hall or camp circle, and other members of the
tribe place contributions on it. In a discussion of contemporary
Arapahoe patterns of exchange, Sara Hunter notes pervasive net-
works of reciprocity reinforced by a high value placed on generos-
ity. "One informant said his grandmother always told him to share
whatever he had: 'If someone comes to your door and wants to
borrow flour, even if you only have a little, share with him. . . .'
Another informant said her grandmother always told her: "Don't
be afraid to give. Even your most prized possession. Something
will always come back to you.' "[20]

The Arapahoe council budgets funds both directly, to aid needy
individuals, and indirectly, to aid other leadership groups to make
distributions. Money is allocated to sodalities to help them to
finance communal feasts and celebrations. This practice in turn
buttresses the leadership status of the sodalities. Tribal celebrations are held at least once a month, at which time money, proper-

ty, and food are given away. (Recipients who are particularly hardpressed may inconspicuously sell or hock property received on these occasions). Each of the clubs—often with aid from the council, occasionally with the help of local non-Indian merchants or with funds they raise themselves from contributions or from such moneymaking ventures as selling soda and coffee at tribal events—is responsible for sponsoring one or more celebrations on such holidays as Christmas, Veterans' Day, and Memorial Day. At a Flag Day celebration recently sponsored by one of the women's auxiliaries, the women purchased and cooked one whole cow; they made potato salad of 100 pounds of potatoes and fourteen dozen eggs; they distributed 150 loaves of bread, several pounds of fried bread, twelve dozen sweet rolls, a large quantity of canned tomatoes, and several gallons of soup, coffee, and fruit punch. A family that attends such a function may accumulate enough groceries to last a day or two.

Individuals may apply to the council for grants for all sorts of personal needs, including groceries, unpaid bills, travel money, health care, school clothing, and funeral expenses. The grants to individuals and families are made by the Welfare Committee, composed of all six councilmen. Families, like clubs, are obligated to make generous periodic distributions to other Arapahoes. Every family sponsors a large giveaway and a feast for the tribe as part of the mortuary ritual for a deceased relative, and holds another giveaway several months after the death as a memorial. Clubs and individuals assist with expenses, but even families with more than average means may go heavily in debt to fulfill the obligation. Families also hold giveaways for relatives who return from military service or who have been honored in some way.

The funds available for the council's loan program are limited, and not every loan request can be met, but the council-appointed members of the Arapahoe Credit Committee attempt to distribute the available money as widely as possible. In General Council meetings, this guideline is periodically reinforced by members of the tribe. At a meeting on September 28, 1968, an Arapahoe expressed dissatisfaction with the committee's failure to approve a loan to every applicant: "The reason why I brought it up was that it appears to me there's a lot of us here that's being deprived of a loan because you're a drunk, you're a gambler, or you have opposed the superintendent or you have opposed the council. It's not right. I think a man, I mean he's going to go out here to, well, supposing if I was a drunk, but I went out here to say, "Well, I think I'm going to go out and get me a loan for cows or a house," well, I believe they should give this guy a loan."[21] When applications for loans are being considered, the spending patterns of applicants or the likelihood of their making repayment are not weighed as heavily as need and reputation.

An additional thrust of council activity is the preservation of the tribe's land base and the allocation of land to members of the tribe so that the majority benefit, rather than the few. It is the policy of the joint council to buy land from individuals who wish to sell their allotments or their portion of land that they have inherited, and thus to prevent the sale of reservation lands to non-Arapahoes or non-Shoshones. Land purchases are made with the funds at the tribes' disposal in the U.S. Treasury, and more recently with additional funds obtained through federal loan programs. When individually owned trust land is put up for sale, the council has the right to match the highest bid and to acquire the property. In fact, the vast majority of reservation land now is owned not individually but in trust by the tribes. The joint council makes assignments of this land for homesites, so that individuals without allotments are not homeless.

In 1976 the Wind River Reservation contained 2,268,000 acres, with 1,778,096 acres (a little over 78 percent) jointly owned in trust status by the Arapahoe and Shoshone tribes. This acreage represents an increase of 4,753 acres since 1968. In 1976 individual Arapahoes and Shoshones owned 106,982 acres in trust status. Non-Indians and a few patent-in-fee Indian owners had 381,626 acres (about 6,582 acres were owned by Indians). Non-Indians own most of the land in the Riverton reclamation area. And 1,296 acres were reserved by the BIA for the agency site at Fort Washakie. The aim of the council is to buy back as much of the fee-patent and non-Indian-owned land as possible. Moreover, the council gives enrolled Indians preference in leasing tribal land for grazing, farming, or business, and non-Indians who obtain leases pay a higher fee. In 1975, 1,752,852 acres were assigned by the joint council to Indians and 18,173 acres to whites. Only a few Arapahoes have grazing leases, and the amount assigned to individuals is adequate for only very small herds. In 1967, for example, 22 Arapahoes owned 1,782 head of cattle (the median number owned was 42), while 10,356 head were owned by 89 Shoshones. A large portion of the range is assigned to the Arapahoe Ranch, where the stock is tribally owned and the profits are divided equally among all Arapahoes.[22]

In all respects, then, the Arapahoe Business Council attempts with the means at its disposal to maximize the tribe's resources, and so far as possible to allocate those resources in roughly equal shares, with priority placed on aiding the most needy. The results are a general leveling process, on the one hand, and the potential for councilmen to wield considerable economic power, on the other.

## Indian-White Relations

The council member's role as an intermediary between the tribe and the white society is colored by the tribe's economic deprivation relative to neighboring whites, periodic threats to cultural and what remains of political autonomy, and challenges to tribal pride. Whites are viewed as adversaries, and the present-day anxieties about the whites' intentions and the expectation that intermediaries must be capable of effective advocacy are reinforced by the elders who describe Arapahoe leaders of the past as men who struggled to prevent, offset, or resist the harm that whites sought to do. One frequently told story about Sharp Nose provides a kind of charter for the councilmen's dealings with whites. When Sharp Nose knew he was dying, he sent for a friend and left with him his last message to the Arapahoes. This is one elderly Arapahoe's version of the story:

"Now you carry what I tell you." He told that to Sitting Eagle, his friend. They're about the same age. "I'm going to tell you about white people. . . . I picked this place to be my reservation. So they bring us up here, but the white people going to watch us; agent, to protect us and learn us what they're doing now. But I tell you, people—tell them—the white people sometimes they get tricky," he said. "They might cheat you out of something and they might cheat you. But always watch out for that tricky stuff. I heard about white people cheating themselves and they going cheat Indians too." And that's happening now. Been happening right along. That's what he told him. And in a couple days, he died.[23]

Today councilmen "watch out" for their constituents against the "tricky" whites in an aggressive and sometimes combative manner, in sharp contrast to the cooperative and counciliatory strategy of earlier times. The income from royalties and bonuses provides the council with the means to intervene effectively on behalf of the tribe. Councilmen vigorously seek to recoup past losses, to strengthen the degree of political independence they have managed to attain, and to augment the benefits that accrue to a federally recognized tribe living on a reservation.

### Reservation Status: The Implications of Legal Separatism

The federal government is charged with preventing the alienation of Indian lands held in trust, with protecting tribal resources, and with providing certain services in the area of land management, health, education, and welfare. Federal agents periodically encourage the tribe's representatives to assume more responsibility, particularly financial responsibility, in providing services. The council pressures the federal government to exercise its reponsibilities more competently and to assume more of the costs of managing the reservation (while at the same time relinquishing authority to the tribe in some areas). Much of the substance of contemporary reservation politics revolves around these maneuverings.

BIA services are looked upon as "treaty obligations," not as gratuities.[24] Councilmen are expected to press the government to fulfill its obligations to the tribe. As one Arapahoe explained to me, "Indians feel they are owed."

Arapahoes often expect unequivocal aid from BIA employees. For example, tribe members occasionally solicit help from the BIA's Road Department to gravel the roads leading from their homes to the highway. The department's policy is to furnish the gravel, equipment, and technical aid, but not the labor. The Arapahoes consider the BIA's refusal to complete the graveling process as typical of the government's failure to meet its obligations to Indians.

The council tries to make sure that the BIA and other federal agencies assume as many as possible of the expenses incurred by the tribe. For example, in response to repeated Indian complaints about health care, in 1969 Public Health Service officials tried to persuade the council members to share the responsibility of planning the health program on the reservation and of explaining the policies and the program to their constituents. The council rejected the proposal. The federal government was bound "by treaty" to assume the full burden for health care, the councilmen contended, and sharing of responsibility would weaken this historic obligation. One Business Council member noted that the council's best strategy was periodically to petition Public Health for additional benefits, and a joint planning program would appreciably weaken its role as petitioner.

New programs often are perceived as long-due "treaty" benefits. In recent years, as part of a general policy to grant Indians more self-determination, the federal government has contracted with tribes for the operation of schools. In 1972 a contract high school was established at Ethete, despite opposition from the Riverton and Lander public school officials, who were wary of losing Indian students and with them the federal funds designated for their education. One elderly Arapahoe man viewed the Wyoming Indian High School as part of the payment due the tribe for land cessions: "The government made a deal with Sharp Nose and Washakie, they's going to be Indian schools built so they could learn talk English and numbers, read and write. . . . And they donate all around pasture, farming land. . . . The treaty was all Indian schools appropriated by the government. Up through first grade, to high school, to college schools. They'd be furnished, appropriated by the government. That's the treaty. . . . Now they [Riverton and Lander] kicking us about that high school. I know they couldn't very well do it. That's Indian money and the treaty says they're going to go through education for all Indians." In the minds of many Arapahoes, the people involved in the effort to acquire the school were pressuring the federal government to honor "the treaties."[25]

Many Arapahoes also viewed the per capita payments as income due them because of their status as Indians. Until recently the per capita checks were issued by the BIA with the consent of the councilmen, who did not wish to bear the administrative expense. The Arapahoes refer to the per capita payment as *chéé'eyóóno*, "what they hand out to you" or "what they issue you." This is the same term that was used to refer to the annuity payments prescribed by treaty in former times. The BIA superintendent is referred to as *cheé'eyeéhinen*, "he who gives [it] out." Councilmen are credited with achieving the distribution of per capita money by "standing up to the government." They mediate between the people and the

202 The Plains Indians of the Twentieth Century

government, and when they are successful, "issue" in various forms is the result.

The Arapahoes conceive of federal benefits and services as "payments" to which they are morally and legally entitled. In contrast, proposals for aid to be extended by private groups or individuals usually are rejected. The councilmen and their constitutents resent "do-gooders."

In expressing the conviction that the Arapahoe people need leaders who are able to resist intimidation and behave aggressively toward non-Indians, one Arapahoe man put it this way: "The people *themselves* won't rock the boat; they'll sit back and take their licks." The controls still exerted by the superintendent and his staff are viewed as irksome and heavy-handed interference. Councilmen are expected to offset BIA interference in their constitutents' personal lives., In one man's words, "We need somebody to get out and go in the white world and not back down."

Under certain circumstances the superintendent of the BIA office at Wind River can withhold funds from the individual Indian money accounts, in which individuals's income from the sale and lease of trust land is deposited. Funds can be withheld for debts to the United States or the tribes, and on the recommendation of the BIA Social Service Department in the case of minors, the elderly, or the mentally handicapped. The superintendent can require an individual to submit a family budget acceptable to BIA staff members before funds from the individual account are released. Moreover, the BIA can institute unpopular conservation measures or limit the number of livestock that can be grazed on reservation lands. The BIA also selects individuals for many job-training programs and administers federal scholarships—activities that frequently raise accusations of unfair treatment.

It is in this context, then, that Arapahoe councilmen personally intercede with the BIA staff on behalf of individual Arapahoes. A "councilman," the Arapahoes say, is "one you can come to with a problem." Councilmen "speak up" for their constituents, and by the grant and loan programs they administer, as well as their watchfulness in relation to per capita payments, they compensate for the uncertainty about access to the money in individual accounts.

The councilmen are generally successful today in offsetting actions of the Fort Washakie BIA which affect the tribe as a whole.

The business councils' procedure is to notify the tribes' attorneys in Washington, D.C., when there is a conflict. These legal representatives then petition BIA officials in the office of the commissioner of Indian affairs or the secretary of the interior. Almost without exception in recent years, controversial regional and local BIA decisions have been reversed. The fact that the Wind River tribes did not organize under the Indian Reorganization Act has resulted in increased flexibility. Because their actions are not limited by by-laws, the attorneys have more room to maneuver to offset policies that the Business Council opposes.[26]

The Council's success in dealing with BIA representatives is also due in part to the fact that the Arapahoe councilmen almost invariably act unanimously. They decide among themselves on a course of action, and, having reached a consensus, approach the BIA staff—or, when necessary, the attorneys—from a position of unity. In matters of interest to the joint council, the Shoshone and Arapahoe business councils often present a solid front, as well—at least in matters defined as "Indian versus white."

Councilmen also work to defend tribal sovereignty in relation to state, Fremont County, and municipal interests. Although most adult Arapahoes avoid face-to-face conflict with neighboring whites, there are periodic court battles over legal jurisdiction. The trust status of reservation lands—exempt from local property taxes—is irksome to many local whites, and they eye reservation resources with interest and hope to profit from the needs of Indians as consumers. Whites view the federal protection of Indian lands as unfair, and particularly resent the fact that Indians do not "use" or "develop" the land. One Lander resident whose family settled in that area in the mid-nineteenth century expressed his frustration thus: "They [nomadic Indians] were in [this part of] Wyoming two or three weeks out of the year, and the most three months out of the year. Whereas my family at that time was here the whole year round. When they talk about indigenous and things like that, it's ridiculous."

Local and state interests frequently conflict with tribal interests. The council has been successful in holding local whites at bay by means of the legal assistance furnished by its attorneys; in former times, when the federal government was the tribe's only recourse, they were less successful. One recent conflict involved the joint council's suit to overrule the country's issue of a liquor license to a prominent white businessman who wanted to operate a bar on the reservation. The businessman's repeated disregard of council instructions about health problems angered the councilmen, and in 1974 they took the issue to court to establish their jurisdiction on the reservation. The attorneys argued successfully that the county could not grant a license to a business in the reservation community, even though it was on nontrust land. In a similar case not yet settled, the Shoshone and Arapahoe tribes claim jurisdiction in a right-to-access dispute involving a business that was established on fee-patent land but which claims access from the public highway through land held in trust.[27] A currrent concern is the issue of water rights. The tribes are seeking to prevent the state from attaining control over the use and allocation of the water from the rivers that rise in the mountains in the western sector of the reservation.

### *"Don't Tell Them White People about It":* ### *The Implications of Social Separatism*

The conflict over jurisdiction reinforces and is conditioned by the strained relations and misunderstandings between Indians and whites in general. There are white families living on the reservation and in two adjacent towns, but there is little contact on a personal level: few friendships are formed and no joint activities take place. Each group clings to stereotypes and assails the moral worth of the other. Blatant economic exploitation, social discrimination, and prejudice against Indians is countered by Arapahoe leaders—both councilmen and elders—on a number of levels.

Arapahoes have about 434 non-Indian neighbors on their section of the reservation. Some operate small farms and live among the Arapahoes, and some are members of the staffs of the two elementary schools and live in the school compounds. Few whites have married Arapahoes and move onto the reservation. A handful of Indian Public Health Service and white BIA employees reside in the government compound at Fort Washakie. There is virtually no social interaction on a personal level between the adult Arapahoe and white residents of Wind River. Both Indians and whites pick up mail at the post offices and attend the mission churches, but they usually do not visit each other's homes or attend weddings or funerals together. From time to time friendships are formed with transient whites—in recent years a few Public Health physicians and their families and occasionally a teacher. These ties are looked at askance by the other whites. Many of the white children attend the elementary schools at Ethete and Arapahoe, and in recent years there has been occasional conflict between white and Indian children.

Riverton, with a population of about 10,000, is actually within the reservation boundary, but the 100 or so Arapahoes who live there consider themselves "off the reservation." Most of these families intend only temporary residence in Riverton and frequently move back to Ethete or Arapahoe. Lander has a population of about 8,000 including about 40 Arapahoes. A few Arapahoe and Shoshone young people commute to attend high school, and reservation residents do their shopping in these towns, but Indians do not attend the churches there or join their social clubs. Indian patients are admitted to hospitals in the two towns, with Public Health assuming the cost, although Indians and Public Health officials have complained of discrimination. Indians and whites rarely visit with each other on the street or in the stores. Despite physical proximity, the two groups keep to themselves.

Local whites assail the moral worth of Indians in innumerable ways, thereby justifying their differential treatment of Indians and whites.[28] Indians are categorized as financially irresponsible. Local whites call the per capita payment a "dole," implying that it is unearned and therefore immoral. Although townspeople are repeatedly informed that the payments come from proceeds of the tribes' own resources, comparable to the stock dividends received by many non-Indians, they continue to cite the Indians' acceptance of the payments as evidence of their lack of moral fiber. Indian values and attitudes in regard to work differ from those of whites. Employment is valued, but reporting for work does not take precedence over family or ceremonial commitments. When sharing is a moral imperative, saving is not possible, and therefore when families come to town with money, they have little incentive to refrain from spending it. To whites, these aspects of Indian behavior are clear evidence that Indians are lazy and improvident. Some local businessmen do not hesitate to overcharge an Indian when they know he has just received his per capita payment or a tribal grant or loan. And some merchants encourage Indians to buy on lay-away or pawn property, knowing that the debt may not be paid and thus the initial payment or property may be forfeited.

While such practices may be regarded as immoral in transactions with whites, Indians are fair game.

As the yards around Indian homes usually lack landscaping and are used as storage areas, the homes themselves are described by whites as "dirty." In the view of whites, Indian families are "disorganized" and parents do not "discipline" their children. Actually, child care is shared by many relatives, with young cousins ("brothers" and "sisters," as they are called and thought of by Arapahoes) frequently rotating their residence from one household to another. Adults usually employ indirect methods of correction and often delegate older children to look after younger ones.

Drinking behavior is another area of conflict. Indians sometimes drink to excess in town and are unable for one reason or another to return the twenty or so miles to the reservation. They are labeled "drunks." Whites who drink to excess usually are quietly escorted by the police to their homes in town.

Compounding these difficulties are the disputes over jurisdiction. The special status of Indian lands and the relationship between the tribe and the federal government are sources of resentment to the whites. Many whites view the Indian status as "anti-American" and feel that Indians should be treated the same as other citizens. Note this comment by one local white: "This idea of saying that because we happen to have a whole band of them who are associated in tribal ancestry, they're different, I just don't buy that. I don't agree with it. . . . There is no more Indian heritage that I can think of to doing anything that they refer to as Indian heritage than there is to cowboy heritage for me to do such things. I don't plan to live in a sheep camp but a large number of my forebears did all their lives." Discriminatory treatment of Indians by whites is justified by whites' categorization of Indians as "different"; yet whites also resent Indians for their special status vis-à-vis the rest of the population.

The Arapahoes are aware of the negative white sterotypes and the resentments. They, in turn, harbor a series of stereotypes about whites. Whites are viewed as "materialistic." They are seen as lacking strong feelings for kin. Whites' emphasis on nuclear-family relationships and on sharing with the immediate family and with lineal sets of relations more often than with collateral kin is viewed as "stinginess." Self-sufficiency and economic independence is seen not in positive terms, but as another indication that a white person "only thinks of himself." Whites are regarded as "pushy" and "mouthy." A person who is outgoing and affable even with strangers is well thought of among whites, but Arapahoes, who view modesty and reticence as central to social harmony, view such a person with suspicion. Thus the moral worth of whites is challenged, and although Indians are not in a position to discriminate in off-reservation contacts, breaches of social norms in relation to whites are more often excused than similar transgressions against other Arapahoes.

Arapahoes also view their own way of life as morally superior to that of whites because of the special tie between the Arapahoes and the Great Mystery. The relationship between the supernatural and whites is more distant. Elders particularly reinforce these sentiments. Note, for example, this account by an elder, who stresses that although whites are disrespectful of Indian religion, they are confounded and worried by it just the same:

That museum over there, there's a lot of stuff in there. I don't know where they got it. But there's some stuff they shouldn't bother. There's a beaver hide and some medicine in there, and this white fellow took it out and had it on display. My grandson told him, "You better put that back in there. It don't belong on that table here." So he put it back in there and they wrapped it up again. . . . In the evening when they turn the lights off in that museum, I think about eight o'clock or nine o'clock, they turn the lights off. Later on, there's light in there again, in the whole building. They said, "They often wonder what causes that." And I told them, I says, "Those people that had those things [the "medicine"] are the ones that turned the lights on again," I told them. "But you don't have to tell them white people about it; they'll find out themselves," I told them.[29]

Elders, in their interpretation of Arapahoe-white relations, perpetuate the values of the Arapahoe way of life and reinforce Arapahoe cultural identity through their stories. One old man told this story to young Arapahoes:

You hear the old people say *nootinei, nootinei*. He married his own daughter. He told his family, "You roll me up and hang me up in a tree." He says, "There's a man coming. His name is *koo'ookunnootinei*, One-Eyed Sioux. And you want to give him our daughter so they'll get married and then he can make a living for you." So he played like he was dead. So they wrapped him up and hanged him on a tree. Then later on he unraveled himself, kept following this camp. They moved one place then another place. Later on, he'd come to the camp and he was trying to talk Sioux, but he couldn't talk very good. But this old lady, his wife, said, "Oh my, when this Sioux is going to come, why he told me to marry my daughter off to him so he could make a living for us.'' So he married this girl that was his own daughter. And then one morning I guess he slept late. But, he put mud on his eye, so he just had one eye. And this girl said, ''Mama, he looks like my dad.'' ''No, your dad died long ago. That ain't him.'' ''No, I think it's him.'' So they went over and looked at him. And it was him! So his wife took a club and started clubbing him. That's where that story comes from. Maybe that's the reason why these white men, you know, marry Indian women. How they put mud in their eye, you know. That's what they say, you know. They tease people that way— ''*koo'ookunnootinei.*'' That's One-Eyed Sioux.[30]

The implication of the story is, first, the whites, like the trickster figure who marries his own daughter in this old Pan Plains story, are exploitive (that is, they marry Indian women in order to profit from economic benefits these women receive from the tribe). And, second, whites, like the trickster, are both powerful and foolish: they violate the moral laws of well-ordered society, and thus, while they may succeed in their deceptions for a time, ultimately their transgressions are exposed.

The councilmen's efforts to bolster pride in Arapahoe cultural identity are evident in several ways. They try to insulate the tribe's members as much as possible from economic exploitation and social embarrassments. A liberal policy regarding grants and loans helps to minimize the need for Arapahoes to seek financial aid from local whites (although such help is sometimes sought). When an Arapahoe mother offers a child for adoption or when a home situation so far deteriorates that Arapahoe leaders acknowledge that the children should be removed, councilmen make sure that whites do not obtain the children. They are placed with Indian families. In the few cases of Indian-white marriage, the council may place limitations on the white parents' access to their children's per capita payments. In cases of divorce, the childern's payments may be placed in a trust account until the children reach adulthood. The council enthusiastically supports and grants funds to clubs that sponsor tribal celebrations; reservation-oriented recreation is considered preferable to exposure to stressful town situations (although Indian families do enjoy trips to town to shop and to patronize drive-in fast-food establishments). Councilmen try to prevent ''insults'' to Indian people, as such incidents reflect adversely on their abilities as protectors.

When councilmen personally represent the tribe in interaction with local whites, they are expected to conduct themselves with skill and dignity. the two local newspapers, the *Riverton Ranger* and the *Wyoming State Journal* (published in Lander), carry the names of the day's arrests in each town. Indian families read these papers regularly and show keen interest in the columns that give the names of people arrested and the charges brought against them. A councilman's arrest for public intoxication or any other legal offense in one of the towns is a most serious breach of trust. Such a thing rarely happens. If councilmen drink socially, they are careful not to do so off the reservation. In fact, councilmen rarely appear at official town functions. Avoidance lessens the chance of a social slight. Councilmen are also charged with controlling the behavior of whites on the reservation. They harass employees who annoy Indians, and they work to prevent the hiring of whites who do not interact graciously with Indians.

In short, local whites' discriminatory behavior and prejudice toward Indians figure in the Indians' expectations in regard to the role of councilman. Today councilmen are more aggressive and less tolerant of slights than they were in past eras.

### Shoshone Neighbors

Despite 100 years of proximity, the Shoshones and the Arapahoes are still socially and culturally distinct. The members of the two tribes have not learned each other's language. There has been no significant diffusion and almost no intermarriage: in 1968, sixty-three Arapahoes were married to Shoshones.[31] While Arapahoes and Shoshones sometimes attend peyote meetings together, strong ties between families are apparently not formed. Forced by circumstances to share limited reservation resources, they have periodic conflicts and harbor resentment and suspicion toward each other.

Shoshone households—nuclear or extended families—are scattered along the tributaries of the Wind and Little Wind. Shoshone homes are much farther apart than those of the Arapahoes. The dispersed settlement pattern accompanies a loose, flexible social organization. In contrast to the Arapahoes, the Shoshones have no cross-cutting institutions (such as sodalities) that mediate kinship divisions, nor do they hold frequent tribal gatherings or tribal giveaways.[32] Reciprocity is found more often within the family. The Shoshone Sun Dance ritual is much more individualistic than the Arapahoe ceremony.[33] And political factionalism corresponds in large part to the resident areas of Trout Creek, South Fork (of the Littlle Wind), North Fork (of the Little Wind), Sage Creek, Morton, Crowheart, and Burris. Often political activity centers on disadvantaging a rival faction. Thus Shoshone sociopolitical organization stands in sharp contrast to the Arapahoe pattern of censensus and consolidation.

Many Shoshones today, as in past generations, marry whites. The tribal census indicates that over three-fourths of the Shoshones have some white ancestry. And many enrolled Shoshones have less than "one-fourth degree" of Shoshone "blood." Shoshones classify themselves as either "full-blood" or "mixed-blood"; these are largely social, not biological, categories. The groups have different life-styles, political strategies, and economic orientations.[34]

In contrast, Arapahoes intermarry very little (in 1968 about seventy Arapahoes were married to whites—few of whom were local residents—and most of these Arapahoes were living off the reservation); about 48 percent are enrolled as full-blood; and while several hundred Arapahoes have some white ancestry, few are classified as mixed-bloods. The Arapahoes, unlike the Shoshones, have not tried to adapt to economic, social, and political discrimination by extensively participating in white institutions or by intermarriage with local whites. And individual or family ranching is much more common among Shoshone families—who are not morally obliged to participate in intratribal sharing—than among  Arapahoes, for whom wage work is more practical in view of the leveling mechanisms operating in the tribe's economics.

Given the nature of the relationships between these two tribes, each perceives the other as a potential threat to its own political and economic well-being. Shoshones still on occasion refer to Arapahoes as "trespassers," and periodically talk of trying to put them off the reservation. Continued resentment toward Arapahoes is abetted by the Shoshones' awareness of the growing numerical strength of the enrolled Arapahoes. At the time of settlement, the Shoshones outnumbered the Arapahoes, but today there are three Arapahoes for every two Shoshones, even though Shoshone criteria for enrollment are less stringent.[35] Shoshone women can enroll their children in the tribe even if the father is not Shoshone. Moreover, approval of applicants is sometimes based on political considerations, rather than conformity to the established criteria. The Shoshones also view the increase in political and economic strength of the Arapahoes as a challenge to their continued well-being.

Similarly, the Arapahoes' anxiety about their own economic predicament is intensified by the Shoshone presence. Despite their smaller population, the Shoshones share equally in all reservation resources including BIA and tribal jobs. Thus the Shoshones per capita payment is $135, considerably higher than the $90 paid to Arapahoes. The Arapahoes sometimes are denied work when the Arapahoe job quota (by a "gentlemen's agreement" among joint council members) is filled, even though there may not be enough Shoshone applicants to fill the available jobs. Range assignments are an additional source of conflict. Shoshones who wish to expand their cattle operations are thwarted by the large acreage assigned to the Arapahoe Ranch.

In joint council proceedings, Arapahoe councilmen generally vote as a block. The Shoshones are aware of this tendency and often are anxious about the potential damage to their interests. If the Shoshone vote splits along factional lines, as it often does, the Arapahoe councilmen can dominate the procedings. Moreover, since the time of Nell Scott's service on the council, the Arapahoes have increasingly tended to assume an assertive stance in relation to whites, no longer allowing Shoshone "mixed-bloods" the principal spokesman role. These considerations increase the insecurity that the Shoshones feel in regard to sharing Wind River with the Arapahoes. Yet the Arapahoes frequently forbear to take advantage of Shoshone factionalism; they sometimes compromise in order to maintain long-range cooperative relations, so that in conflicts with whites the two tribes' resentment of each other does not work against their joint interests. In this spirit, by custom the chairmen of the councils alternate the job of presiding over joint council meetings.[36]

## POLITICAL STRATEGIES

In manipulating the symbols surrounding the "protector" and the "provider" aspects of council leadership, councilmen minimize dissent and generate support for policies and programs. As advocates for the tribe vis-à-vis the federal government, they seek to

212 of the Twentieth Century

demonstrate their vigilance in furthering tribal interests. For example, in 1969 the Arapahoe Business Council refused to allow the BIA Law and Order Department to use the tribe's motor vehicles. If BIA personnel were to drive the cars owned by the tribe, constituents would have felt that the council was sharing responsibilities that at that time belonged to the federal government. Moreover, individual councilmen sometimes make a point of ridiculing or berating the agency superintendent in public places where their Arapahoe constitutents can watch. A few minutes later, the two may be amicably talking about agency business in an office out of public view.[37]

In 1968 problems between local whites and Indians caught the attention of the governor of Wyoming, and he established the Governor's Advisory Council, a committee of reservation people to act as liaison between the tribes and his office. From names submitted by the superintendent at the request of the council, three Arapahoes and three Shoshones were chosen by the joint council to serve on the committee. Several BIA employees urged that the people selected should be, in one official's words, "educated people who could talk, rather than accepted Indians in the community. . . . Indians can't express themselves." The superintendent suggested two councilmen and one former councilman as the Arapahoe members of the committee. Actually, the Arapahoes were extremely reluctant to serve, and two of the three resigned shortly after their appointment because of "conflict of interest." One of the replacements was considered to be loyal to Arapahoe interests and concerns; the other was a "mixed-blood" who had little contact with or understanding of the tribal community.

For the most part, the committee worked to attain state welfare benefits for Indians without jeopardizing the trust status of Indian lands. By 1969 the Arapahoe Business Council was wary of the group. The councilmen objected to the Advisory Council's efforts to deal independently with state officials and to seek benefits for Arapahoes. They also feared that involvement with the state might weaken the tribe's claims on federal aid. Success on the part of the advisers would undercut the position of the councilmen as intermediaries. Councilmen began to remark to their constituents that there was no "full-bloods" on the committee, that the members were not "doing any good," and that "they might want to take on too much." In other words, they could not be trusted and they would abuse their authority. At a meeting on April 16, 1969, one Advisory Council member pessimistically said, "I question what the council would give us the authority to talk about. . . . Too many times the Business Council can slant things and get a scapegoat." Soon after that, Arapahoe participation on the committee declined.

During a Shoshone General Council meeting in 1968, A Shoshone game warden made several derogatory remarks about Arapahoes, and word of the episode soon circulated through the Arapahoe community. At that time there were two other game wardens, both Arapahoes. Subsequently, in a joint business meeting, the Arapahoe council retaliated by proposing that the man's job be abolished—officially for disobedience to the council order, actually for insulting the Arapahoes. Five Arapahoes (one other was acting as chairman) and two Shoshones, who were members of a faction hostile to the same warden and his relatives, voted to abolish his job. The action put a tremendous strain on intertribal relations. For a time it was rumored that one of the two Arapahoe wardens would be fired in order to even things out. Eventually the council hired a Shoshone as the man's replacement and appointed him supervisor over the two Arapahoes. In this way the Arapahoe councilmen avenged the slight to their constituents' satisfaction, yet repaired their relations with the Shoshones.

Arapahoe councilmen frequently suggest that individuals who oppose their policies and decisions endanger the security of the tribe by inviting interference not only from whites but also from Shoshones. To gain support against their critics, the councilmen call them "radicals" and either suggest that they are dangerous deviants or tell anecdotes that hold the critics up to ridicule.

Councilmen can also circumvent criticism by attributing to Shoshone or non-Indian influence any decision that displeases individual Arapahoes. They are quite adept not only at manipulating federal officials into accepting responsibility but also at using these officials to better relations with their constituents. For example, when the Arapahoe Credit Committee was organized to act on applications for moderate and large loans, the council asked the BIA superintendent to sit on the committee with veto power. When a would-be borrower is considered to be a bad risk, the superintendent's veto can be blamed for the denial of the loan, while the Arapahoe committee members—and the councilmen who appointed them—avoid criticims. The superintendent wields his veto power very sparingly and takes into account the wishes of the committee in selecting those applications to be denied.

Constituents may apply some of the same tactics to influence the behavior of the councilmen. In 1970 several Arapahoe men, leaders in a peer group of men in their late thirties who were eager to gain political influence, began to generate support for a contract high school and pressured the federal government to finance it. The councilmen initially opposed the efforts of these ambitious "youths." But as the elders began to favor the plan and local whites and Shoshones opposed it, the councilmen changed their position. As soon as the proposal generated opposition from parties hostile to the tribe, the council felt obliged to assume a protective stance. The supporters of the school manipulated the opposition, even organizing a "camp-in" at the state capitol and releasing statements to the local press that provoked negative reaction from whites. The councilmen's reputations soon were linked with the success of the proposal to establish the school, and they supported the venture.

Councilmen also attempted to demonstrate their efficacy as providers by personally delivering council services so that they as individuals are associated in their constituents' minds with specific benefits. Old people who are granted a sum of money by the council may be presented with the authorization in person by one of the councilmen. Councilmen also may drive individuals to the agency and help them to deal with their difficulties with the superintendent.

Because the council carefully guards its prerogative to provide for its constituents' welfare, the councilmen were wary of the community health representatives or CHRs—three members of each tribe who, beginning in 1969, served as liaison between the Indian community and their employer, the Indian Health Service. When the CHRs solicited toys from local merchants to be used as prizes in a children's toothbrushing contest, the Arapahoe councilmen told them to stick to their job. The councilmen consider the distribution of goods—toys or anything else—to be their task; they may delegate it, but they do not look kindly on those who assume it unasked. Similarly, when a club established by Arapahoe men in their thirties began to distribute firewood to elders, the council again took effective action to prevent infringement on a service customarily provided by the council.

Constituents are constantly alert for any failure on the part of the council to fulfill its responsibilities. In the spring of 1969 some people criticized the council's agreement to provide a trailer to be staffed by a Public Health physician and used as a first-aid station at tribal gatherings. Critics remarked, "We shouldn't have to furnish the trailer. That's Public Health's job. The council shouldn't have agreed to that." In order to avoid criticism while publicly displaying their accomplishments as providers, Arapahoe councilmen have to walk a very fine line indeed.

Finally, councilmen seek to manipulate the Arapahoes' negative attitudes toward the Shoshones in ways that buttress their pride in their cultural identity as Arapahoes. Since they are in frequent contact with Shoshones at Fort Washakie, they may entertain their constituents with tales of Shoshone ineptitude at the agency or Tribal Office and with reports of comments from outsiders about the richness of Arapahoe tradition in comparison with the Shoshone cultural tradition.

In sum, Arapahoe adaptation to a precarious socioeconomic situation results in a relationship between council and constituency that in some respects is a patron-client relationship. Councilmen are obliged to intercede for and provide for a constituency that in return is obligated to support the council's actions. As one councilman commented, "A tribal employee has no business not backing up the council." Recipients of any form of aid are similarly expected to be loyal. During the last generation, the Business Council has had unquestioned authority in secular matters. Opposition is checked, and factional divisions are circumvented, both by the councilmen's economic levers and by their skill in keeping the Shoshone and white communities sufficiently at bay so as to minimize the anxiety of their constituents.

At the root of the council's legitimacy is the fact that the tribe's elders sanction its authority in the secular realm. Of equal importance are the cultural constraints on abuse of the council's powers. To be recognized and supported as a councilman (or a leader in one of the soldalities), an individual must manage to acquire a reputation that reassures other Arapahoes of his social and moral fitness for the position. An indivdual who aspires to leadership must "make a name for himself."

# Notes

1. Unless otherwise indicated, quotations and facts cited in this chapter are from my field notes taken during 1967–78.

2. Before 1972 the required age for political participation, including the right to vote, was 21.

3. A few Arapahoes living in the Kinnear area, a few miles east of Morton, are considered to be residents of Ethete.

4. These figures, as well as those on the Shoshones and the subsequent estimates on white population, are computed by the Bureau of Indian Affairs (hereafter BIA) and the Tribal Office.

5. See Loretta Fowler, "Arapahoe Migrants" (unpublished manuscript, 1971), pp. 5–8.

6. Data from an unpublished report of Hurlbut, Kershich, and McCullough, consulting engineers ("Inventory of Water Resources: Wind River Indian Reservation, Wyoming"), cited in Veronica Evaneshko, *Exploring Recruitment and Retention of Indian Nursing Students* (Laramie, Wyo.: Commission for Nursing and Nursing Education, 1976), p. 50.

7. Additional income from sources other than joint tribal resources may be credited to one tribe only, as in the case of the 1964 claim award to the Arapahoe tribe. The Business Council budgets must be approved by a delegated representative of the secretary of the interior; his approval is normally routine.

8. Royalties ranging from 12.5 to 30 percent have been obtained in these negotiations.

9. Minutes of Joint Business Council meeting, April 30, 1969, Records of the BIA, Fort Washakie, Wyo. The Arapahoe tribe recently invested money in an industrial park; the tribe has had great difficulty attracting industry to the site.

10. See Ann Sawyier Straus, "Being Human in the Cheyenne Way," (Ph.D. diss., University of Chicago, 1976); Katherine Weist, "The Northern Cheyennes: Diversity in a Loosely Structured Society," (Ph.D. diss., University of California, Berkeley, 1969); Thomas H. Johnson, "The Enos Family and Wind River Shoshone Society; A Historical Analysis," Ph.D. diss., University of Illinois, 1975).

11. *Sarah Jean Chamberlain Slattery* v. *Arapahoe Tribal Council and Secretary of the Interior, Walter J. Hickel, Federal Reporter*, 2d ser., vol. 453, p. 278. In this case, the federal court refused jurisdiction.

12. *Riverton Ranger*, letter to editor, October 14, 1969.

13. *Riverton Ranger*, October 16, 1969.

14. Labor Force Reports, 1968 and 1975, BIA, Fort Washakie. These statistics count only women who are not classified as "housewives" as part of the available work force. The superintendent's Report to the Commissioner for 1964 stated that 25 percent were permanently employed during that year.

15. Evaneshko, *Exploring Recruitment*, p. 5.

16. See Loretta Fowler, "The Arapahoe Ranch: An Experiment in Cultural Change and Economic Development," *Economic Development and Cultural Change* 21, no. 3 (1973): 446–64, 35–36.

17. Bureau of the Census, *Census of Population, 1970*, vol. 2, "Subject Report, American Indian," p. 143; Evaneshko, *Exploring Recruitment*, p. 21.

18. Sara Hunter, "Northern Arapahoe Grandparents: Traditional Concepts and Contemporary Socio-Economics," (Master's thesis, Indiana University, 1977), pp. 47, 55.

19. Ibid., p. 50.

20. Ibid., p. 25.

21. Minutes of Arapahoe General Council meeting, September 28, 1968, Office of the BIA, Fort Washakie.

22. Office of Land Operations, BIA, Fort Washakie. The Riverton reclamation project is administered by the U.S. Bureau of Reclamation. In 1953 the lands in the reclamation project that were not being used were restored to the tribes; in 1958 the mineral rights to the reclamation area were restored.

23. Interview with Orio Amos, May 28, 1975, author's field tapes.

24. See also Hunter,'' Northern Arapahoe Grandparents,'' pp. 44–45.

25. See Loretta Fowler, ''Arapahoe Political Activists: 'Radical' Change within a Conservative System,'' paper read at American Anthropolitical Association meetings, November 20, 1976, Washington, D.C.; interview with Orio Amos, August 13, 1975, author's field tapes.

26. Interview with the tribe's attorney, Glenn Wilkinson.

27. *U.S.* v. *Mazurie et al.*, Supreme Court, *United States Reports*, vol. 419, p. 544; *Dry Creek Lodge, Inc.* v. *United States*, *Federal Reporter*, 2d ser., vol. 515, p. 926, and *Dry Creek Lodge, Inc.* v. *Arapahoe and Shoshone Tribes*, *Federal Reporter*, 2d. ser., vol., 623, p. 682.

28. Niels Winther Braroe, *Indian and White: Self-Image and Interaction in a Canadian Community* (Stanford, Calilf.: Stanford University Press, 1975). Braroe has discussed in detail white definitions of Cree Indians as ''profane'' persons whose ''dignity may be assaulted with impunity'' (p. 35). His study focuses on Cree and white attempts to construct morally defensible self-images in a socially stratified community. Braroe concludes that such an adaptive strategy enables the Cree to cope with their subordinate status and that whites, ''in large part through ignorance, are able to maintain an image of Indians as profane persons'' which ''justified a special treatment of band members that violates the usual norms governing interpersonal behavior'' (p. 183).

29. Interview with Nickerson Shakespeare, August 21, 1975, author's field tapes.

30. Ibid.; see also George A. Dorsey and Alfred L. Kroeber, *Traditions of the Arapahoe*, Field Columbian Museum Publications, No. 75, Anthropological Series, No. 5, Chicago, 1903, pp. 82–86.

31. Since 1968 there have been marriages between Arapahoes and Shoshones, but the exact number I do not know.

32. There is an American Legion post whose members are Shoshones and whites who live on the reservation. There is one powwow to which other tribes are invited. On this occasion the Arapahoe drum groups are invited to perform.

33. The Shoshone dancers are permitted much more autonomy than the Arapahoes; for example, Shoshone dancers paint themselves according to a personal vision rather than according to the direction of ritual leaders, and their dance styles vary. When the religious symbolism of the dance is explained to the Shoshone dancers by the Sun Dance chief, other shamans may offer different interpretations. See Joseph G. Jorgensen, *The Sun Dance Religion: Power for the Powerless* (Chicago: University of Chicago Press, 1972).

34. See Johnson, ''The Enos Family and Wind River Shoshone Society.''

35. Ibid.

36. This description of Shoshone culture and social organization is based on observations and interviews made during my fieldwork between 1967 and 1978; most of my contacts with Shoshones were limited to councilmen. I made no intensive study of Shoshone life.

37. These observations pertain to the years before 1977; in 1977 a Cheyenne replaced the white superintendent at the Wind River Agency.

# CHAPTER 9

# Tribal Leaders and the Demand
# for Natural Energy Resources
# on Reservation Lands

## BY DONALD L. FIXICO

*Donald Fixico's article, published here for the first time, was origi-
nally presented in 1979 as a paper for a conference on relationships
between people and their land at the Institute of Indian Studies of the
University of South Dakota. Fixico's analysis has been revised specifically for this anthology, with additional emphasis placed on contemporary Plains Indians.*

*As Fowler's description of the Wind River Reservation has already
made clear, one of the critical challenges facing Indian people in the
region is the development of a viable economy. Many reservations in
the Plains contain sizable mineral resources, and how those resources
might or might not be used has been the subject of considerable debate
among tribal leaders and their constituents. While Fixico's analysis
includes some pertinent examples drawn from neighboring Indian
lands of the Southwest, his primary attention is given to people such as
the Northern Cheyennes and the Crows of Montana.*

*As recently as a generation ago Indians often made agreements
with powerful companies that seized control over the mining of their
resources and denied Indians proper compensation for their minerals.
Federal officials, local boosters, and others have often encouraged
tribal leaders to assent to leases that proved not to be in the best
interest of their peoples. Energy development provided neither the
projected number of jobs nor the revenue promised to the tribal
treasuries.*

*Although Fixico observes that serious problems remain, he shows
that Indian peoples now have a more informed sense of what those
problems are and consequently a sharper picture of the advantages
and disadvantages attending this form of economic development. As*

*the damming of the Missouri revealed, the demands and needs of the larger society cannot help but infringe upon Indian rights and Indian well-being. Fixico notes that "ironically, today's Indian leaders are negotiating with white Americans and the federal government for tribal lands as their ancestors did more than 100 years ago." The full impact of those negotiations cannot yet be discerned, but we may be sure that it will be felt for generations to come.*

MORE than one hundred years ago Indian tribal leaders were forced to negotiate with white Americans and the United States government for possession of Indian lands. Today's tribal leaders face a similar situation owing to the growing energy crisis and increased demands for natural resources. Depletion of our country's mineral reserves has caused energy companies to look toward reservation lands to replenish needed oil, coal, gas, and uranium. Even water has become a precious resource for transporting coal in slurry pipelines. In almost every western state Indian and white interests are competing for this pricelss commodity.[1] As a result of the increasing demand for natural resources, relations between tribal reservation leaders and white Americans have intensified.

Today more than half of the nation's coal fields are west of the Mississippi River.[2] One-third of the western coal fields exist on lands of 22 tribes.[3] Large portions of the reservations of most of these tribes will be disrupted during mining operations. The Northern Cheyennes, whose 440,000-acre reservation stands over a rich coal vein in southeastern Montana, will have approximately 56 percent of their land mined.[4] The Crow Reservation, adjacent to the Cheyennes' will suffer similar disturbances, including reduction of land available for the Crows' own use. In Montana and North Dakota coal fields are estimated to contain 15 times the energy reserves of the Alaska North Slope oil and gas fields. The Jicarilla Apache Reservation, in New Mexico, contains 154 million barrels of oil and 2 trillion cubic feet of gas. Overall, geologists report that 25 to 40 percent of this nation's uranium, one-third of its coal, and approximately 5 percent of its oil and gas are on Indian reservations in the West.[5]

Mining operations on Indian lands can be monetarily beneficial; tribes bestowed with large mineral deposits on their reservations receive large royalty payments. Such revenue enables the tribes to promote various programs and to improve their economies. The western tribes faced a grave dilemma, however: Should they allow mining development on their reservations? In 1977, Peter Mac-Donald, chairperson of the Navajo Nation, said in a speech before the Western Attorney Generals in Seattle, Washington: "The history of Indian resource development reaches far into our past. Before the white man came to our lands, Indians developed their resources for their own needs. Our people used only what they needed, and they were very careful not to destroy the land." The mining situation has changed drastically, however. "Pipelines, railroads, trucks and powerlines transport this material [resources] off the reservation to provide Americans with a better life," said MacDonald. "At the same time, most Indians still live in poverty, without such 'luxuries' as water and electricity, which most Americans regard as the barest necessities of life."[6]

The Indians' reaction to the demand for their energy resources is twofold: one is a reluctance to allow the mining operations to continue, and the other is a progressive attitude toward increased mining to help develop tribal programs. Among the western tribes factions for and against mining have developed among the native peoples. Some tribespeople who are conservative traditionalists oppose mining. Those who favor mining are the progressives, especially tribal leaders, but they are in the minority. Nevertheless, tribal leaders control their tribes' affairs, and they sometimes negotiate with energy companies without their people's consent.

Generally the conservative blocs consist of the tribal elders. They see their traditional cultures threatened, leading them to believe that after the mining companies are gone, their lands will never be the same. David Strange Owl, one of the thirty-six Northern Cheyennes on a fact-finding mission, visited the mining operations on the Navajo reservation. He confessed, "Before, I didn't know much about coal." Observing the mining operations aroused in him of feelings of repugnance: "What I've seen between the Navajo and Hopi is a sad thing, to see the strip-mining, on their reservations . . . because it's going to hurt a lot of lives of the [our] reservation—our lives, our culture."[7] Possessing a deep attachment to the land, traditionalists view themselves as part of it. According to native tradition the earth is mother to all, and no harm should come to her; The "mother Earth" concept is one of the few universal concepts among American Indians. Those who still hold to this concept say that these tribal members who want to exploit the land are no longer Indians.[8]

Over the next thirty years more than 250,000 acres of Plains soil will be torn up by huge steam-powered shovel machines called draglines, as tall as sixteen-story buildings, weighing 27 million pounds, and able to move 220 cubic yards (325 tons) of "overburden"—earth—in a single pass. In the path of the draglines are croplands, wildlife refuges, and former residental areas. On the average the steam shovels rip down through 100 and 150 feet of soil just to recover the coal veins.[9]

Many traditionalists bitterly oppose energy companies wanting to exploit their lands. They do not understand or care about the growing energy crisis. One young Hopi Indian's reaction to the demand for reservation resources to solve the crisis was, "Don't tell me about an energy crisis. I don't even have electricity in my village."[10]

Mining operations are lending credence to the traditionalists' fears. Aside from harming Mother Earth and jeopardizing the relationship between nature and mankind, the companies bring more non-Indians onto the reservation. Soon the non-Indians may outnumber the native people on their own lands. In one instance, if the mining operations continue on the Northern Cheyenne Reservation, twenty non-Indians will be brought in for every Cheyenne living on the reservation.[11] Many Indians do not want this to happen and charge that tribal leaders are allowing the abuse of their people, homelands, and culture by cooperating with energy companies.

Conversely, tribal leaders believe that they can improve the welfare of their people by generating revenues and programs from mining arrangements. They deem that now is the time to take advantage of energy companies. With increasing demands for natural resources there is no doubt that revenue received from mining companies will mean further changes in Indian life-styles. For some native people social changes are already taking place. Residents of reservations who work at off-reservation jobs, for instance, are familiar with the mainstream society.[12]

The progressive Indian nations have elected to improve their situation socially, politically, and economically. Peter MacDonald asserted that his people have chosen to change:

We are an emerging nation. Like other underdeveloped countries with rich but exhaustible supplies of fuel and minerals, we realize we must use our natural resources to create jobs for our people and put us on the road to economic self-sufficiency. Otherwise, we will not have anything left when our resources are gone. That's why we are demanding more from the people who want to exploit our wealth.[13]

Speaking on behalf of the 4,500 members of the Crow tribe whose reservation possesses some 14 to 18 billion tons of coal, former Chairperson Patrick Stands Over Bull said, "I'm for coal development, but I'm for control."[14] Stands Over Bull asserted that his tribe needed time to develop plans for land use and to pass zoning regulations and tax laws.

Navajo and Crow tribal members hesitate to allow mining companies onto their lands. In fact, many do not trust their own leaders, some of whom, they allege, have put tribal monies into their own pockets. Moreover, lack of knowledge about mining, techniques, operations, and legalities has made tribal members suspicious of their leaders. How to estimate the resources on their lands and how to judge their value are problems beyond the expertise of most reservation residents. Instances of mismanagement have upset them. Even though tribal members themselves do not understand the intricacies of mining, they blame their officials for any mishaps, especially long-term leases that force the tribes to "give away" reservation minerals to mining companies.

Tribal leaders have been forced to rely heavily upon non-Indian lawyers and non-Indian advisers who are experts in energy development areas and the legalities of leasing contracts. This dependency has been reduced in recent years as the number of trained Indian lawyers has grown, but lawyers still demand large fees for their services. Past relations with attorneys and non-Indian experts have caused tribal members to be distrustful of everyone.

Even without the support of their tribespeople Indian leaders are confident that they can supervise mining operations and develop their own tribal mining companies. The lack of training and, especially, of capital has hindered and sometimes discouraged them. Addressing the Indians's lack of knowledge of mining, the late John Woodenlegs, a Northern Cheyenne, said, "Coal has been under the Cheyenne reservation a long time, and it can stay there until we know the best thing to do."[15]

Tribal leaders protest that the royalty payments from leases are too low and that they are locked into poorly negotiated leases for long periods of time. Because the secretary of the interior is empowered by law to approve leases, the energy companies can control Indian lands. Supposedly the tribes would benefit from the agreement, but Indians criticize the government for failing to advise tribes correctly and not protecting them from being victimized. Lack of proper supervision by the Bureau of Indian Affairs to protect Indian interests and the bureau's urging of tribes to accept inadequate leases have angered the energy-endowed tribes.[16]

The Northern Cheyennes have alleged that from 1969 to 1971 the United States government misadvised them. Peabody, Amax, and Chevron were given exploration and mining leases for over half of the reservation's 450,000 acres. The tribe did not realize how unfair the ill-advised agreements were until 1972, when Consolidation Coal Company offered the tribe $35 an acre, a royalty rate of 25 cents, and a $1.5 million community health center. After further investigation the Cheyenne Tribal Council charged the federal government with thirty-six violations of leasing procedures.[17]

The tribe petitioned Rogers Morton, then secretary of the interior, to cancel all of their leases with energy companies. Instead the secretary suspended the leases until a "mutual agreement" was worked out between the companies and the tribe. But the Northern Cheyennes demanded cancellation. "We don't negotiate with the companies until they tear those leases up in front of us and burn them," said Tribal Chairman Allen Rowland. "And we can start over on our terms, not theirs."[18]

Government and industry officials have responded that, although some mistakes have been made, most leases were negotiated fairly. In 1974, Secretary of the Interior Rogers Morton, told Northern Cheyenne leaders that they would have to abide by lease agreements with Peabody, Consolidation, and other companies. Later that same year, however, Northern Cheyenne leases were suspended, and leasing was conducted by negotiation or competitive bidding.[19]

The Crows have charged the secretary of the interior with violating the National Environmental Policy Act and have said that as a result their coal leases do not comply with federal regulations. Since the government represents the tribes, through the BIA and the secretary of the interior, there are conflicting attitudes within the federal government, and the tribes are caught in between. The Omnibus Tribal Leasing Act of 1938 authorized the Department of the Interior to approve leases between the tribes and the mining companies.[20] "The government is the trustee of the Indians and the coordinator of national energy policy. That is a conflict of interests," stated Thomas J. Lynaugh, an attorney for the Crow Tribe.[21] In summation Hopi Chairperson Abbott Sekaquaptewa commented, "The energy situation has put us in a much better posture. We are going to make our decisions on whether to develop our resources, when it will be done, and how."[22]

Indian leaders are currently taking a more active role in the negotiations for their natural resources. In some instances tribal officials are suing against long-term leases that underpay their tribes; the American dollar has shrunk since these leases were originally signed. The Crow Indians are trying to regain control of some 30,000 acres in southeastern Montana leased to Shell Oil Company and 14,000 acres held by Amax Coal Company. In addition Peabody Coal Company controls 86,122 acres of Crow land, and Gulf Oil Company holds 73,293.[23] If the Crows are successful in obtaining a favorable decision from the courts, new leases will benefit their tribal economy tremendously.

Another alternative for the Crows is a possible joint ownership with an energy firm. Instead of accepting the traditional royalty payments, Crow tribal leaders are asking for a percentage of the production results in raw material or profit. On April 4, 1983, Secretary of the Interior James Watt approved a coal-mining agreement between the Crows and Shell Oil Company to mine an estimated 210 million tons of coal from the reservation's Youngs Creek area. The tribe will receive $12 million in preproduction and royalty payments. The agreement also gives the tribe a 50 percent participation in a profit-sharing plan to be implemented after twenty years of mining operations.[24]

The Indian Mineral Act of 1982 allows tribes to enter into joint agreements to establish companies for developing oil, gas, and other mineral resources. The measure was passed during a lame-duck session of Congress with the expectation that President Ronald Reagan would sign the bill into law. Energy-endowed tribes could now venture into business enterprises to develop their resources.[25] A contract between the Assiniboines, the Sioux, and the U.S. Energy Corporation was the first approved joint company under the new legislation. Assistant Secretary of the Interior Ken Smith stated that the contract "accords perfectly with President's recently issued Indian policy which calls for the development of reservation economies and the strengthening of tribal governments." Under this particular agreement the company will bear the entire cost of drilling and operating the first well; afterward the company and the tribes will share the net proceeds from production.[26]

In another case the Blackfeet Nation formed a joint ownership with Damson Oil Corporation, a small energy firm. After the company strikes gas on the Blackfeet reservation, the tribe will receive 58 percent of the profits after paying operational expenses.[27] In addition the Blackfeet recently entered into another agreement, forming a joint company with Blocker Drilling Ltd. Distribution of the drilling company's profits will be based upon the tribe's 51 percent ownership and Blocker's 49 percent, with the understanding that 90 percent of the company's net cash flow will first be used for purchasing equipment for the company to operate. The agreement also includes an on-the-job training program for tribal members in both roughneck work and management.[28]

The Chippewa-Cree Indians and other native groups are exploring the joint venture idea, yet some tribes want to form their own energy companies someday. "Up to now, we've always been satisfied in exchange for mineral rights," said Navajo leader Peter MacDonald. "That is no longer enough. We want a share of the income instead of the royalties. Eventually, we plan to go it alone in development of our natural resources."[29]

In an effort to protect reservation resources leaders of twenty-five western Indian tribes united in 1976 to form the Council of Energy Resource Tribes (CERT).[30] CERT is controlled by an executive board consisting of eight tribal chairpersons and a ninth chairperson who serves as the executive director of CERT. With one-third of all coal in the West located on Indian lands, CERT takes an agressive business approach toward energy firms to bargain in the best interests of the tribes. CERT sought advice from several OPEC nations over the United States government's disapproval. To halt further OPEC assistance, the federal government awarded CERT grants totaling $1,997,000 from the Department of Energy, the BIA, and the Department of Health, Education and

Welfare. Initially CERT opened offices in Denver, Colorado, and Washington, D.C., but closed the doors of the Washington Office when its 1982 budget of $6 million was cut to $3.1 million in 1983.[31] The council educates tribes in evaluating their energy sources, in the technology of mining natural resources, and in the development of human resources and provides management studies and computer services.[32] To prevent further exploitation of Indian lands, CERT has established a broad Indian policy "so that energy companies won't be able to pick us off one by one" according to Charles Lohah, the Acting Secretary for CERT.[33]

It should be added that, despite its success, the organization has hardly been immune from criticism. In recent years CERT has been severely criticized by Indians who charge that it is too "prodevelopment" regarding reservation resources. CERT has also been accused of holding "glittery, black-tie galas for federal officials and energy company brass."[34]

Today coal is foreseen as a key natural resource to meet the recurring energy crises, and mining companies are eager to develop reservation minerals. The nation's energy resources east of the Mississippi have been severely depleted, and mining firms look to the West for new fields of coal and other natural resources. Economic reasons have also forced companies westward, because strip mining is more economical than shaft mining in the East. Vast reserves of coal beds to up one hundred feet thick lie just below the surface, and over half of the 225 billion tons of coal in the West is available by strip mining. In the west draglines can strip-mine 100 tons of coal per man-day of labor, more than eight times the rate from the deep Appalachian shaft mines. Health and safety conditions are also more favorable in western strip mining, allowing coal to be mined at $3 to $5 per ton as compared with $9 to $14 in the East.[35]

The list of corporations on Indian lands in the West is long. In the Black Hills of South Dakota alone, twenty-seven multinational corporations have obtained state prospecting leases for over one million acres. The corporations are Union Carbide, Gulf, Exxon, Wyoming Minerals (owned by Westinghouse), Mobil, Endicott Copper, Nokota Company, John Mansfield, Cyprus Exploration, International Nickle, Power Resources, Mineral Exploration, Century Mining, Kerr-McGee, American Copper, Chevron, Natrona Service, Energy Resources, Energy Transportation System, Peter

Kewitt, Rio Agum, M&M Iron Co., Pittsburgh Pacific, Colorado Fuel and Iron, United Nuclear Homestake, Western Geophysical, and Shell. In response to the mining in the Black Hills, Indian and white residents of the area formed the Black Hills Alliance in 1979 as a survival effort to protect the environment and their homes. The alliance, which has between 250 and 300 members, discusses development for the area and seeks out information about newly employed mining techniques that may be hazardous to the Black Hills.[36]

Until recent years energy firms have had easy access to western coal fields. The Department of the Interior could persuade tribal officials to lease lands to companies, thereby easing the exploitation of Indian lands. As a result, the Utah International Company has been mining the Four Corners Region, now the largest strip-mining operation in the world, on Navajo land.[37] Today, however, as they conduct intense negotiations with energy company officials, tribal leaders are developing a new image for themselves. Today's Indian tribal leaders are unlike their forefathers, who did not understand the complexities of handling land negotiations. Company and government officials have noticed the transition from the old tribal leadership, which is adamant about demands and cognizant of white ways of dealing for land.

Reservation leaders have become more successful in negotiations, and the future looks brighter for Plains and Southwest tribes. With the increased knowledge and understanding of white ways, tribal leaders are also initiating and developing new programs to help their people. It may be appropriate here to cite the advice of the Sioux leader Sitting Bull. When the mighty Sioux Nation was in decline, mostly because of white influence, Sitting Bull warned: ''Take the best of the white man's road, pick it up and take it with you. That which is bad, leave it alone, cast it away. Take the best of the old Indian ways—always keep them. They have been proven for thousands of years. Do not let them die.''[38]

The younger tribal leaders of the western reservations are making tremendous strides in improving their tribes' status. From the level of third-world nations, Indian groups are progressing rapidly toward parity with white American society. With competent leadership and additional aid from the Bureau of Indian Affairs, energy-endowed tribes have been able to develop successful industries. Federal funds have been appropriated to finance such tribal ventures as Yatay Industries, Sandia Indian Industries, Apache Indian Industries, and Ute Fabricating, Ltd.[39] Other tribal industries include Northern Pueblo Enterprises, Navajo Indian Wood Products, Zuni Enterprises, and White Eagle Industries. These business ventures are the work of careful planning and exemplify the entrepreneurlike quality of modern Indian achievement.

Partly because such new tribal programs are highly visible, a resurgence of Indian nationalism is developing among western tribal nations. Damson Oil President Barrie M. Damson contends that this native nationalism will grow and that energy companies need to recognize this.[40]

As Indian Americans enter the 1980s, some problems remain unresolved. A seventy-two-page report from the Minerals Management Service of the Department of the Interior stated that $119.2 million in royalties had reportedly been paid to Indians in 1980. The next year some $161.4 million in royalties went to Indians.[41] Unfortunately, in one known case the royalty checks never reached the people. In Wyoming, seventy allottees from the Wind River Reservation have filed a lawsuit against Amoco Production Company for not paying royalties on 1.3 million barrels of crude oil taken from the Lander Oil Field between 1971 and 1982. The allottees, who have coalesced into the Wind River Allottees Association, petitioned their case to a federal court because they felt that the government would not act soon enough on their behalf. The group seeks either a return of the oil or payment at the current value, an estimated $41 million, plus compensation for punitive damages.[42]

An area of new importance opened after a court decision of 1982 in which the U.S. Supreme Court ruled that the Jicarilla Apaches could charge energy companies a severance tax for mining on their land. Two other tribes, the Shoshone and Arapahoe of Wyoming, are attempting to impose a 4 percent severance tax on oil and gas, pending approval by the secretary of the interior. With state government also taxing the mining companies, the energy firms now face double taxation. Although the state taxes are generally higher, the energy companies are challenging the right of the tribes to tax them.[43] The 1982 ruling has opened up a new avenue for tribal income, but it is one that reservation leader will have to fight to keep.

Many tribal leaders and reservation peoples, however, face serious problems. Some Americans assume that Indians are getting rich from royalty payments, though actually only 15 percent of the Indian population has natural resources on tribal lands. In 1982 the BIA reported that royalties on reservations totaled more than $396 million—a large sum, but if the royalties were distributed to the entire Indian population of 1.3 million (1980 census), the per captia payment would be only $290 for each person. For their oil tribes received on the average $2 a barrel in royalties at a time when OPEC nations were demanding and receiving $40 a barrel. Four of the largest energy resource deposits are on the Blackfeet, Crow, Fort Peck and Wind River reservations in Montana and Wyoming. In 1980 more than 1,200 wells on the four Plains reservations produced 6.1 million barrels of oil. As for coal, in early 1981, when American coal was being sold to foreign buyers for $70 a ton, the Navajo were receiving only 15 cents a ton from Utah International Mining company and 37.5 cents a ton from Pittsburgh Midway Coal Company. These two companies negotiated leases with the Navajos in 1953, 1964, and 1966.[44]

In negotiations with the energy companies tribal leaders are at a disadvantage. Their governments usually cannot pay for equipment to evaluate their natural resources. The requisite trained personnel and exploratory data are in short supply, forcing tribes to give up a major share of their potential wealth by leasing their lands or entering into joint ventures with energy companies.

To compound the dilemma, Indian affairs have low priority in Washington. the entire budget appropriated for Indian affairs would buy just one aircraft carrier. Worse the BIA is a frequent hindrance to tribal leaders because it also lacks the expertise that the mining firms possess in the highly competitive business of energy development. For example, on January 25, 1982, ruling in favor of the Jicarilla Apaches, the Supreme Court maintained that Indian tribes ''have the inherent power'' to impose severance taxes. Nevertheless, a few months later the BIA wrote regulations for the severance taxation, and in doing so it invited the opinions of representatives from the oil-and-gas industry. Indian criticism forced the BIA to withdraw its regulations, and guidelines were substituted. The bureau's actions' prompted additional criticism from U.S. Representative Sidney Yates, who chaired the House Appropriations subcommittee that handles Indian Affairs. Yates chided, ''Tell me why an oil and gas industry association should be allowed to formulate guidelines by which the tribes will be able to tax members of that industry.''[45]

Tribal leaders, unlike their ancestral leaders, have had to take on a hurried ''get-tough'' attitude in a businesslike modern, ''ruthless'' way. Such behavior is foreign to the traditional nature of Indian leadership, and it has been an obstacle that tribal representatives have had to overcome if their people are to survive. Although the leaders can probably use more expertise in running their reservation governments like corporations, they know how to hire such expertise. In a very short time they have become educated in the high finance business world and are experienced in dealing with the bureaucracy of the federal government.[46] Contemporary Indian leaders are sophisticated and forceful in order to protect their people and their reservations—lands that were deemed worthless in the nineteenth century.

The energy crises and the industrial demand for natural resources on Indian lands imply serious repercussions for the tribes' future. The anticipated outcomes are both positive and negative and will have tremendous impact on Indian leaders, tribal members and reservation lands. The mining operations, gasification plants to convert coal into gas, and the production of electricity are extensive and cover large areas of land; as a result, reservation supplies of nonreplaceable natural resources are being severely depleted. In addition, land formations that had religious significance to the people are permanently damaged. Even with reclamation attempts to restore the land to its original state, it will never be the same to the traditional Indians.

Perhaps the fears of the tribal elders who oppose the mining of Mother Earth are justified. While tribal leaders are trying to improve their tribes' economies through new programs, schools, and jobs, perhaps a greater harm will come to them. Aside from the exploitation of their lands, the trend to adopt white ways may also mean that much of the tribal cultures will be forgotten.

Or can Indians live with one foot in the traditional world and the other in the white world? Many are doing it now, but how much of their tribal heritage do they remember, and how successfully have they assimilated into white American society? Currently more Indians than ever are receiving the same education as whites and are moving rapidly into the mainstream society. Indians who live on reservations are becoming more aware of the functions of white society as they travel to and from their reservations. In place of their previous poverty many native people have rasied their economic level and have become successful American citizens according to white standards. Perhaps it is premature to judge whether the Indian has acquired social change at the loss of native identity. Certainly the next generation will provide better answers.

At the present time the growing demand for natural resources on Indian lands has acted as a catalyst in forcing Indians, especially tribal leaders, to choose a life-style for their peoples. They are confronted with the dilemma of a social transition from the traditional world to the white man's life-style. Within all of this turmoil, it is ironic that today's Indian leaders are negotiating with white Americans and the federal government for tribal lands as their ancestors did more than one hundred years ago.

# Notes

1. Dennis Williams, Gerald C. Lubenow, and William J. Cook, "Where Coal is not a Problem," *Newsweek*, March 20, 1878, p. 35. See also William H. Veeder, "Water Rights in the Coal Fields of the Yellowstone River Basin," *Law and Contemporary Problems* 40 (1976); 77–96.

2. Richard Boeth, Jeff B. Copeland, Mary Hager, and Phyllis Malamund, "A Paleface Uprising," *Newsweek*, April 10, 1978, p. 40.

3. "Indians Want a Bigger Share of Their Wealth," *Business Week*, May 3, 1976, p. 101; "A Crow Indian Threat to Western Strip Mines," *Business Week*, October 13, 1975, p. 37.

4. Melinda Beck, Jeff B. Copeland, and Merril Sheils, "Resources: The Rich Indians," *Newsweek*, March 20, 1978, p. 61.

5. "A Crow Indian Threat to Western Mines," *Business Week*, October 13, 1975, p. 37; "The Black Hills Alliance," *Akwesasne Notes* (Mohawk Reservation, N.Y.) 2, No. 2 (May, 1979).

6. "Energy and Land Use Questions on Indian Lands," *Wassaja* (San Francisco, Calif.) 5, no. 6 (September, 1977), originally stated in "A Major Statement to the Annual Meeting of Western Attorney Generals," Seattle, Washington, August 9, 1977, by Navajo Chairperson Peter MacDonald.

7. "Killing the Earth, Air, Water," *Akwesasne Notes* 9, no. 1 (Early Spring, 1977).

8. Clyde Kluckholn and Dorothea Leighton, *The Navaho* (Cambridge, Mass.: Harvard University Press, 1958), pp. 227–228; Philip Reno, "The Navajos: High, Dry and Penniless," *Nation*, March 29, 1975, p. 359.

9. Michael Garity, "The Pending Energy Wars, America's Final Act of Genocide," *Akwesasne Notes* 11, no. 5 (December, 1979).

10. Fred Harris and LaDonna Harris, "Indians, Coal, and the Big Sky," *Progressive*, December, 1974, p. 25.

11. "Indians Want a Bigger Share of Their Wealth," p. 102.

12. Imre Sutton, *Indian Land Tenure: Bibliogaphical Essays and a Guide to the Literature* (New York and Paris: Clearwater Publishing Co., 1975), p. 201.

13. "American Indians Bargain 'Arab Style' to Cash in on Resources," *U.S. News and World Report*, June 3, 1974, p. 53.

14. "A Crow Indian Threat to Western Strip Mines," p. 37.

15. David R. Zimmerman, "Can Indians and Environmentalists Find Common Ground?" *Progressive*, December, 1976, p. 28.

16. "An 'OPEC' Right in America's Own Back Yard," *U.S. News and World Report*, August 2, 1976, p. 29; Zimmerman, "Can Indians and Environmentalists Find Common Ground?" p. 28.

17. "The Black Hills Alliance."

18. "The Northern Cheyenne . . . Defending the Last Retreat . . ." *Akwesasne Notes* 10, no. 1 (Early Spring, 1978).

19. "An 'OPEC' Right in America's Own Back yard." p. 29; Harris and Harris, "Indians, Coal, and the Big Sky," p. 23; "Tribes Being Plundered," *Wassaja* 6, no. 11 (December, 1978).

20. Omnibus Tribal Leasing Act of 1938, May 3, 25, USCS—396a et seq., 52 *U.S. Stat.* 347.

21. "A Crow Indian Threat to Western Strip Mines," p. 37.

22. "Indians Want a Bigger Share of Their Wealth," p. 100.

23. "A Crow Indian Threat to Western Strip Mines," p. 37.

24. "Watt Approves Coal Mining Agreement," *Lakota Times* (Rosebud, S. Dak.), April 14, 1983.

25. "Indian Mineral Development Act," *Lakota Times*, January 6, 1983. The act is Public Law 97–382, December 22, 1982, 96 *U.S. Stat.* 1938.

26. "Ft. Peck Sioux Sign Agreement on Oil & Gas," *Lakota Times*, April 22, 1983.

27. "Indians Want a Bigger Share of Their Wealth," p. 100.

28. "Blackfeet Tribe Forms New Company," *Akwesasne Notes* 2, no. 9 (November 23, 1983). An insightful study of contemporary intra-Blackfeet social interaction among mixed-bloods and full-bloods, tribal values and new tribesmen's status from mining royalties is in Malcolm McFee, *Modern Blackfeet: Montanans on a Reservation* (New York: Holt, Rinehart and Winston, 1972).

29. "American Indians Bargain 'Arab Style' to Cash in on Resources," *U.S. News and World Report*, June 3, 1974, p. 53.

30. "Indians Want A Bigger Share of Their Wealth," p. 101.

31. Beck et al., "Rich Indians," *Newsweek*, March 20, 1978, p. 63; Marjane Ambler, "Controversial Speech Draws Ire at CERT Convention," *Lakota Times*, November 9, 1983.

32. See note 30 above. CERT sponsors Tribal Resource Institute in Business, Engineering, and Science (TRIBES), a college scholarship program to educate Indian youths who will likely help their tribes; "Rosebud Chairman Elected to CERT Executive Board," *Lakota Times*, December 9, 1982; "$2 Million for Tribes' CERT," *Wassaja* 6, nos. 9–10 (October–November, 1978); "Rosebud Chairman Elected to CERT Executive Board," *Lakota Times*, December 9, 1982.

33. "Indians Want a Bigger Share of Their Wealth," p. 101.

34. John A. Farrell, "Empty Promises, Misplaced Trust," New Indian Wars Series, *Denver Post*, November 20, 1983.

35. Thomas Brom, "The Southwest: America's New Appalachia," *Ramparts*, November, 1974, pp. 17–18.

36. "The Black Hills Alliance."

37. The Four Corners Power plant located on the shore of Lake Powell occupies, 1,021 acres, plus 765 more for storing fly ash. The stacks tower to a height of 800 feet, dispersing daily more than 600 tons of sulfur dioxide, nitrogen oxides, and ash from about 23,000 tons of coal into the atmosphere. An estimated 40,000 acre-feet of water will be consumed annually to flow through the cooling towers at a rate of 270,000 gallons per minute. The plant has cost $328 million, plus another $178 million for the transmission lines to carry away its output. "The Southwest: America's New Appalachia," p. 18.

38. Harris and Harris, "Indians, Coal, and the Big Sky," p. 22.

39. "An 'OPEC' Right in America's Own Back yard," p. 30.

40. "Indians Want a Bigger Share of Their Wealth," p. 102; "An American 'Nation' is Gaining Unity, Respect—and Results," *U.S. News and World Report*, February 25, 1974, pp. 60–61.

41. "Indians received $161.4 Million in Minerals Royalties in 1981," *Lakota Times*, November 18, 1982.

42. Marjane Ambler, "The Forgotten People," *Lakota Times*, November 2, 1983.

43. Marjane Ambler, "Victories for Tribes in Tax Cases," *Lakota Times*, September 14, 1983. The tribes may be able to use inherent sovereign powers to continue taxing non-Indian lease holders of mining rights on reservations. See Jim Noble Jr., "Tribal Power to Tax Non-Indian Mineral Leases," *National Resource*

*Journal* 19 (October, 1979): 969–95. Two articles that cover the legal extent of tribal taxation of non-Indians are Carol E. Goldberg, "a Dynamic View of Tribal Jurisdiction to Tax Non-Indians," *Law and Contemporary Problems* 40 (1976): 166–89; and Quentin M. Jones, "Mineral Resources: Tribal Development of Reservation Oil and Gas Resources Through the Use of a Nontaxation-Based Tribal Joint Development Program," *American Indian Law Review* 9, no. 1 (1983): 161–94. On state taxes conflicting with tribal taxes, see Sharon E. Claassen, "Taxation: State Transaction Privilege Tax: An Interference with Tribal Self-Government," *American Indian Law Review* 7 no. 2 (1979): 317–33.

44. John A. Farrell, "Empty Promises, Misplaced Trust."

45. Ibid. The right of the tribes to impose a severance tax is based on the combined cases of *J. Gregory Merrion and Robert L. Bayless, et al., and Amoco Production Company and Marathon Oil Company* v. *Jicarilla Apache Indian Tribe*, January 25, 1982, 455 U.S. 130, 71 L. Ed. 2d 21, 102 S.C. 894 in *U.S. Supreme Court Reports*, Lawyers' Edition, vol. 71.

46. Daniel H. Israel, "The Reemergence of Tribal Nationalism and Its Impact on Reservation Development," *University of Colorado Law Review* 47 (Summer, 1976): 617–52; Pattie Palmer McGee, "Indian Lands: Coal Development: Environmental/Economic Dilemma for the Modern Indian," *American Indain Law Review* 4, no. 2 (1976): 279–88.

# CHAPTER 10

# The Distinctive Status of Indian Rights

## BY VINE DELORIA, JR.

*The Indian people of the Plains are both a part of and apart from the United States. As Sioux attorney and activist Vine Deloria, Jr., reminds us in a new essay contributed for this volume, Indians have a right to own their lands, to determine their own tribal memberships, and to have their own governments, codes of conduct, and courts. Even if they reside on a reservation, non-Indians are limited in their ability to participate in Indian life.*

*This continuing separation, termed by some anthropologists a "working ethnic boundary" produces an inevitable tension between Indians and the larger American society. Thus the particular legal status of Indians is as important as it is complex. There are, of course, different interpretations of that status, and not everyone would subscribe to Deloria's view that Indians are extraconstitutional.*

*Certain issues between whites and Indians have proved especially troubling. One of the most emotionally charged issues has been religion. The ideals of religious freedom and separation of church and state have not been embraced in federal Indian policy. Indian religions have been discouraged or prohibited; conversion to Christianity has been encouraged or imposed. While federal policy at times has been less heavy-handed and more enlightened than at other times, the tension—born of deep-rooted convictions about the desirability and inevitability of assimilation—has nevertheless remained.*

*Not all Indians of the Plains or elsewhere believe in or practice traditional tribal religions or more contemporary forms of worship such as the Native American Church. Religious freedom, however, represents an integral part of self-definition and self-determination; that is why Deloria and others emphasize it. In the pages that follow, a*

237

*leading spokesman addresses the continuing importance of religion in*
*Plains Indian life within the larger framework of a careful analysis of*
*the unique place of American Indians in this country.*

IN 1978, Congress passed the American Indian Religious Freedom
Resolution (92 *U.S. Stat.* 469), which expressed a growing national concern to provide protection for and understanding of traditional Indian religious practices. In the half decade since the enactment
of that resolution, there has been a significant amount of litigation
dealing with Indian religious rights. Unfortunately, in recent years
Indians have lost most of the cases involving those rights, suggesting that the resolution failed to clarify and protect the unique
religious practices of American Indians. In five such decisions the
issue concerned the right of Indians to practice their religion on
land under federal control.[1] In every case except one the Indians
lost.[2]

On balance, the difficulty of defining the rights of religious
freedom for Indians appears to lie in accommodating the free-
exercise clause and the establishing clause so that Indians will have
sufficient leeway to exercise their rights without falling under one
of the traditional categories of prohibition. We must learn how to
phrase questions of Indian religious freedom so that we can begin
to achieve the proper results. We must first raise fundamental
questions regarding the nature of all Indian rights: social, political,
economic, educational, and religious. We must ask how Indians
received these rights, why they differ in degree and kind from the
civil rights of other American citizens, and how they can be
clarified and thereby protected and enforced.

In every area of federal Indian law there seems to be an inevitable reference to Chief Justice John Marshall's remark that

> the condition of the Indians in relation to the United States is perhaps
> unlike that of any other two people in existence. In general, nations not
> owning a common allegiance are foreign to each other. But the relation of
> the Indians to the United States is marked by peculiar and cardinal
> distinctions which exist nowhere else.[3]

The most noteworthy aspect of this peculiar relationship, Marshall
wrote, was that the Indians

and their country are considered by foreign nations, as well as by ourselves, as being so completely under the sovereignty and domination of the United States, that any attempt to acquire their lands, or to form a political connection with them, would be considered by all as an invasion of our territory and an act of hostility.[4]

Although Marshall's words are frequently cited, they are not really taken seriously as an aid to describing the actual nature of the relationship which Indians enjoy with the United States ("enjoy" is here a technical word of legal language, not a realistic description of the effects of the relationship). Basically, Marshall tells us that Indians exist comfortably within the protective reach of the United States *with respect to foreign nations*, but Indians are not themselves part of the United States. The relationship between Indian tribes and the United States has always been a political relationship that is foreign in every sense. This foreign relationship entails certain basic guarantees of political existence. Tribes have a right to their lands and cannot be removed without their consent under most ordinary conditions. Tribes determine their own memberships. Within a broad spectrum of alternatives tribes have their own forms of government. Tribes have their own codes of conduct and their own courts, and they have the power to govern the lands under their jurisdiction according to certain prerogatives which have been theirs since a time before the adoption of the United States Constitution. Although tribes do not now have jurisdiction over non-Indians (a decline in status over the past two centuries), non-Indians cannot participate in any tribal functions or activities without the permission and grace of the tribe.

Because there is this unbridgeable gulf between Indian tribes and their institutions, on the one hand, and American society and its citizens, on the other, we cannot and should not assume that this gap does not exist at every point at which Indians and Indian matters are tangent to non-Indian American society. Whatever happens within an Indian reservation or tribe does not affect those outside the Indian sphere of influence, and by the same token whatever happens outside an Indian community does not, unless Congress specifically permits it, affect Indians living in tribal relations. Although we know of no clear, bold statement separating Indians and non-Indians made at the beginning of the republic, all evidence suggests that the Founding Fathers intended Indian Affairs to be a distinct field outside American domestic law and governed by extraordinary responsibilities vested in the federal government. The Ordinance of 1787 clearly states the principles under which Congress will govern its relations with the Indians:

The utmost good faith shall always be observed toward the Indians; their land and property shall never be taken from them without their consent; and in their property rights, and liberty, they never shall be invaded or disturbed unless in just and lawful wars authorized by Congress but laws founded in justice and humanity shall from time to time be made, for preventing wrongs being done to them, and for preserving peace and friendship with them.[5]

This delineation of policy attempts to provide for Indian tribes a protection equivalent to that offered American citizens under the Constitution and Bill of Rights. The status of Indians as a foreign political entity, however, is unquestionable. Nowhere in the Constitution does Congress have the power to wage just wars on its citizens or any subdivision of the state or national governments.

Indians receive the protection of the federal government precisely because they are outside the protections of the Constitution; they need and receive special consideration when the federal government interacts with them and handles their affairs. We have often called the government's power to accomplish this task "plenary" because we supposed that it needed to be immune from ordinary challenges which might otherwise hamper the wise administration of the affairs of Indians. Unfortunately, this plenary power has been used more often to deny them protection for their property, for their undisturbed social life, and for the practice of their religions than to assist them. The plenary power has no apparent limitation except the moral sensibility of Congress, which is a slender reed at best.

When discussing federal Indian law, we often overlook the fact that Indians are extraconstitutional. We suppose, wholly without foundation, that the ordinary legal doctrines and procedures used in ordinary American domestic law apply in Indian cases just as they apply in non-Indian matters. On the contrary, federal Indian law contains so many exceptions to traditional Anglo-Saxon jurisprudence as to constitute a field qualitatively and procedurally distinct from it. One reason that we fail to understand the role of federal Indian law in American jurisprudence is that the expositors of the subject stress the power of the federal government in respect to Indian affairs almost to the exclusion of the actual structure of federal Indian law. Two doctrines—plenary power and trust responsibility—completely overshadow all other considerations of what might be the substance of federal Indian law. Consequently, we fail to see that federal Indian law is a separate, indeed isolated, field, with few analogies to other fields of law and with a logical consistency all its own. The logical consistency is built upon the premise that Indian matters are politically foreign to the rest of American domestic law and hence constitute a separate discipline or subject area. This area is always extraconstitutional.

If we could reorganize our present view of federal Indian law according to the distinctions made above, we would see that one of the fundamental doctrines of the correct interpretation, that *general national legislation has no application to Indians unless they are* ✱ *Deloria* *specifically mentioned,* becomes the cornerstone of a new way of arranging the rights and responsibilities of both the Indian tribes and the federal government. We would come to understand that what we have called the "trust responsibility" of the federal government toward Indian tribes is mandated by the fact that Indians are extraconstitutional. No constitutional protections exist for Indians in either a tribal or an individual sense, and hence the need for special rules and regulations, special administrative discretionary authority, and special exemptions. This special body of law replaces the constitutional protections granted to other members of American society. Let us examine several areas in which Indian rights are tangent to the rights of other Americans and see how federal law and its interpretations have affected Indians.

### INDIANS AND THE CONSTITUTION

Indians are mentioned twice in the Constitution as it was originally adopted. In Article I, section 2, clause 3, Indians "not taxed" are not to be counted when determining the population for the purpose of apportioning taxes and representatives to the Congress among the states. In Article I, section 8, clause 3, Congress is authorized to "regulate Commerce with foreign Nations, and among the several States, and with Indian Tribes." *The Federalist Papers* may mention Indians in discussing the powers of the national government, but they do not elaborate on the status of Indians within the constitutional framework; Indians are always perceived as outside the constitutional setting.

The Bill of Rights does not mention Indians, and the subsequent historic treatment of Indians by the federal government testifies that Indians were perceived to have no constitutional rights at all. How else could we justify holding the Chiricahua Apaches first in a federal prison and later at Fort Sill for a generation? How else could we explain the prohibition of Indian religious ceremonials by officials of the Bureau of Indian Affairs or the prohibition of the speaking of Indian languages in government schools? Until *United States* ex. rel. *Standing Bear* v. *Crook*[6] (25 Fed. Cas. 695, C.C.D. Neb. 1879), Indians were not even perceived to be persons under the domestic law of the United States.

Later constitutional amendments deomonstrate that Indians have always been beyond constitutional reach. We read in our casebooks and legal treatises that the Thirteenth Amendment prohibited slavery and involuntary servitude within the limits of lands controlled by the United States. This amendment apparently did not, however, apply to American Indians. On July 27, 1868, Congress passed Joint Resolution No. 83, which prohibited the peonage of women and children of the Navajo tribe.[7] Had the Thirteenth Amendment applied to American Indians, it presumably would have covered this situation.

The Fourteenth Amendment repeated the prohibition against enumerating "Indians not taxed" but extended the rights of citizenship to "all persons born or naturalized in the United States." In *Elk* v. *Wilkins* the Supreme Court seized the opportunity to determine whether this amendment applied to Indians and delivered an exhaustive analysis on the status of Indians in the United States:

The alien and dependent condition of the members of Indian tribes could not be put off at their own will, without the action or assent of the United States. They were never deemed citizens of the United States, except under explicit provisions of treaty or statute to that effect, either declaring a certain tribe, or such members of it as chose to remain behind on the removal of the tribe westward, to be citizens, or authorizing individuals of particular tribes to become citizens on application to a court of the United States for naturalization.[8]

It is important in this respect to note that the Nebraska statute under which John Elk sought to vote did not require him to be a citizen but required him only to intend to become a citizen. Nevertheless, he was denied even the basic right of personal political decision. Elk and other Indians were not regarded as citizens because they were not born "subject to the jurisdiction of the United States," and therefore the Fifteenth Amendment provided no relief, and no rights either.

The Sixteenth Amendment finally became law in 1913, after a decade of efforts to empower the federal government to raise the revenues needed by a modern nation. This amendment gave Congress the "power to lay and collect taxes on incomes, from whatever source derived, without apportionment among the several States, and without regard to any census or enumeration." The language of this amendment leaves little question and, until Congress began to meddle with it, few loopholes or escape clauses: income "from whatever source derived." It did not, however, touch income derived by Indians from ownership of their lands or in some instances from activities conducted on their lands. In tax cases the question always arises whether or not Congress intended to tax Indian income, and insofar as the income has been derived from property or activities specifically involved in Indian matters, the immunity has always been upheld. If any constitutional amendment appears to include Indians, the Sixteenth Amendment, because it involves revenue, has come closest to bringing Indians within the constitutional fold.

In 1924, Congress, in a very short and concise statute, granted citizenship to those Indians who had not previously received it "That all non-citizen Indians born within the territorial limits of the United States be, and they are hereby, declared to be citizens of the United States: *Provided, That the granting of such citizenship shall not in any manner impair or otherwise affect the right of any Indian to tribal or other property.*"[9] The granting of full citizenship and the preservation of rights to tribal property should have resolved the many legal entanglements which Indians suffered. Many Indians had previously received some form of citizenship but had learned, much to their dismay, and contrary to the apparently clear language of the General Allotment Act of 1887,[10] that citizenship did not include the freedom to dispose of their property as they wished. In *United States* v. *Nice* the Supreme Court declared that "citizenship is not incompatible with tribal existence or continued guardianship, and so may be conferred without completely emancipating the Indians or placing them beyond the reach of congressional regulations adopted for their protection."[11]

If certain forms of property guardianship were believed compatible with citizenship for Indians, that protection fell well within the traditional area of federal responsibility assumed under numerous treaties. Additionally, as we learn in *Johnson* v. *McIntosh*,[12] the United States believed land title to be most closely associated with its claims of sovereignty over Indian tribes. The federal officials believed that their most profound responsibility to Indians was to see that non-Indians did not cheat them in land transactions and that foreigners did not attempt to purchase their lands without seeking the permission of the United States. Hence it was natural for the Supreme Court to assume that some form of property trust could be made compatible with the citizenship rights of individual Indians.

What effect did citizenship have on the exercise of civil rights by Indians? It did not, apparently, give them the rights that other American citizens received in the Bill of Rights. No freedom of religion existed on the reservations until the New Deal, a decade after the granting of citizenship to Indians. The Eighteenth Amendment, prohibiting the manufacture, sale, or transportation of intoxicating liquors, was adopted before passage of the Indian Citizenship Act, but the Twenty-first Amendment, adopted in 1933, repealed the provisions of the Eighteenth Amendment. Although these amendments applied to commercial activity in alcoholic beverages, their impact on the populace was first to prohibit consumption of liquor and then to allow it. Neither amendment had any effect on Indians. They had been prohibited from drinking under the provisions of various treaties and agreements, and more generally by a national act passed by Congress on July 23, 1892,[13] which was also phrased as a prohibition of commerce in alcoholic beverages and not a prohibition against individual Indians consuming alcoholic drinks. It was not until 1953 that Congress repealed the Indian liquor laws providing for local reservation option regarding liquor sales and consumption on the reservations.[14]

We can summarize the relationship of American Indians to constitutional rights and protections very simply: No matter what the actual conditions or needs of Indians were and no matter what the justice of the situation required, in those instances where the  Constitution or its amendments might have been applied to Indians, it did not, and Congress always handled Indian matters through special legislative enactment. Citizenship for Indians did not entail a single new right (with the possible exception of the right to vote in some states) until Congress had granted Indians specific new responsibilities or the exercise of specific new rights. We come, then, to the question of religious freedom for American Indians.

## AMERICAN INDIAN RELIGIOUS FREEDOM

We have described the current problem in protecting Indian religious freedom as a matter of tip-toeing between two constitutional phrases which delimit questions of the exercise of religious freedom: the free-exercise clause and the establishment clause. The history of these two provisions of the Constitution provides us with an insight into the development of the question of religious freedom in American jurisprudence.

The earliest settlers fled Europe because of two kinds of religious persecution. First, people could be prohibited from practicing their religion by a monarchy or other government that had instituted an official state religion. Second, people could be forced to help support an official religious body that is dominant over their own religion. To prevent the state from installing any particular religious institution as the official and favored one, the Founding Fathers neatly restricted the powers of the national government regarding its entanglement with religion through the free-exercise clause and the establishment clause.

In its treatment of Indian religions the federal government did not obey the prohibition against a state-sponsored religion, and it  did not allow the free exercise of religious practices by Indians. From the earliest period of Indian administration, Christian church bodies and their missionaries received favored treatment from the federal government. To ensure that the members of the different tribes gave the Christian religion its due, traditional tribal ceremonies were forbidden. The questions of constitutional protection for traditional tribal religions and the constitutional prohibition against an established religion among Indians never reached the federal courts at any time before the enactment of the American Indian Religious Freedom Resolution in 1978 (the decisions upholding the Indian religious use of peyote do not apply here because they were primarily state court decisions; in this instance the state courts were far ahead of the federal judiciary).

Following the enactment of the American Indian Religious Freedom Resolution, Indians began taking cases to the federal courts, seeking protection from intrusions and unwarranted actions by federal officials that inhibited or prohibited the free exercise of their traditional religions. Indians have been told that interests must be balanced and that any meaningful authorization of the practice of traditional religions would be an establishment of a special and favored religion or the creation of a special shrine to which other citizens could not come. In making this statement, federal courts have acted as though the American Indian Religious Freedom Resolution did nothing more than ensure that Indians enjoyed the same protections from the same evils which the earliest settlers had feared and that nothing more was intended by Congress.

We have seen this kind of argument before in other areas of Indian law. Chief Justice Marshall himself used it in deciding *Cherokee Nation* v. *Georgia*, when he interpreted a treaty provision allowing the United States to assume control of the trade relations of the Cherokees as the surrendering of their powers of self-government. Fortunately he reversed himself in *Worcester* v. *Georgia*,[15] admitting that no political body of people would willingly and knowingly surrender their powers of government and political existence. We have also seen this kind of logic in the arguments by the states of Washington and Oregon to the effect that the treaty phrase ''fishing in common with other citizens'' only gave the Indians of the Pacific Northwest the right to fish under state supervision along with whites. The federal courts rejected that argument because it meant that no bargain was in fact consummated; the courts remarked that the Indians would certainly not bargain for a right which was theirs anyway under all circumstances.

The basic question we face in protecting the free exercise of Indian religions is whether or not congressional acts dealing with  Indians have any intent and substance or whether they simply affirm for Indians the rights which other Americans already enjoy under the Constitution. In a sense they do enfranchise Indians with rights which have long been denied them. Yet the fact that Congress has always spelled out specific provisions for the exercise of any Indian rights—because Indians occupy a politically foreign status—always means the aggressive and specific application of protection for whatever rights Indians are authorized to exercise.

There may indeed be some kind of establishment of religious freedom for American Indians. If so, it is because Congress has dealt with the question of the practice of Indian religions and felt it to be necessary to extend the protection of federal laws further in the case of Indians than the Constitution allows it to extend to ordinary citizens. In this instance Indians are not to be regarded as "supercitizens"; rather, the practice of Indian religion is to be regarded as under the special protection of the federal government in the same way that Indian water rights, land titles, and self-government are protected.

Congress has always dealt with Indians in a special manner; that is why Congress and the federal courts cherish and nourish the doctrine of plenary powers in the field of Indian affairs. To say that the American Indian Religious Freedom Resolution gives Indians no further protection than that given other citizens by the Constitution is simply to say that Congress passes frivolous legislation which has no content or meaning. In view of the long history of special congressional acts outlining and articulating Indian rights, and in view of the persistent omission of Indians from the Constitution and its amendments (to be followed later by specific legislation describing the times, manner, and scope of Indian exercise of certain civil functions and personal freedoms), it seems apparent that the American Indian Religious Freedom Resolution clothes  the practice of Indian religions with a massive, protective federal cloak which the federal courts must recognize and uphold. In efforts to clarify and expand the scope of Indian religious freedom we must ensure that it is seen in the full light of the history of the federal-Indian relationship.

From the very beginning of the Republic that relationship has been understood as having a foreign aspect that could not be denied. The fact that Indians are politically foreign to the ordinary and routine operation of American domestic law requires that whenever Congress wishes Indians to participate more fully in American life it must make provisions for them to do so by special legislation. The American Indian Religious Freedom Resolution is as much a part of that legislative-political history as is H.C.R. 108 or any other congressional resolution that has been woven into the fabric of federal Indian policy.

# NOTES

1. The cases were *Sequoyah* v. *T.V.A.*, 620 F.2d. 1159 (6 Cir. 1980; cert. den., 449 U.S. 953 [1980]; *Badoni* v. *Higginson*, 638 F. 2d. 172 (10 Cir. 1980; cert. den., 452 U.S. 954, 1981), *Fools Crow* v. *Gullet*, 541 F. Supp. 785, aff'd., 706 F. 2d 856 (8 Cir. 1983; cert. den.—U.S.—, 104 U.S. 413 [1983]; *Wilson* v. *Block*, 708 F. 2d 735 (D.C. Cir. 1983; cert. den.—U.S.—, 104 U.S. 37, 1983); *Northwest Indian Cemetery Protective Association* v. *Peterson*, 565 F. Supp. 586 (1983).
2. The one exception was the *Northwest Cemetery* case.
3. *Cherokee Nation* v. *Georgia*, 5 Pet. 16 (1831).
4. Ibid., 5 Pet. 17 (1831).
5. 1 *U.S. Stat.* 50 (1787).
6. 25 Fed. Cas. 695, C. C. D. Neb. (1879).
7. 15 *U.S. Stat.* 264 (1868).
8. 112 U.S. 100 (1884).
9. 43 *U.S. Stat.* 253 (1924). Italics added.
10. 24 *U.S. Stat.* 388 (1887).
11. 241 U.S. 591, 598 (1916).
12. 8 Wheat. 543 (1823).
13. 27 *U.S. Stat.* 260 (1892).
14. 67 *U.S. Stat.* 586 (1953).
15. 6 Pet. 515 (1832).

# CHAPTER 11

# Power for New Days

## BY PETER J. POWELL

*For many years Peter J. Powell, an Anglican priest, has spent*
*summers with the Cheyennes, who have accorded him an unusual*
*place within their active religious life. He, in turn, has been impressed*
*by what he calls the beauty, the power, and the holiness of the*
*Cheyenne Way.*

*The Sacred Mountain described in the following chapter from*
*Powell's* Sweet Medicine *is known to most people as Bear Butte, a*
*remarkable land formation in western South Dakota. Bear Butte,*
*or Nowah'wus, has a special significance in Cheyenne history and*
*religion. It is the place where the Cheyenne culture hero Sweet*
*Medicine obtained the Sacred Arrows and received instruction on*
*how the people must live. Ever since, the Sacred Mountain has*
*represented Cheyenne strength and continuity, Powell's words*
*speak to the power of that place: "For those who climb*
*Nowah'wus, glimpses of the Cheyenne past still lie all around. A*
*man can look out to where the horizon seems to begin. The prairie*
*colors flow toward the four directions where the Sacred Persons*
*dwell."*

*Powell's chapter addresses the integral importance of tradition*
*and the persistence of Plains Indian life. Strange new days surely*
*do lie ahead, but they always have. In the land and in the sky of the*
*Plains, within themselves and from each other, Plains Indian*
*peoples find sustenance for the present and for the future.*

From Peter J. Powell, *Sweet Medicine: The Continuing Role of the Sacred Arrows, the Sun Dance, and the Sacred Buffalo Hat in Northern Cheyenne History*, 2 vols. (Norman: University of Oklahoma Press, 1969): 412–28. Reprinted by permission.

THROUGHOUT the passing years, Nowah'wus, the Sacred Mountain, has remained the heart of Cheyenne worship and life. The tipis of Mahuts and Is'siwun open in the direction of the Mountain. So does the Arrow Renewal Lodge and the Medicine Lodge at Sun Dance time. Even the doors of the new prefabricated houses springing up around Lame Deer, Busby, Birney, and Ashland face Nowah'wus and the East. Whenever power is needed for new days, the Cheyennes return to the Sacred Mountain.

Little Wolf's band had paused near Nowah'wus on their way north in 1879. It was at the end of that bitter winter, and they had left the sheltered valley near the forks of the Niobrara to head toward the Yellowstone once more. Little Wolf himself climbed the Sacred Mountain, carrying the Chiefs' bundle back to the Arrows' home. There the Sweet Medicine Chief fasted and prayed for the few Cheyennes left in his care, this remnant who must face the hard, new road ahead. Then Little Wolf and his people moved on toward the Yellowstone and surrender to White Hat Clark.[1]

Little Chief's people camped in the shadow of the Sacred Mountain during their journey to Indian Territory in 1878. Prisoners of war then, they all the more deeply needed the power that flows from Nowah'wus. Some of the people fasted there. Others left offering cloths to flutter from the branches of the stunted trees growing on the Mountain. As always, each Cheyenne who visited there left a stone behind. Then Little Chief's band turned their faces toward the humid south country.

Not until the winter of 1890–91 would the hearts of Little Chief's people again be gladdened by the sight of the Sacred Mountain.[2] The bands of Little Chief and Standing Elk did not join in the Ghost Dance troubles at Pine Ridge, so Agent Royer finally granted them a pass to Fort Keogh. The Cheyennes started out in the dead of winter with nearly four hundred miles of travel ahead of them. There were 276 people in all, and the journey took them almost two months. When they finally reached Keogh, they were detained there, within a hundred miles of their relatives and friends. They had expected that the military would move them to Tongue River Agency, but their passes read to Fort Keogh, and it appeared for a time that they might have to stay there. John Tulley, the newest agent at Lame Deer, wrote many letters on their behalf. However, the government red tape dragged on, and it was not until October 3, 1891, that the waiting ended and Little Chief's people joyfully

moved on to Lame Deer. There they were finally enrolled on
Tongue River reservation. Now all the Northern Cheyennes were
home.[3]

The dreary reservation years followed. A long succession of
agents discouraged Cheyenne roaming and the sacred ceremonies
themselves. Small parties occasionally managed to slip away to the
Sacred Mountain, to fast and pray there briefly. Four Cheyennes
fasted there during World War I. August Spotted Tail's Sioux
grandfather fasted there in 1913. But it was not until the 1930's that
the return to Nowah'wus gained new impetus.

Early in the 1930s Whistling Elk received a message from the
Sacred Mountain. The meaning was not clear:

The white man is going to make something that isn't big; but it is very
powerful. He is going to be known for it. Once that thing goes off, all the
world is going to know about it.

That was all the Maiyun said. Neither Whistling Elk nor his
family understood—until the bomb was dropped on Hiroshima.[4]

Then late in September, 1939, four old Cheyennes led the first
pilgrimage to the Sacred Mountain since World War I. Yellow
Nose, the warrior who captured the Custer guidon, was the oldest
member of the group. He and Low Dog had been the first Cheyennes to cross the Big Horn and face Custer's men. They had
ridden back and forth before the soldiers, slowing down their
approach. In the quieter years that followed, Yellow Nose had
become respected for his healing power.[5]

Three other old warriors were with him: Nelson Medicine Bird,
the Keeper of the Elk Society bundle; John Black Wolf; and
Charles Spotted Elk, who had told Black Bird to open Is'siwun for
Hugh Scott. There were younger men, too. Most of them were
members of the Northern Cheyenne Tribal Council: Eugene
Fisher, the president; John Stands in Timber, then a judge of the
tribal court; Rufus Wallowing, the chief of police at Lame Deer;
Eugene Limpy, Pat Spotted Wolf, and Dallas Wolf Black, all
members of the Council. Most of the men were members of the
warrior societies as well. James Fisher, Eugene Fisher's son, came
along also.

Eugene Fisher stated that the purpose of this pilgrimage was to
assist a local committee in determining Bear Butte's history, especially as it related to the Indians who had lived there before 1876.

The local committee was hoping to have Bear Butte designated a national monument.[6] However, the main purpose of the Cheyenne visit was to allow the old men to worship on the Sacred Mountain once more.[7]

A drizzling rain prevented their ascent on September 28.[8] Instead, the four older Cheyennes spent hours at the base of Nowah'wus, praying and meditating upon the holiness of the place. They smiled when they discovered, near the western base of the butte, the stone tipi rings of earlier camps. They also found an eagle pit, and they recalled the old-time ceremony of capturing the bird who is so close to Thunder himself. Near Fort Meade they located sandstone boulders scarred with deep grooves in which arrowheads and spearheads had been sharpened. One of the men used his cane to overturn several stones which marked the location of a sweat lodge.

These discoveries were greeted almost silently, for the solemnity of this return filled the thoughts of all the men. Later they described Sweet Medicine's pilgrimage to the Sacred Mountain. They also said that it was from this mountain that the people had received the Buffalo Hat. Now the old Suhtai mountain in the north also had become identified with Nowah'wus. Yellow Nose and the others hunted for the door through which Sweet Medicine had entered the lodge in the mountain, but they were unable to find it.

The old men also spoke of the Cheyenne claim to the Black Hills. They said that the Cheyennes controlled the region until about 1850. Then the Sioux started gaining control of the land through treaties with the whites, and finally the Cheyennes themselves were forced to leave the area.

On September 29, Nelson Medicine Bird climbed to the summit of the Sacred Mountain. He stood there praying, asking Maheo to bless the nation and all the people who lived in it. Then Medicine Bird left an offering cloth behind. When the Cheyennes left for Tongue River Agency, they promised to return the next year.

Then World War II came. At the beginning of the war years David Deafy, a younger man, had a dream. In his dream he saw four men standing in a row, one behind the other. The men were naked, and their bodies were covered with yellow paint. They stood motionless as they prayed. Deafy was too young to have gone on the old pilgrimages to the Sacred Mountain. Therefore, he carried a pipe to Whistling Elk, asking to interpret the dream.

In August, 1944, the dream was repeated. This time a voice
spoke to Deafy. Deafy said nothing about this until he had carried
the pipe to Whistling Elk again. Whistling Elk replied that this was
the way Sweet Medicine had said it would be. The Sacred Powers
wanted four men to go to Nowah'wus, because the Cheyennes
were troubled and were attempting to find a way to end the war.

When Deafy heard this, he vowed that he would go to the Sacred
Mountain.[9]

Even in Northern Cheyenne country, the hardships of the faraway war were being felt in new ways. John Stands in Timber
wrote to the Chamber of Commerce at Sturgis, South Dakota, the
city located near the Sacred Mountain. He asked for food and other
help for the Cheyennes while they were camped near Bear Butte.
The Chamber of Commerce promised to help, but again government red tape blocked the Cheyennes. This time the Office of Price
Administration refused to give them the gasoline ration stamps
needed to buy fuel for the journey. Deafy's pilgrimage was delayed
another year.

Even after a year, it seemed that Deafy would have to climb the
Sacred Mountain by himself. However, the day before he planned
to leave the reservation, three other men volunteered to fast with
him. They were Bert Two Moon, grandson of the old Chief; Albert
Tall Bull; and Mike Little Wolf. Whistling Elk was their instructor.
John Stands in Timber went along to interpret. Twenty-one people
made their trip altogether.

The four fasters started up the Sacred Mountain the first week in
June, 1945. Whistling Elk had told them to pray hard for all the
boys in the armed services, for all the boys who had lost their lives,
and for all the people of America. He reminded Deafy and his
companions that Sweet Medicine had first brought the Sacred
Arrows from this mountain, and that the Prophet had told the
Cheyennes to fast there in order to receive blessings.[10]

An afternoon storm had sprung up that day. However, it had
passed by the time the party of twenty-one Cheyennes left the foot
of the Sacred Mountain. Halfway up they paused on a prominent
point. Bedrolls were spread for the men who would be fasting; two
on the south side, two more on the southwest.

Deafy and his companions stripped to their breechclouts. Then
Whistling Elk painted their bodies yellow, the old Sun color. As
sunset arrived, he told them to form a line—just as Deafy had seen

the men standing in his dream. Whistling Elk climbed to a spot just above them, and the other Cheyennes moved down below, where they stood looking at the fasters. As darkness drew on, the air became crisp. Some eight hundred feet below, blinking lights marked the automobiles on the road and the scattered homes and ranches in the distance.

The four men stood there for over an hour, constantly praying. Then, as darkness all but hid them, the fasters moved up higher on Nowah'wus. They were wrapped in their blankets, and each man carried a pipe. Meanwhile, the other Cheyennes moved down the steep side of the butte to the camp below.

Deafy described the fast afterward. "We never rested. We prayed every minute of every hour for four days, and suffered awful without food, but especially without water."[11]

On the morning of the second day, Mike Little Wolf noticed black marks on the back of Deafy's hands. The marks were triangular, like the shape of the Sacred Mountain itself. Deafy had no idea how the marks had gotten there.

It was on the morning of the fourth day that the vision came. Deafy saw a rider on top of the Sacred Mountain. The rider was facing east. Suddenly he charged. His horse galloped past Deafy at full speed, and on down the side of the mountain. However, nothing happened to either horse or rider.

Soon the horse and rider appeared again. Once more the horse charged down toward the foot of the mountain. As they went by, Deafy noticed that there was a boy sitting behind the rider. Again, they reached the bottom safely.

When evening of the fourth day arrived, Deafy and his companions moved down to the camp below. Whistling Elk was waiting for them there. Each man took a swallow of water every fifteen minutes during the first hour, four swallows in all. Next, food was offered to the Sacred Persons and to Maheo. Then the fasters ate a little food every fifteen minutes. Thus they ate four times during the first hour after their fast ended.

Whistling Elk listened quietly as Deafy spoke of his vision. Then the priest interpreted it. The first rider was the first nation American fought—Germany. "We have beaten them," the priest said. Two riders appeared the second time. They represented the second country that America was fighting—Japan. "When the wild strawberries get ripe; that is when we will lick the Japanese,"

Whistling Elk said. He also interpreted the black marks on Deafy's hands. They were the color of the old black charcoal paint used to cover the faces of victorious warriors in the old days. So they, also, showed that America would win the war.[12]

Deafy's vision came in June, 1945, a month after Germany had surrendered. In August, Japan also fell.

In September, 1945, Baldwin Twins, Keeper of Mahuts, led a pilgrimage to the Arrows' home. A tipi was erected near the base of Nowah'wus. The Arrow bundle was opened, and Mahuts were exposed upon a bed of sacred white sage and offering cloths. The Keeper offered prayers of thanksgiving for the peace that had come to the nation.[13]

The old pattern of Cheyenne worship at the Sacred Mountain had been restored.

By the fall of 1950, the Korean war was raging, and the nation once more needed prayers. So David Deafy returned to the Sacred Mountain. Thirteen Cheyennes made the trip with him, all of them piled into one old car. Among them was Deafy's son, who had vowed to fast with his father.[14]

Again camp was made at the foot of the Sacred Mountain. The fasters' bodies were painted yellow, and they offered the pipe to the Sacred Persons and to Maheo. Deafy and his son climbed up the mountain. They were carrying their pipes and about seventy-five offering cloths—gifts from the Cheyennes who were not able to come.

The men fasted for two days. Each morning and evening they offered their pipes to Maheo and the Sacred Persons. The cloths also were offered above and to the four directions. Then the men tied them to the stunted trees and bushes growing around them. They first tied a loose knot in each cloth, offering a prayer as they did so. After that, a second knot was tied and pulled tight. This was a prayer for long life for the person who had sent the offering cloth.

While Deafy and his son lay fasting, they were stretched out upon beds of white sage. They were permitted to lie face up or face down, but they had to keep the position all day long. At morning and at nightfall, they sat up long enough to offer the pipe to Maheo and the Maheyuno. They were praying continually; for the soldiers in Korea, for the Cheyennes in the hospital, for the boys in the penitentiary, and for all the Cheyenne people.

Once, while Deafy was praying with the pipe, a bird sat nearby.

Deafy told his son that this was a Maiyun who had come to listen. Then the bird flew down into the side of Nowah'wus, into the entrance to the Sacred Mountain itself.

There was no vision this time. However, Deafy's son who was fighting in Korea returned, and so did the other Cheyenne soldiers.

In June, 1951, Whistling Elk again instructed fasters on the Sacred Mountain. Again four men came with him. Albert Tall Bull and Bert Two Moon had fasted there before. Charles White Dirt and Willis Medicine Bull had come to fast there for the first time. They were coming to fast for peace.

On June 7, the four men stripped to their breechclouts and Whistling Elk painted them. Wrapped in their robes, with pipes in their hands, they climbed Nowah'wus to begin their fast. They stayed there without food or water four days. At the foot of the mountain, some forty of the people watched and prayed.

When the fasters came down, Whistling Elk again listened to their experiences. Two Moon had seen a vision of many people. White Dirt said that a blue cloud and blue flame had appeared before him. Albert Tall Bull said that while he was listening to a Maiyun's voice, his partner coughed and he missed the message. Medicine Bull did not see a vision, but he left the mountain with a good feeling. However, after he returned to Birney, he dreamed that the war talk would go on, but the war itself gradually would go away. "I did not hear a voice. But it came to my mind in a dream afterward," he said.[15]

Whistling Elk's interpretation of the fasters' experiences was that the Korean War would end before four months had passed or before the snow would fall.[16]

Throughout later years, Whistling Elk's reputation as a priest had grown among the Northern Cheyennes. It was he who instructed many of the men who offered a solitary sacrifice of their bodies in the pine hills. He was the man to whom the fasters on the Sacred Mountain first carried the pipe. He was a Sun Dance priest, and younger priests often asked his guidance during the Medicine Lodge ceremonies. He and his family were prominent Crazy Dogs. The Cheyennes also respected him for his understanding of the animals, birds, and natural forces.

Old Brady was Whistling Elk's father. During the long years of government suppression of the sacred ways, Brady often spoke longingly of Nowah'wus. "When I die, I am going to the Sacred

Mountain. I am going to be a servant there,'' the old warrior told his family. Brady was over ninety-five years old when he died in 1936.[17] Whistling Elk himself died in 1958. It is said that Whistling Elk, the man who once stood against Thunder, joined his father in fulfilling that wish to return to the Sacred Mountain.

When Mike Little Wolf and George Elk Shoulder vowed to fast on Nowah'wus in 1961, they carried the pipe to Willis Medicine Bull. The long-haired Medicine Bull was a Sun Dance Instructor, and, as a young man, he had taken part in the Contrary dances. He was respected as a man of good disposition, one who possessed power in the sacred ways.

Their ascent of Nowah'wus was a quiet one.[18] One of the men carried the buffalo skull, as well as sage and a pipe. They paused part way up the mountain. There Medicine Bull filled the pipe and offered it. He called upon the Sacred Powers, begging their blessings upon the two men who had vowed this fast. He asked the Maiyun to bless the families of Little Wolf and Elk Shoulder and to give them good health. Then he prayed for all people, including the white people. ''Now we beg you Powers to renew all the things that have been almost forgotten, through these men who are going to fast. Carry them through the next four days,'' he begged.

Medicine Bull painted the two men with the yellow paint. He told them to keep in mind the purpose of their fast, the bringing of blessings to the Cheyenne people and to their own immediate relatives. ''Fill the pipe. Offer it to Maheo and to Sweet Medicine,'' he told Little Wolf and Elk Shoulder. Then the two men moved on up the Sacred Mountain.

Shortly after sunrise of the fourth day, Medicine Bull heard a whistling sound. He looked up and saw something coming down like a bullet. It was a swift hawk. ''I told them that this was the power that they had asked for through four days and nights. Both of them felt good. After they got through the ceremonies, they ate and drank and left for Sheridan the same day,'' he later recounted.

Four years later, in August, 1965, Cheyenne pilgrims again traveled to the Sacred Mountain. This time a new Arrow Keeper was among them. He was James Medicine Elk, a Northerner who had married among the Southern Cheyennes. As a boy he had taken part in the Massaum ceremony in Oklahoma, and the people there respected him as an Arrow Lodge priest. He had been chosen Keeper several years before.

Jay Black Kettle's eyesight had been growing bad. Finally, in 1963, he had asked the Southern Chiefs and military leaders to choose a new Keeper.[19] Again there was trouble finding a man. The chiefs had offered the position to three persons, and each had refused it. James Medicine Elk and his family had cared for Jay Black Kettle during the past several years, and Medicine Elk told the Chiefs that he would care for Mahuts until they found a permanent Keeper.

Again there had been rumors, this time that Mahuts were to be placed in a museum in Oklahoma City. This news disturbed Medicine Elk. One Sunday morning he said to his wife Jennie and to her sister, Bertha Little Coyote:

You are women, but I will tell you this: I am taking this tipi this fine morning. I will be the Keeper. I love this sacred way, and I don't want Mahuts to be put in a museum. They were brought to us from the Sacred Mountain, and we should take care of them.

I am from the north, but they belong to you Southerners. I say this: I love you all. I feel I am one of you now. I have a family here.

. . . I want everybody to be happy and well, for I will be Keeper now. I will go inside [the sacred tipi], make a fire and smoke the pipe.

The women cried a little when they heard that. Their tears were part joy, part sorrow. The Arrow Keeper must stay home always—he can no longer go out to work. Now Jennie Medicine Elk was worried about how they would live. However, Bertha Little Coyote comforted her. She said to her brother-in-law, "I am happy over it. I am sure the Almighty can see that you know what you are doing, and that you will never be without food."

Medicine Elk vowed that someday he would go to the Sacred Mountain. "I will report that I look after this tipi, and I will tell our Grandfathers [the Sacred Powers] that I am Keeper," he told the women.

In June, 1965, Medicine Elk had traveled north to Lame Deer in an attempt to get his claims funds there. Jay Black guarded the Arrows while he was away. One day while Medicine Elk was in Lame Deer, Charles White Dirt called him over to Alex Brady's house. Alex was Whistling Elk's youngest brother. The two men told the Keeper that they were going to fast on Nowah'wus. Medicine Elk replied that he would be happy to go with them, so he could fulfill his promise to report to the Grandfathers there.

However, no date was set for the fast, and Medicine Elk finally returned to Oklahoma. Late in August, he received word from Sturgis that the Cheyennes were going to fast on the Sacred Mountain soon. When he heard that, the Arrow Keeper, his wife, and his sister-in-law hurried back to Lame Deer. There Mike Little Wolf told Medicine Elk what he would need in the way of preparations for the fast, and he offered to supply the Keeper with everything necessary for fulfilling his vow.

They reached the Sacred Mountain late in the afternoon of August 26. Willis Medicine Bull had been chosen the chief instructor by the Northern Cheyennes. Mike Little Wolf and George Elk Shoulder were assisting him. Albert Tall Bull had joined the Keeper, White Dirt, and Brady, making four fasters, the sacred number. Brady's nephew, Henry Tall Bull, came along to interpret. So did Sam Buffalo, the Southern Cheyenne leader who assisted in returning Mahuts to Oklahoma in 1957. There were some forty Cheyennes altogether. Most of them camped in a ravine near the foot of the butte, with the Northern and Southern people in separate camps.

Medicine Bull asked the Arrow Keeper to take the lead. As the sun lay low over the Sacred Mountain, the four fasters, their families, and the instructors started up the southern face of Nowah'wus. They stopped on a small knoll. Medicine Elk and his companions spread their robes upon beds of white "man" sage.

The fasters stripped to their breechclouts, and Medicine Bull, Little Wolf, and Elk Shoulder began to paint their bodies yellow.[20] Mike Little Wolf painted the Arrow Keeper first and took care of him throughout the preparations for the ascent. Medicine Bull painted Brady and Tall Bull. George Elk Shoulder painted White Dirt. After the yellow paint had been rubbed on, the Sun symbol was painted on each faster's chest and the Moon symbol on each man's right shoulder blade. A dark lightning mark was traced around each faster's face, and a lizard was painted on either side of each man's nose. This design represented the Maiyun who takes the form of this tiny reptile, which has great power to resist the elements.

Medicine Bull prepared the buffalo skull, the sacred symbol of Is'siwun's presence among the people. He offered the prayers, made the four forward motions, and moved the skull so that it faced where the fasters would rest. Now Is'siwun would be watching them and blessing them in their sacrifice.

The priests and fasters seated themselves in a half circle around the buffalo head. A cold wind was rising, and the four men pulled their blankets around them. The pipe was filled and offered. Prayers were offered to Maheo and to the Sacred Persons at the four directions. Medicine Bull rested the pipe bowl upon the earth, while the Arrow Keeper and his three companions inhaled smoke from it four times. The fasters made the purifying gestures, covering their limbs, bodies, and heads with smoke from the pipe that never fails to bring a blessing. Then the pipe was passed around the half circle four times.

While these ceremonies continued, the other Cheyennes stood looking on from a respectful distance. When the smoking ended, the relatives returned to the camp below. A number of Sioux families had driven up from Rapid City to join their old-time allies in the prayers and waiting. White spectators also were looking on. On the side of the Sacred Mountain above them, the Arrow Keeper and his companions were beginning their fast. They were praying for peace in Vietnam, for all the Cheyenne people, and for the nation as a whole. Henry Tall Bull had said, "We all realize the seriousness of the war, and this is our way of helping."

The third night, the men had offered the pipes, smoked, and gone to bed. Medicine Elk was lying there in the darkness, thinking. It was very quiet, and he thought that he was the only one who was awake. Then a voice spoke from the head of his bed, from the north. It sounded like the voice of an older man. "You are going to get blessings," the voice said. Just then White Dirt spoke, and the Arrow Keeper did not hear any more. Then Medicine Elk sat up and loaded his pipe. He wept as he sat there praying.[21]

Shortly after sunrise of the fourth day, Willis Medicine Bull led the fasters down from the mountain. It was Sunday, August 29. They reached the bottom at about the same time astronauts Gordon Cooper and Charles Conrad came back to earth from outer space.[22] Mike Little Wolf removed the Arrow Keeper's paint with sacred sage. Medicine Bull and Elk Shoulder did the same for the other men. Each man first was given his four mouthfuls of water, with an interval between each drink. Jennie Medicine Elk and Bertha Little Coyote had prepared food for the Arrow Keeper. The relatives of the other men had done the same. Mike Little Wolf offered the first food to the Sacred Persons and to Maheo for Medicine Elk. Then the Keeper ate, and the other men broke their fast at the same time.

That afternoon a public program was held in honor of the Cheyennes. Richard B. Williams, the interpretive specialist at Bear Butte State Park, introduced the fasters and instructors.

Henry Tall Bull told the crowd that the four men had related their experiences to Medicine Bull, and that it would take some time before the experiences could be properly interpreted. "They came here to pray for peace, not by guided missiles, but by guided men," he said. "The medicine man told me to withhold a prediction at this time as their dreams or visions will be explained at a later date. It takes time to interpret their meaning."[23]

For those who climb Nowah'wus, glimpses of the Cheyenne past still lie all around. A man can look out to where the horizon seems to begin. The prairie colors flow toward the four directions where the Sacred Persons dwell. In late August the greens, blues, yellows, and browns of summer are tinted by the shades of the autumn that comes early in the north country. The old Cheyenne sites lie below. The remains of the eagle-catching pit were there when Medicine Elk fasted on Nowah'wus. So was the spring from which the people once dug blue clay—the clay used to paint the old-time parfleches which, like so many other beautiful objects, perished in the fires of Morning Star's burning camp. Much of Cheyenne history still can be traced around the Sacred Mountain, if a man knows where to look.

Today there are new sights that mingle with the old. Now the Cheyennes can see the impression of a narrow trail that stretches around much of the base of the Sacred Mountain. Now, to the north, the west, and the northeast, Minuteman missiles lie hidden beneath the earth. Their wires encircle Nowah'wus, the ancient source of new life for the Cheyenne people.

Henry Tall Bull has spoken of the messages that still reach Cheyennes who have the ears to listen:

The Above Powers have sent a sign from the Sacred Mountain saying that someone must return there. There are three or four men who have the feeling they should go.

They are going to get another thing from there—something that will save the Cheyennes from this new destructive power the white people have developed.

Whistling Elk used to be the man who make the pilgrimages. Now he is gone. Now the people feel it is necessary for someone to go back. They feel that time is an important factor now.

Someone is being selected who has a lot of faith. . . .[24]

In their first ancient days of despair, Maheo sent his People the Sacred Arrows that, for some of them at least, remain the soul of Cheyenne tribal existence. Since then, in nearly every generation the Cheyennes have known that someone must return to Nowah'wus; someone must represent the People on the windblown sides of the Sacred Mountain. For power in abundance awaits the Cheyennes there; strength like the power flowing from Mahuts themselves.

Blessed by the Sacred Arrows, the Sacred Buffalo Hat, and the strength that pours from Nowah'wus, the Sacred Mountain, all will be well for Maheo's People, even in the strange new days that lie ahead.

# NOTES

1. Mari Sandoz, *Cheyenne Autumn* (New York: McGraw-Hill, 1953), pp. 258–59.

2. Yellow Nose, Spotted Elk, Medicine Bird, et al., are quoted as saying that *all* the Northern Cheyennes made the pilgrimage in 1891. This is extremely unlikely, in view of the unsettled conditions at that time. Most of Yellow Nose's party had been with Little Chief's band, and all of that band had stopped there on the way back to Keogh.
Cf. Thomas E. Odell, *Mato Paha, The Story of Bear Butte* (Spearfish, S. Dak.: n.p., 1942), p. 150.

3. "Census of the Pine Ridge Northern Cheyenne Indians Transferred from Fort Keogh, Mont., to Tongue River Agency, Mont., October 3rd, 1891," Tongue River Agency papers, National Archives. Cf. Verne Dusenberry, "The Northern Cheyenne," *Montana Heritage Series* (Helena, Mont.: State Historical Society Press, n.d.), pp. 16–18. Standing Elk's band had been transferred from Indian Territory to Pine Ridge in 1883.

4. Whistling Elk to his nephew, Henry Tall Bull. Tall Bull to the author, 1959.

5. John Stands in Timber to the author, 1957. Cf. "Crayon Drawings of Cheyenne Ceremonial Customs and Implements," Daniel Little Chief, Drawing 11, MS 2016–A, National Anthropological Archives, Smithsonian Institution.

6. Odell, *Mato Paha*, p. 140.

7. John Stands in Timber and Rufus Wallowing to the author, 1958.

8. The account of the ascent is from Odell, *Mato Paha*, pp. 141–43. Cf. *Rapid City Daily Journal*, September 29, 1939.

9. *Sturgis Tribune*, June 7, 1945.

10. John Stands in Timber to the author, 1958.

11. *Sturgis Tribune*, June 7, 1945.

12. Details of the vision are from Henry Tall Bull and John Stands in Timber, 1958–59. The *Sturgis Tribune* gave a different version. It stated that the black marks on Deafy's hands represented the old black color of victory. The mark on the left hand was the fainter of the two. It showed the defeat of Germany. The darker mark on the right hand showed that Japan soon would be beaten. The two appearances of the horseman were symbols of victory. The rider and child represented safety for the American people—both old and young.

13. See *Sweet Medicine*, chap. 27, "The Sacred Arrows Come North"; Cf. *Sturgis Tribune*, September 13, 1945.

14. This account is from Deafy's son to the author, during the 1961 Sun Dance. Cf. "Lame Deer Indians Fast, Pray for Peace on South Dakota Mountain," *The Billings Gazette*, October 8, 1850.

15. Willis Medicine Bull to the author, 1961.

16. Ibid. Whistling Elk's prediction was announced to the United States forces in Korea via a headline in the *Stars and Stripes*. The headline said: "War End? Ugh!" *Sturgis Tribune*, July 5, 1951.

17. Henry Tall Bull, grandson of Brady, to the author, 1961.

18. This account is from Willis Medicine Bull to the author, 1961.

19. James Medicine Elk to the author, March 1967.

20. These details are from James Medicine Elk and Sam Buffalo to the author, 1965. Also, *Rapid City Daily Journal*, August 27, 1965; *Black Hills* (Sturgis) *Press*, August 28, 1965; *Sturgis Tribune*, September 1, 1965.

21. James Medicine Elk to the author, March 1967.

22. This observation by Richard B. Williams, the interpretive specialist at Bear Butte State Park. He had long assisted the Cheyennes during their pilgrimages to the Sacred Mountain.

23. *Sturgis Tribune*, September 1, 1965.

24. To the author, August 1959; repeated in August, 1969.

# The Contributors

DONALD J. BERTHRONG is Chairman of the Department of History and Professor of History in Purdue University. He received the Ph.D. from the University of Wisconsin. He is continuing his study of the Cheyenne-Arapahoes of Oklahoma and is the author of *The Southern Cheyennes* and *The Cheyenne and Arapaho Ordeal: Reservation and Agency Life in the Indian Territory, 1875–1907*, both published by the University of Oklahoma Press. Berthrong has been a Fulbright professor and has served as an expert witness in court cases for the Cheyennes.

JOSEPH H. CASH is Dean of the College of Arts and Sciences in the University of South Dakota. He received the Ph.D. from the University of Iowa. At the University of South Dakota, he directed the Doris Duke Indian Oral History Project. Among his publications is *The Mandan, Arikara, and Hidatsa People*.

VINE DELORIA, JR. (Standing Rock Sioux), is Professor of Political Science in the University of Arizona. He received the J.D. from the University of Colorado. He is the author of many books, including *Custer Died for Your Sins, God Is Red*, and *Behind the Trail of Broken Treaties: An Indian Declaration of Independence*. Formerly Executive Director of the National Congress of American Indians, Deloria is a leading spokesman on contemporary Indian affairs.

DONALD L. FIXICO (Creek, Seminole, Sac and Fox, Shawnee) is Assistant Professor of History in the University of Wisconsin, Milwaukee. He received the Ph.D. from the University of Oklahoma and is completing for publication a revision of his dissertation, "Termination and Relocation: Federal Indian Policy, 1945–1960." Fixico has held fellowships at the Newberry Library's D'Arcy McNickle Center for the History of the American Indian and at the University of California, Los Angeles, American Indian Studies Center.

LORETTA FOWLER is Associate Professor of Anthropology in the City College of New York and Senior Research Associate of the Institute for the Study of Human Issues. She received the Ph.D. from the University of Illinois. She is the author of *Arapahoe Politics, 1851–1978: Symbols in Crises of Authority*, winner of the Erminie Wheeler-Voegelin Prize for 1982, presented by the American Society for Ethnohistory. Fowler has also carried out extensive research in Gros Ventre history.

WILLIAM T. HAGAN is Distinguished Professor of History in the State University of New York College at Fredonia. He received the Ph.D. from the University of Wisconsin. He is the author of many books, including *The Sac and Fox Indians* (published by the University of Oklahoma Press), *United States-Comanche Relations: The Reservation Years*, and *The Indian Rights Association: The Herbert Welsh Years, 1882–1904*. He is past president of the Western History Association and the American Society for Ethnohistory.

TOM HOLM (Cherokee and Creek) is Assistant Professor of Political Science in the University of Arizona. He received the Ph.D. from the University of Oklahoma; his dissertation is entitled "Indians and Progressives: Indian-White Relations, 1898–1922." He is coeditor of *Indian Leaders: Oklahoma's First Statesmen* and has contributed to many journals.

HERBERT T. HOOVER is Professor of History in the University of South Dakota and has served as Acting Director of the Newberry Library's Indian History Center. He received the Ph.D. from the University of Oklahoma. He was Research Associate for the Doris Duke Indian Oral History Project at the University of South Dakota and is the author of *To Be an Indian* and *The Chitimacha People*, and is the coauthor of *Bibliography of the Sioux*.

FREDERICK HOXIE is Director of the D'Arcy McNickle Center for the History of the American Indian at the Newberry Library.

He received the Ph.D. from Brandeis University. He is the author of *A Final Promise: The Campaign to Assimilate the Indians, 1880–1920*. Aided by a Rockefeller Foundation fellowship, he is currently working on a study of Crow life in Montana in the late nineteenth and early twentieth centuries.

NORRIS HUNDLEY, JR., is Professor of History in the University of California, Los Angeles, and Managing Editor of the *Pacific Historical Review*. He received the Ph.D. from the University of California at Los Angeles. He is the author of several books, including *Water and the West: The Colorado River Compact and the Politics of Water in the American West*. He is a recipient of a Guggenheim Foundation fellowship and is currently working on a history of Indian water rights.

PETER IVERSON, Professor of History in the University of Wyoming, received the Ph.D. from the University of Wisconsin. He is the author of *The Navajo Nation* and *Carlos Montezuma and the Changing World of American Indians*. He has held fellowships from the National Endowment for the Humanities and the W. K. Kellogg Foundation and is now working on a study of modern relations between white ranchers and Indians.

MICHAEL L. LAWSON is Staff Historian with the Bureau of Indian Affairs in Washington, D.C. He holds the Ph.D. from the University of New Mexico and is the author of *Dammed Indians: The Pick-Sloan Plan and the Missouri River Sioux, 1944–1980*, published by the University of Oklahoma Press in 1982. His article ''Indian Heirship Lands: The Lake Traverse Experience'' earned the Ray A. Billington Award of the Western History Association in 1983.

PETER J. POWELL is an Anglican priest with the Saint Augustine's Indian Center in Chicago and is a Research Associate of the Newberry Library. He is the author of *Sweet Medicine: The Continuing Role of the Sacred Arrows, the Sun Dance, and the Sacred Buffalo Hat in Northern Cheyenne History* (published by the University of Oklahoma Press in 1969) and *People of the Sacred Mountain: A History of the Northern Cheyenne Chiefs and Warrior Societies, 1830–1879, with an Epilogue, 1969–1974*. The latter received the American Book Award for history in 1982.

# INDEX

Allen, Edgar A.: 40
Allotment: on Comanche, Kiowa, and Kiowa-Apache Reservation, 13–15, 19, 21, 24, 27–28; on Cheyenne River Reservation, 62; *see also* General Allotment Act
Amax Coal Company: 224–25
American Association on Indian Affairs: 162
American Copper: 227
*American Indian* Magazine: 162
American Indian Religious Freedom Resolution: 238, 245–47
Amoco Production Company: 229
Anadarko, Okla.: 21–26, 125, 141
Annapolis, Md.: 155
Apache Indian Industries: 229
Apache John: 13
Apiatan (Kiowa chief): 13–14
Appalachia: 227
Arapahoe, Wyo.: 205
Arapahoe Business Council, on Wind River Reservation: 187–89, 192–204, 208–15
Arapahoe Ranch (Wind River Reservation): 199, 211
Arapahoes, Northern: 146–47; on Wind River Reservation, 187–215; mineral resources of, 229
Arapahoes, Southern: 140; allotment policy for, 31–35, 38–49
Arikara Indians: 172
Arkansas: 181
Armstrong, O. K.: 161–63

Arrow Keeper (Cheyenne): 257–60
Arrow Renewal Lodge (Cheyenne): 250, 257
Ashland, Mont.: 250
Assiniboine Indians: 77, 79–80, 225

Bailey, Joseph: 16–17
Baldwin, Frank; 14
Bear Butte, S.Dak.: 249, 251–53, 261; *see also* Nowah'wus, S.Dak.
Beatty, Willard: 116
Berry, E. Y.: 176
Big Bend Dam (South Dakota): 169, 171–72, 177
Big Horn River: 251
Big Pasture (Oklahoma): 15–16, 23, 26
Big Wolf: 38
Bill of Rights, U.S. Constitution: 152, 240–42, 244
Birney, Mont.: 250, 256
Black, Ernie: 47
Black Bird: 251
Black Eagle, Oliver: 66
Blackfoot Indians: creation of reservation for, 80; water rights of, 88; participation in World War II by, 149, 160; mineral resources of, 226, 230
Blackfoot band (Sioux): 58–60
Black Hills (South Dakota): 57, 227–28, 252
Black Hills Alliance: 228
Black Kettle, Jay: 258
Blackman, John P.: 27–28
Blacks: 153, 158
Black Wolf, John: 251
Blaine County, Okla.: 35, 46
Blocker Drilling, Ltd.: 226

Blue Sky Hall (Wind River Reservation): 190
Board of Indian Commissioners: 37, 48
Bonnin, Gertrude: 6
Brady, Alex: 258–59
Brady, Old: 256–57
Broken Arrow, Okla.: 154
Bruner, Joseph: 107
Buffalo, Sam: 259
Buffalo hat (Cheyenne): 252, 262
Burke Act: 31, 37, 43
Burnett, Samuel B.: 16–17
Burris, Wyo.: 190, 210
Busby, Mont.: 250

California: 130, 143, 145
Canada: 86
Cantonment Agncy: 39, 41–42, 47, 140
Carlisle Indian Industrial School (Pennsylvania): 5, 13, 22–23, 39, 43–44, 47
Carnegie, Okla.: 4
Carter, Thomas: 86
Cashmere, Wash.: 153
Century Mining Corp.: 227
Chandler, Joseph: 15
Charger's Camp (Cheyenne River Reservation): 59
Cherokee Commission: 11
Cherokee Indians: 155, 246
*Cherokee Nation* v. *Georgia*: 90, 246
Cherry Creek, S.Dak.: 58–61, 63, 66, 69–70
Chevron Corp.: 224, 227
Cheyenne and Arapaho Competency Board: 47

269

Cheyenne-Arapaho Reservation: 31, 33–35
Cheyenne River Reservation: 133, 136; response of, to Americanization era, 55, 57–72; in Indian New Deal, 113; affected by Pick-Sloan Plan, 171–73, 176, 178
Cheyennes: and World War II, 149; and Nowah'wus, 249–55, 259–62; see also Northern Cheyennes, Southern Cheyennes
Cheyennes, Northern: enrollment in tribe, 193; mineral resources of, 219–24; and Nowah'wus, 251, 253, 256–57, 259
Cheyennes, Southern: consequences of allotment policy for, 31–36, 38–49, 55; and Nowah'wus, 257–59
Chickasaw Indians: 3
Chickasha, Okla.: 12
Chilocco Indian School (Oklahoma): 8, 22, 44
Chinook, Mont.: 81
*Chinook Opinion*: 90, 95
Chippewa-Crees: 226
Chiricahua Apache Indians: 242
Choctaw Indians: 13
*Christian Century*: 160
Christianity: in Americanization era, 4, 6, 32–33, 35, 58; in new Deal, 124; on Wind River Reservation, 190–91; and federal policy, 245
Citizenship: 151–52, 243–44
Civil War: 154
Clark, Joseph J. ("Jocko"): 155
Clark, White Hat: 250
Claymore, Bazile: 66
Cleveland, Pres. Grover: 81
Cloud Chief (Cheyenne): 38
Cohen, Felix: 120–21
Collier, John: program of, 6–7, 175, 188; im-

pact of program in Dakotas, 107, 110–11, 114, 120–21, 123–26; and World War II, 152–54; criticism of, by non-Indians, 160–61, 163
Colorado Fuel and Iron Corp.: 228
Colorado River Reservation: 157
Comanches: 135, 141,143; opening of reservation, 11–12, 15–16, 18–23, 26–28
Comprehensive Employment and Training Act: 195
Concho Agency: 43, 45
Congressional Medal of Honor: 154
Conover, George W.: 15
Conrad, Charles: 260
*Conrad* v. *U.S.*: 88
Consolidation Coal Corp.: 224
Contraries (Cheyennes): 257
Coolidge, Sherman: 6
Cooper, Gordon: 260
Council of Energy Resource Tribes (CERT): 226–27
Court of Indian Offenses: 14, 59
Cox, Emmett: 15
Crazy Dogs (Cheyennes): 256
Creek Indians: 107, 154
Crow Creek Reservation: 142; and Indian New Deal 111, 113; affected by Pick-Sloan, 171–73, 176–77
Crow Feather, James: 63–64, 66
Crowheart, Wyo.: 190. 210
Crows: 137–39; and World War II, 156; mineral resources of, 219–20, 223–25, 230
Curtis, Charles: 16
Custer, George: 251
Cyprus Exploration: 227

Damson, Barrie L.: 229
Damson Oil Corp.: 226, 229

Darlington Agency: 38, 40–41
Datel Co.: 192–93
Davis, Charles: 68
Dawes, Henry L.: and General Allotment Act, 4; and leasing of Cheyenne-Arapaho lands, 34; and Great Sioux Agreement of 1889, 56–57, 59, 65
Dawes Act: see General Allotment Act
Dawes Commission: 154
Deafy, David: 252–56
Denver, Colo.: 227
Dewey, John: 116
Dewey County, S.Dak.: 70
Diker, Fred: 120–21
Distinguished Service Cross: 154
Dog Soldiers (Cheyennes): 38
Douglas Aircraft Co.: 143
Downs, Randolph C.: 163
DuBray, Alfred: 108, 125–32
Ducheneaux, Frank: 176
Duncan, Okla.: 17, 28
Dupree, S.Dak.: 71

Eagle Butte, S.Dak.: 4
Eastman, Dr. Charles: 6
Economic Development Administration: 179, 192–93
Education: in Americanization era, 22–23, 59–60, 69–71; in Indian New Deal, 114, 116–17, 120, 126–28; in contemporary era, 194–95, 201, 205, 214
Eels, Walter C.: 163
Eighteenth Amendment, U.S. Constitution: 244
Eisenhower administration: 7
Elk, John: 242
Elk Shoulder, George: 257, 259–60
*Elk* v. *Wilkins*: 242
El Reno, Okla.: 18
Emerson, Haven: 162–63
Endicott Copper Corp.: 227

*End of the Trail* (statue): 56
Energy Resources Co.: 227
Energy Transportation Systems, Inc.: 181, 227
English language: 4, 112, 201
Eschiti, and opening of Comanche, Kiowa, Kiowa-Apache lands: 12–14, 23–24, 27
Ethete, Wyo.: 147, 189–91, 201, 205
Europe: 245
Exxon Corp.: 227

Faith, S.Dak.: 4
Farming: on Comanche, Kiowa, and Kiowa-Apache lands, 15; on Cheyenne-Arapaho lands, 32, 25, 39–42, 48; on Cheyenne River Reservation, 58–62, 68–71; on Fort Belknap Reservation, 81–82, 86–87, 92–93, 96, 98–99; on Sioux lands during Indian New Deal, 114–15, 122, 126–28; on Wind River Reservation, 194
*Federalist Papers*: 241
Ferguson, Thompson: 46
Fielder, Allen: 63
Fifteenth Amendment, U.S. Constitution: 243
Fisher, Charles: 251
Fisher, James: 251
*Fletcher* v. *Peck*: 89–90
Flood Control Act of 1944: 171, 178, 180
Fort Belknap Reservation, and *Winters* v. U.S.: 77, 79–82, 84–85, 87–88, 92, 94–99
Fort Bennett, S.Dak.: 58, 60
Fort Berthold Reservation: 144, 172
Fort Keogh, Mont.: 250
Fort Laramie Treaty of 1868: 57
Fort Meade, S.Dak.: 252
Fort Peck Reservation: 80, 230

Fort Peck Dam (Montana): 172
Fort Randall Dam (South Dakota): 169, 171–72, 177
Fort Sill, Okla.: 18, 23, 27, 242
Fort Washakie, Wyo. 190, 198, 202, 204
Four Corners region: 228
Fourteenth Amendment, U.S. Constitution: 242
France: 154
Fraser, James: 56
Fremont County, Wyo.: 194, 203
Fresno Dam (Montana): 98
Frisco Railroad: 36

Gamble, Robert, and Cheyenne River Reservation: 63, 65, 67–68, 72
Gandy, Henry L.: 72
Garrison Dam (North Dakota): 144, 172, 178
General Allotment Act: 4, 11, 56, 243; effect of, upon Cheyennes and Arapahoes, 31–38, 48; relationship of, to citizenship, 151
Germany: 150, 154, 157–58, 254–55
Ghost Dance: 250
Governor's Advisory Council (Wyoming): 212–13
Grass Rope Unit (Lower Brulé Sioux): 179
Great Britain: 98
Great Northern Railroad: 81
Great Plains Hall (Wind River Reservation): 190
Green, R. H.: 47
Green Grass, S.Dak.: 59
Gros Ventres Indians: 77, 79–80; *see also* Fort Belknap Reservation
Gulf Oil Corp.: 225, 227

Hall, Philo: 63
Hampton Institute (Virginia): 44

Harlem, Mont.: 81, 95
Harrington, Frank: 39
Harvard University: 108
Haskell Indian School (Kansas): 43–44
Havre, Mont.: 81
*Havre Herald*: 87, 95
*Havre Plain Dealer*: 87
Hawaii: 154
Hayes, Darwin: 36
Hayes, Ira: 155
Hays, Luke C.: 83
Headley, Arnold: 146
Health Care: *see* U.S. Indian Health Service
Heap of Birds, Alfrich: 43
Hidatsa Indians: 172
Hill, John T.: 13
Hiroshima, Japan: 251
Hitchcock, Ethan A.: 82
Hitler, Adolf: 157
Holidays, on Wind River Reservation: 197
Hoover, Pres. Herbert: 164
Hoover Commission: 164
Hopi Indians: 180, 221–22, 225
Hunkpapa band (Sioux): 160
Hunt, William F., and *Winters* v. U.S.: 83–89, 91, 94–99
Hunter, Sara: 196

Ickes, Harold: 115, 153, 156
Illinois: 13
Indian Appropriation Acts: 33, 36–37, 44
Indian Citizenship Act: 244
Indian Mineral Act of 1982: 225
Indian New Deal: 7, 141, 175; effect of, upon the Sioux, 107, 116, 126; criticism of, 161–63; *see also* John Collier
Indian police: 138; on Cheyenne River Reservation, 59, 61, 68–72
Indian Reorganzation Act: general effect of, 6–7, 161; effect of, upon Sioux, 107–11, 113, 117–23, 125–27;

and Wind River
Reservation, 188, 203
Indian Rights Associa-
tion: 24–25, 63
*Indian's Friend* (news-
letter): 151, 153
Indian Territory: 11, 13,
32–33, 250
*Indian Wardship*
(pamphlet): 161
Individual Indian
Account: 45
International Nickle
Corp.: 227
Iron Lightning, S.Dak.:
60
Iroquois, League of:
157–58
Is'siwun (Cheyenne):
250–51, 259
Italy: 154, 157–58
Iwo Jima: 155

Japan: 155, 157–58
Japanese-Americans:
153, 156–57
Jennings, Joe: 110
Jerome, David A.: 11, 33
Jerome Agreement,
effect of, upon Co-
manches, Kiowas, and
Kiowa-Apaches: 11–
13, 15, 17, 24
Jerome Commission: 33
Jewett, Charles: 67
Jicarilla Apache Indians:
220, 229–30
John Mansfield Corp.:
227
*Johnson* v. *McIntosh*:
244
Joint Resolution 83
(U.S. Cong., 1868):
242
Jones, William A.: 14,
35

Kansas: 16, 165
Kansas City, Mo.: 178
Keeper of the Elk Soci-
ety (Cheyennes): 251
Kelly, Josephine: 176
Kerr-McGee Corp.: 227
King (superintendent):
69
Kinman, William: 18
Kinney, Clesson S.: 93
Kiowa-Apache Indians:
11, 15, 18, 21, 23,
26–28, 141

Kiowa County, Okla.:
21
Kiowa Indians: 141;
opening of lands of,
11–15, 18, 21, 23,
26–28; and World
War II, 149, 160
Klamath Indians: 165
Korea: 255–56

La Farge, Oliver: 163
La Flesche, Francis: 6
La Flesche, Susan: 6
La Flesche, Susette: 6
Lake Mohonk Con-
ferences: 24–25, 37
Lame Deer, Mont.: 250,
258–59
Lander, Wyo.: 188,
190, 201, 203, 205,
209
Lander Oil Field, Wyo.:
229
Land sales: on Coman-
che, Kiowa, and
Kiowa lands, 26–28;
on Cheyenne and
Arapaho lands, 33,
36–43, 45–49; on
Cheyenne River
Reservation, 57, 62–
67; *see also* leasing of
Indian lands
Lane, Franklin K.: 42
La Plant, Charles: 66
Last Man, John: 66
Lawton, Okla.: 18–19,
21–22
Leasing of Indian lands:
Comanche, Kiowa,
and Kiowa-Apache,
11, 15–17, 21, 26–28;
Cheyenne and Arapa-
ho, 34–35, 39–42; *see
also* farming, ranch-
ing, mineral resources
*Leavenworth* v. *U.S.*: 90
Leupp, Francis E.: 25–
26, 82
Limpy, Eugene: 251
Little, Eugene: 121
Little Bear (Cheyenne
chief): 38
Little Chief (Cheyenne):
250
Little Coyote, Bertha:
258, 260
Little Eagle, S.Dak.:
160

Little Raven (Arapaho):
39
Little Wind River: 209–
10
Little Wolf (Cheyenne):
250
Little Wolf, Mike: and
Nowah'wus, 253–54,
257, 259–60
Logan, William R., and
*Winters* v. *U.S.*: 80–
85, 91, 94–95, 99
Lohah, Charles: 227
Lone Wolf: 12–14, 23–
24
Lone Wolf, Delos: 13–
14
Lone Wolf, Okla.: 4
*Lone Wolf* v. *Hitchcock*:
effect of, upon Co-
manches, Kiowas, and
Kiowa-Apaches, 12,
24, 27; effect of, upon
Cheyenne River
Sioux, 62
Lookout, Fred: 6
Los Angeles, Calif.: 132
Louisiana: 181
Lovell, Wyo.: 147
Low Dog: 251
Lower Arapahoe, Wyo.:
189–91
Lower Brulé Reserva-
tion: in Americaniza-
tion era, 57; in Indian
New Deal, 113;
effects of Pick-Sloan
upon, 171–73, 176,
179
Lynaugh, Thomas J.: 225

MacArthur, Gen Doug-
las: 157
MacDonald, Peter: 221–
23, 226
McGregor, James H.:
110
McKenna, Joseph: 91,
93
McKinley, Pres. Wil-
liam: 13–14
McLaughlin, James:
134; and Comanches,
Kiowas, and Kiowa-
Apaches, 25; and
Cheyenne River
Sioux, 63–67
McNickle, D'Arcy: 7
Maheo (Cheyennes):
252, 257, 260, 262

Mahuts (Cheyennes): 250, 255, 258–59, 262
M&M Iron Co.: 228
Mandan Indians: 172
Marshall, Chief Justice, John: opinion of, in *Fletcher* v. *Peck*, 89–90; opinion of, in *Worcester* v. *Georgia*, 97–98; 246; opinion of, in *Cherokee Nation* v. *Georgia*, 238–39, 246
Martinez, Clifford: 143
Massachusetts: 4
Massaum ceremony (Cheyenne): 257
Medicine Bird, Nelson: 251–52
Medicine Bull, Willis, and Nowah'wus: 256–57, 259–61
Medicine Elk, James, and Nowah'wus: 257–61
Medicine Elk, Jennie, and Nowah'wus: 258–60
Medicine lodge (Cheyenne): 250, 256
Medicine Lodge, Treaty of: 15, 28
Menominee Indians: 165
Meriam Report: 115–17
Meritt, E. B.: 43
Mexico: 121
Midway, Battle of: 154
Milk River and *Winters* v. *U.S.*: 81–88, 90–91, 94–95, 97–98
Milk River United Irrigation Association: 90
*Milk River Valley News*: 95
Mineral Exploration Corp.: 227
Mineral resources: on Wind River reservation, 191–92, 194, 229; development of on Indian lands, 219–32
Minerals Management Service: 229
Minneconjou band (Sioux): 59–60
Mississippi River: 220, 227

Missouri: 48
Missouri Basin Inter-Agency Committee: 173–74
Missouri River: 144; and Cheyenne River Sioux, 57, 59; and Pick-Sloan Plan 171–72, 177–82, 220
Missouri River basin: and Pick-Sloan Plan, 169–74, 177–78, 180–81
Missouri Valley Authority: 171, 173–74
Mitchell, S.Dak.: 125
Mobil Oil Corp.: 227
Montana: 4, 111, 156; and *Winters* v. *U.S.*, 77, 79–84, 86, 89; Supreme Court, 89; and mineral resources, 220, 225
Moody, William: 82
Moreau River: 58–59
Morton, Rogers: 224
Morton, Wyo.: 190, 210
Mosqueda, Imogene Lincoln: 140
"Mother Earth" concept: 221–22, 231
Mount Suribachi, Iwo Jima: 155
Mower (Dog Soldier chief): 38
Muskogee, Okla.: 125

Names, imposition of Anglo-Saxon: 4
Nance, Thomas J.: 36
National Congress of American Indians: 164
National Environmental Policy Act: 224
National Progressive Education Association: 116
Native American church: 6, 32, 124, 237
Natrona Service: 227
Navajo Codetalkers: 155
Navajo Indians: and Indian New Deal, 109, 116–17; and World War II, 155–56, 159, 163; and federal assistance, 180; and mineral resources, 221, 226, 228, 230, 242

Navajo Indian Wood Products: 229
Navy Cross: 154
Nazis: 150, 157–58, 163
Nebraska: and termination era, 108, 125, 128; and Indian New Deal, 111; and *Elk* v. *Wilkins*, 242
Nestell, John: 15
New Deal: and Sioux, 113–16, 125; criticism of, 163; and freedom of Indian religion, 244; *see also* John Collier
New Dealers: 111–12
New Mexico: 107, 220
Ninth U.S. Circuit Court and *Winters* v. *U.S.*: 87–91, 93, 95–97, 99
Niobrara River: 250
Noble, John: 57
Nokota Co.: 227
Normandy: 154
North Dakota: 144–45; and Indian New Deal, 111; photographs relating to, 144–45; and Missouri River dams, 169, 178–79; mineral resources of, 220
Northern Pueblo Enterprises: 229
North Fork of Little Wind River (Wyoming): 210
North Slope (Alaska): 220
No-wa-hi (Cheyenne): 36
Nowah'wus (Sacred Mountain, South Dakota): 148; importance of, to Cheyennes, 249–57, 261–62

Oahe, S.Dak.: 59
Oahe Dam (South Dakota), and Pick-Sloan: 169, 171–72, 178, 181
Oglala, S.Dak.: 108
Oklahoma: 3–6, 125; opening of Comanche, Kiowa, and Kiowa-Apache lands in, 17, 55; opening of

Cheyenne-Arapaho lands in, 32, 43, 47–48, 55; and Indian New Deal, 107–108; and World War II, 154, 159; and energy development, 181; and Nowah'wus, 257, 259

Oklahoma City, Okla.: 258

Oklahoma Territory: 33, 35, 46; Supreme Court, 14

"Old Dealers" oppposition of, to Indian New Deal, 11–13, 121–24

Omaha Indians: 6, 128, 132, 149, 154

Omnibus Tribal Leasing Act: 225

On the Trees, S.Dak.: 58

Ordinance of 1787: 240

Oregon: 165, 246

Osage Indians: 5–6, 149, 154

"Outsider, The" (film ): 155

Pacific Northwest: 246

Pacific Ocean: 155

Parker, Harold: 24

Parker, Quanah: see Quanah

Parker, Wanda: 23

Peabody Coal Co.: 224–25

Pearl Harbor, Hawaii: 152, 154

Pedrick, Laura: 14

Pedrick, William E.: 14

Peter Kewitt Corp.: 227–28

Peyote: 124, 135; see also Native American church

Phillips, Percy: 63, 66–67

Pick, Lewis A.: 171

Pick-Sloan Plan, and Missouri River dams: 169–82

Pierre, S.Dak.: 59, 63, 111

*Pierre Daily Capital-Journal*: 68

Pimas: 155

Pine Ridge Reservation: and Americanization era, 57; and Indian

New Deal, 108–109, 111, 113–14, 118; and Alfred DuBray, 125; and termination era, 130; and Pick-Sloan Plan, 180; and factionalism, 187

Pittsburgh Midway Coal Co.: 230

Pittsburgh Pacific Corp.: 228

Plains: and Americanization era, 4–6; and Indian New Deal, 6–7, 107–108; and termination era, 7; mineral resources of, 8, 219, 222, 228, 230; Indian life in, 8, 249; and tribalism, 128, and World War II, 149, 153, 159; and Missouri River dams, 169; and tribal government, 187–88; and Indian religious rights, 237–38

Politics, tribal: among Comanches, Kiowas, and Kiowa-Apaches, 12–14, 22–24; among Cheyennes and Arapahoes, 38–39, 42–44; among Cheyenne River Sioux, 61, 63–68, 70–74; among Sioux in Indian New Deal, 117–26; and Pick-Sloan Plan, 175–76; and to contemporary mineral resources, 220–32; see also Arapahoe Business Council

Power Resources Corp.: 227

Pueblo Indians: 107

Purple Heart: 154

Quanah (Parker): 135; and opening of Comanche lands, 12–13, 15, 22–24

Quay, Matthew S.: 25

Ranching: on Comanche, Kiowa, and Kiowa-Apache lands, 11, 14–17, 20, 26–28;

on Cheyenne River Reservation, 58, 60–62, 70; on Fort Belknap Reservation, 81–82, 87; on Sioux lands during Indian New Deal, 121, 126; on Wind River Reservation, 202; see also farming, land sales, leasing

Randlett, James F., and opening of Comanche, Kiowa, and Kiowa-Apache lands: 12–19, 21–27

Rapid City, S.Dak.: 59, 110, 260

Rasch, Carl: 82–85

*Reader's Digest*: 161

Reagan, Pres. Ronald: 225–26

Redman, Alfred: 147

Red Plume (Cheyenne): 36

Red River: 15–16, 26

Red Scaffold, S.Dak.: 60

Red Shirt Table, S.Dak.: 114

Reifel, Ben: 108–20, 126–27

Relocation during termination era: 108, 130–32, 144

Rio Agum Corp.: 228

Riverside Indian school (Oklahoma): 141

Riverton, Wyo., and Northern Arapahoes: 188, 190–93, 201, 205

*Riverton Ranger*: 193, 209

Riverton Reclamation Area: 198

Rock Island Railroad: 12, 16, 36

Roman Catholic church: 124, 190–91

Roosevelt, Pres. Franklin D.: and Indian New Deal, 6, 111, 125; and World War II, 157, 159

Roosevelt, Pres. Theodore: and opening of Comanche, Kiowa, and Kiowa-Apache lands, 19, 23–25, 27–

28; and Cheyenne and Arapaho lands, 42, 48; and Cheyenne River Sioux Reservation, 64
Rosebud Reservation: and Americanization era, 57, 62 and Indian New Deal, 108, 113, 120–27
Roubideaux, Antoine: 108, 120–24
Rowland, Allen: 224
Royer, Daniel: 250
Ryan, Carson: 116

Sacred Arrows (Cheyenne): 249, 262
Sacred Persons (Cheyenne): 255, 260–61
Sage Creek (Wyoming): 210
Saint Mary River: 86, 98
Saint Michael's Mission (Ethete, Wyo.): 190–91
Saint Stephen's Church (Ethete, Wyo.): 190–91
Sandia Indian Industries: 229
San Francisco, Calif.: 87, 132, 181
San Jose, Calif.: 145
Sans Arc band (Sioux): 58–60
Santa Monica, Calif.: 143
Santee Sioux: 6
*Saturday Evening Post*: 150
Schools, *see* education
Scission, Kenneth: 153–54
Scott, Hugh: 251
Scott, Nell: 211
Scott, W. W.: 45
Seattle, Wash.: 221
Seger Agency: 43, 45
Sekaquaptewa, Abott: 225
Sells, Cato: 42–48
Sharp Nose (Arapaho): 199, 201
Shell, C. E.: 40
Shelley, W. C.: 14–15
Shell Oil Corp.: 225, 228

Sheridan, Wyo.: 257
Shoshones: at Wind River Reservation, 187, 189–93, 195, 198–99, 203–205, 209–15; mineral resources of, 229
Silberstein, Asher: 16
Silver Star: 154
Sioux: and Americanization era, 3, 55–59; and Indian New Deal, 111; and World War II, 149, 153, 159; and Missouri River dams, 169, 182; and mineral resources, 225, 228; *see also* Cheyenne River, Crow Creek, Lower Brulé, Pine Ridge, Rosebud, Sisseton, Standing Rock, Yankton reservations
Sioux Agreement of 1889: 55–56, 58, 62, 70
Sioux City, Iowa: 128, 178
Sioux Falls, S.Dak.: 142
Sisseton Reservation: 111
Sitting Bull (Sioux): 59, 228
Sixteenth Amendment (U.S. Constitution): 243
Sloan, William Glenn: 171
Smiley, Albert K.: 37–38
Smith, C. W.: 45
Smith, Ken: 226
Society of American Indians: 6
South Dakota: 4, 133–34, 136, 142, 148; in Americanization era, 3, 5, 55, 57, 62–63, 65, 67, 69–70; and Indian New Deal, 108, 110–11, 125; and World War II, 153; and Missouri River dams, 169, 171, 176, 178–79, 181; mineral resources of, 227
*South Dakota v. Rippling Water Ranch*: 181
South Fork (Little Wind River, Wyoming): 210

Spotted Elk, Charles: 251
Spotted Elk, August: 251
Spotted Wolf, Pat: 251
Springer, William M.: 13–14, 24
Stabler, Robert: 154
Stalin, Joseph: 157
Standing Elk: 250
Standing Rock Reservation: and Americanization era, 57, 59, 67; and Indian New Deal, 113; and Pick-Sloan Plan, 171–72, 176
Stands in Timber, John: 251, 253
Stands Over Bull, Patrick: 223
Stephens, John H.: 26–27
Straight Head: 67
Strange Owl, David: 221
Sturgis, S.Dak.: 253, 259
Sugg, E. C.: 16
Sun Dance: prohibition of, 5, 124; on Wind River Reservation, 190, 209–210; Cheyenne, 250, 256–57
Swan, Ed: 63, 66–67
Sweet Medicine (Cheyenne): 252–53, 257

Taft, Pres. William Howard: 42, 48
Takes-his-gun (Sioux): 160
Tall Bull, Albert: 253, 256, 259–61
Tecumseh, Kiutus: 153
Tennessee Valley Authority: 171
Termination era: 108, 130–32, 144–45, 149–50, 160–65
Teton Sioux: 56, 62
Texas: 16–17, 26
Thirteenth Amendment (U.S. Constitution): 242
Three Affiliated Tribes: 144, 172
Thunder Butte, S.Dak.: 59–61, 66

Tia-piah Gourd Dance
Society: 160
Tinker, Clarence L.: 154
Tivis, William: 13
Tomasa (wife of Joseph
Chandler): 15
Tongue River: 250
Tongue River Reserva-
tion: 251–52
Traylor, H. S.: 47
Tribal Land Enterprise:
114–15, 125
Trout Creek (Wyoming):
210
Tulley, John: 250
Turner, Frederick Jack-
son: 3
Twenty-first Amendment
(U.S. Constitution):
244
Twins, Baldwin: 255
Two Kettle band
(Sioux): 58, 60
Two Moon, Bert: 253,
256

Union Carbide Co.: 227
United Nuclear Home-
stake: 228
U.S. Army Corps of
Engineers: 169, 171–
81
U.S. Army: 151–52,
154
U.S. Bureau of Indian
Affairs: and Chey-
enne-Arapahoes, 36–
38; and Cheyenne
River Sioux, 67, 69–
70; and termination,
108, 145, 161–64;
and New
Deal, 114, 116, 124–
28; and Northern Ara-
pahoes, 187, 190,
193–95, 198, 200–
204, 211–12; and
mineral resources,
224, 226, 228, 230;
and Indian religions,
242
U.S. Bureau of
Reclamation: 99; in-
volvement of, in Mis-
souri River basin,
169, 171, 177–78,
180–81
U.S. Civilian Conserva-
tion Corps: 122

U.S. Coast Guard: 152
U.S. Congress: and
Comanches, Kiowas,
and Kiowa-Apaches,
12, 14–15, 20, 24,
26–27; and Cheyenne-
Arapahoes, 32–36, 40;
and Cheyenne River
Sioux, 62, 64–65, 67;
and Fort Belknap
Reservation, 81, 89,
93; and Indian New
Deal, 109–10, 112,
119, 125; and ter-
mination, 131, 162,
164; and Indian rights,
152, 328–40, 242–47;
and flood control,
171; and Missouri
River basin, 174–80
U.S. Constitution: 239–
44, 246–47
U.S. Department of En-
ergy: 178, 226
U.S. Department of
Health, Education,
and Welfare: 226–27
U.S. Department of the
Interior: and Coman-
ches, Kiowas, and
Kiowa-Apaches, 19–
20; and Indian water
rights, 98; and Indian
New Deal, 120, 123;
and Missouri River
basin, 175; and Indian
mineral resources,
225, 228–29
U.S. Energy Corpora-
tion: 226
U.S. ex rel Standing
Bear v. Crook: 242
U.S. General Land Of-
fice: 18
U.S. House Concurrent
Resolution 108: 164,
247; see also termina-
tion
U.S. House Indian
Affairs Committee:
64, 164–65, 230
U.S. Indian Claims
Commission: 164
U.S. Indian Health Ser-
vice: on Wind River
reservation, 190, 194–
95, 200–201, 204–
205, 214–15
U.S. Indian Office: 40,

64–65, 67, 91; see
also U.S. Bureau of
Indian Affairs Indian
police: 138; on
Cheyenne River
Reservation, 59, 61,
68–72
U.S. Indian Service: 14,
38, 161; see also U.S.
Bureau of Indian
Affairs
U.S. Marine Corps:
151–52, 155
U.S. Navy: 151–52
U.S. Office of Price Ad-
ministration: 253
U.S. Reclamation Ser-
vice: 86–87, 98; see
also U.S. Bureau of
Reclamation
U.S. Senate Indian
Affairs Committee:
64, 164–65
U.S. Supreme Court:
and Lone Wolf v.
Hitchcock, 13, 24, 62;
and Winters v. U.S.,
77–78, 89–99, 180;
and Fletcher v. Peck,
89–90; and U.S. v.
Rio Grande Dam and
Irrigation Company,
89, 93; and U.S. v.
Winans, 93; and
Worcester v. Georgia,
97–98; and Indian
court system, 118; and
condemnation of In-
dian land, 176; and
severance taxes for
mining on Indian
land, 229–30; and
Cherokee Nation v.
Georgia, 238–39,
246; and U.S. ex rel.
Standing Bear v.
Crook, 242; and Elk
v. Wilkins, 242–43;
and U.S. v. Nice,
243; and Johnson v.
McIntosh, 244
U.S. v. Nice: 243
U.S. v. Rio Grande
Dam and Irrigation
Company: 89, 93
U.S. v. Winans: 93
U.S.War Relocation Au-
thority: 156–57
Utah: 165

Utah International Corp.: 228, 230
Ute Fabricating, Ltd.: 229

Valentine, R. G.: 39, 41
Vernon, Texas: 26
Vestal, Stanley (Walter S. Campbell): 153
Vietnam: 260
Villard, Oswald Garrison: 160–62

Waggoner, Daniel: 16
Waggoner, Tom: 16–17
Wallowing, Rufus: 251
Warden, Cleaver: 39
Washakie: 201
Washington, D.C.: and opening of Comanche, Kiowa, and Kiowa-Apache lands, 13, 16, 19, 27; and Cheyenne and Arapaho lands, 38, 47; and Cheyenne River Reservation, 64–67; and *Winters* v. *U.S.*, 81–82; and Indian New Deal, 111, 120, 125; and termination era, 164; and Wind River Reservation, 203; and mineral resources, 227, 230; *see also* U.S. Bureau of Indian Affairs
Washington, state of: 221, 246
Water rights: *see Winters* v. *U.S.*, Pick-Sloan Plan
Watkins, Arthur V.: 165
Watonga, Okla.: 35, 46
*Watonga Republican*: 46
Watt, James: 225
West, Walter G.: 41–42
West Coast: 129
Western Geophysical Corp.: 228

Westinghouse Corp.: 227
Whistling Elk and Nowah'wus: 251–58
White Dirt, Charles: 256, 258–60
White Eagle Industries: 229
White Horse, S.Dak.: 59–61, 63, 66–67
Whitlock (superintendent): 114–15
Wichita Mountains (Oklahoma): 15, 17–19
Williams, Richard B.: 261
Willkie, Wendell: 157
Wilson, Horace G.: 43, 48
Wilson, Pres. Woodrow: 42, 44
Wind River: 209–10
Wind River Allottees Association: 229
Wind River Reservation: 146–47; contemporary conditions on, 187–215; mineral resources of, 219, 229–30; *see also* Northern Arapahoes, Shoshones
Winnebago Reservation: 108; Alfred DuBray on, 125, 127–32
Winner, S.Dak.: 125
*Winters* v. *U.S.*: 77–79, 81–88, 94–99; relation of, to contemporary Indian water rights, 180–81
Wisconsin: 165
Wisdom, W. W.: 47
Wolf Black, Dallas: 251
Wolf Chief (Cheyenne): 43
Woodenlegs, John: 223
*Worcester* v. *Georgia*: 97, 246

World War I: and Cheyenne River Reservation, 68, 70; Indian participation in, 151, 153, 159; and Northern Cheyennes, 251
World War II: Indian participation in, 7, 142–44, 149–50, 152–60, 170; and Sioux, 108, 114, 122; and Northern Cheyennes, 252
Wounded Knee (South Dakota): 3, 55, 58, 170
Wyatt, William: 15
Wyoming: 3, 146–47; mineral resources of, 181, 229–30; and Wind River reservation, 189, 194, 203, 212
Wyoming Department of Public Assistance and Social Services: 195
Wyoming Indian High School: 147, 201, 214
Wyoming Minerals Co.: 227
*Wyoming State Journal*: 209

Yankton Reservation: 111, 171–72, 176
Yankton Sioux: 6
Yatay Industries: 229
Yates, Sidney: 230–31
Yellow Nose: 251–52
Yellowstone River: 250
Young Creek (Montana): 225
Yuwipi (Sioux): 124

Zuni Enterprises: 229

*The Plains Indians of the Twentieth Century*,

designed by Bill Cason, was set in various sizes of Times Roman by the University of Oklahoma Printing Services and printed offset on 55-pound Glatfelter Smooth Antique B-31 by Cushing-Malloy, Inc., with case binding by John H. Dekker & Sons.